CHRISTIAN

IDENTITY &

RELIGIOUS

PLURALISM

RELIGIONS IN CONVERSATION

Michael Barnes

Abingdon Press/Nashville

95

1989

CHRISTIAN IDENTITY AND RELIGIOUS PLURALISM:
RELIGIONS IN CONVERSATION

Copyright © 1989 by Michael Barnes

This book is printed on acid-free paper.

First published in Great Britain 1989 by SPCK, Holy Trinity Church, Maryle-
bone Road, London NW1 4DU

Abingdon Press edition published 1989

Library of Congress Cataloging-in-Publication Data

BARNES, MICHAEL, 1947–
    Christian identity and religious pluralism:
religions in conversation / Michael Barnes.
        p. cm.
    Bibliography: p.
    Includes index.
    ISBN 0-687-07219-0 (alk. paper)
        1. Christianity and other religions. 2. Religions.
3. Religious pluralism. I. Title.
    BR127.B33   1989
261.2—dc19   88-36437
                                                                                CIP

To my mother and father
with love and gratitude

MANUFACTURED BY THE PARTHENON PRESS AT
NASHVILLE, TENNESSEE, UNITED STATES OF AMERICA

PREFACE

When I travelled to India in the New Year of 1987 my object was to discover how Christian theologians in that country were coping with the vexed problem of religious pluralism. I very quickly learned that it was a mistake to separate this from other issues, such as liturgy and liberation. The problem of pluralism is only the problem of Christian identity in another guise. This book, therefore, focuses not just on the theology of religions – a recent but increasingly important aspect of the process of Christian reflection – but also on broader and ever more complex themes, including Christology, ecclesiology, the theology of mission and the nature of theology itself.

Any work of theology must be analytic and critical, an attempt to keep in touch with the literature of the subject as much as to enhance the process of reflection on the Christian tradition as a whole. There are thus two parts to this book: the first concerned with the debate about other religions which has engaged the attention of theologians from various Christian communities, the second devoted to the inter-religious encounter, the conversation going on at all levels between Christians and people of other faiths. Some readers, finding detailed discussion of theologians a trifle tedious, may prefer to move straight on to the more systematic part. However, Part Two needs preparation, if only so that my thinking is not seen as idle speculation with little reference to any tradition of theologizing in this area. Part One aims to be an accurate, but necessarily limited, summary of current thinking. I do not intend to rival the work of recent surveys and commentaries, but to make some critical comment, particularly on the current fashion for a threefold paradigm in the theology of religions. My intention here is to negotiate an escape from this somewhat rigid patterning of Christian theology.

My main aim is to contribute to a debate. I hope that students of theology will find my interpretations and suggestions cogent and stimulating. But there is another aim and another audience in mind: those who already feel the need to begin the inter-religious conversation but lack either an adequate theology or (which amounts to the same thing) sufficient motivation. My hope is that readers who persevere with Part One will be stimulated by Part Two to begin the difficult but infinitely rewarding process of building relationships with people of other faiths and thus learning more about their own faith. Theology should be an absorbing activity of personal engagement as well as a subject of study. Should the academic debate be pushed forward a notch or two I will feel well-rewarded; but the aim is to inspire practice, not to achieve the neatness of dogmatic theory.

A complex subject which touches on so many areas is not easily documented. I have not tried to turn the references into an encyclopedia but, making a virtue of necessity, have left them as bare as possible and would ask anyone interested in the literature of the subject to follow up points with the aid of the two bibliographies at the end. Even so, where I felt it important not to interrupt the main argument, some sub-themes and 'asides' have been developed in the form of notes.

Since this is primarily a work of theology it seems appropriate to make minimal use of diacritics in transliteration. Thus, for instance, I have preferred the anglicised Krishna instead of the more strictly accurate *Kṛṣṇa*.

Finally a word about the guiding metaphor behind the work. I have used the term conversation, somewhat inconsistently, to refer to the process by which theology of religions is to be done. I hope that it will overcome something of the formality implied in the term dialogue. Conversation is what happens when people meet and talk, listen and learn, usually in relaxed and friendly circumstances. Dialogue, as it is often used these days, is too reminiscent of heavy conferences. There should be nothing heavy about the inter-faith encounter. Understood in the sense which I propose in this book it can be the source of renewal for people of all faiths and a stimulus to pursue theology, not as an apologetic strategy, but as a genuine service of the Word – listening to what the Spirit may be saying to the Church.

Michael Barnes SJ
Heythrop College, London
September 1988

ACKNOWLEDGEMENTS

I am only too well aware of the multiple debts which must be acknowledged in the writing and production of this book. What began as talks and articles has, I hope, found some coherence in this volume and I am grateful for the support, criticism and enthusiasm of all who have helped me to shape the printed word. The then Jesuit Provincial Superior, Jock Earle, gave me time to make the 1987 trip to India when many ideas fell into place; the present Provincial, Michael Campbell-Johnston, has been no less supportive. It would be impossible to mention all the help I got from people in India – Christians, Hindus and Muslims. I should record one unforgettable evening spent in a village in southern Gujerat which taught me more about the reality, rewards and pains of the inter-faith conversation than a dozen conferences. In addition I must thank the kindness of many of my Jesuit brethren in India, particularly George Soares Prabhu and Salvino Azzopardi of Jnanadeepa Vidyapeeth, near Pune, George Gispert-Sauch, Samuel Rayan and T.K. John, of the Vidyajyoti Institute in Delhi, Michael Amaladoss, now in Rome, Sebastian Painadath, of Kalady, the birthplace of Śankara, and the incomparable Ignatius Hirudayam, of Aikiya Alayam, in Madras.

Friends and colleagues at Heythrop helped me to organize my thoughts and prevented the worst of mistakes. A special word of thanks must go to John McDade for his constantly stimulating comments on various drafts. Thanks too to Bruno Brinkman, Robert Murray, Peter Vardy, Anne Murphy, Joe Laishley, Elizabeth Lord and Gerry Hughes who read all or part of the manuscript and made encouraging noises and not a few invaluable suggestions. The mistakes and infelicities which remain are, of course, no fault of theirs. I should also acknowledge the support of those whose interest has made the project seem worthwhile, among them James Hanvey, Gavin D'Costa, Daniel Faivre and Philip Law of S P C K. Thanks also to Brendan Callaghan, Philip Sheldrake and my Jesuit community in South Woodford who punctuated any incipient pomposity with appropriate good humour, and to the Hengrave community, near Bury St Edmunds, who gave me the space needed to complete the final draft. Last, but by no means least, a special word of thanks to Gwen Griffith Dickson without whose constant interest this book would never have been begun – or finished.

Contents

Part One

THEOLOGIES AND RELIGIONS

But who can know, clearly and well,
The single true source of salvation?

Richard Wagner, *Parsifal*, act 2

1 PROBLEMS AND PARADIGMS

The problem of religious pluralism is the problem of 'the other', the one who dresses differently, behaves differently, perhaps speaks a different language, and whose life seems to be guided by principles very different from our own. Of course on closer acquaintance many of the differences are overcome, usually without any difficulty. Sometimes it comes as a real surprise to learn how much we share in common with people who, whether we like it or not, are our neighbours, despite barriers of creed, colour, race or religion. And it is possible to exaggerate the problem, to surround communication across the age-gap, the culture-gap, the language-gap, with so many problems that no one has the energy to try. Nevertheless, communication does take time and effort. However much we may share in common, the other is also different and, at times, a threat. It is easy to ignore or patronize strangers; it is much more difficult to take them seriously, to accept them on their terms, not just on ours, and to be prepared to live in their world rather than in ours. For as long as we look upon this one world as *our* world and insist on doing things only in *our* way we ignore the fact that we share that world with people who have every right to do things differently, in *their* way.

The problem of religious pluralism is also, more specifically, the problem of religion. Whatever religion is – and enough definitions of religion have been produced to provide the central theme of many a book, including this one – it is clearly something central to our self-understanding as human beings. Religion is the heart of culture, that collection of mores, myths and fundamental beliefs which holds a people together and gives a society a sense of coherence and identity. Even a secular, or secularized, society needs its myths, its collective story. Perhaps more importantly, every society needs a sense of tradition, a common understanding that it is firmly rooted in the past and that that past makes sense for the present and the future. All of us inherit culture. We do not choose it. And to an extent the same can be said for religion. It is true that most people are Christians, Muslims, Hindus or Buddhists because they were born into societies which are Christian, Muslim, Hindu or Buddhist. But that does not mean to say that the traditions which have sustained

3

communities of faith for several hundreds of years cannot claim to teach something which has universal significance. In fact all the major religions in their different ways do precisely that. Many people change their allegiance, of course, being converted to a faith which they find intellectually or emotionally more satisfying, but many more grow up in conscious commitment to the faith of their birth. That is the true meaning of conversion. Indeed if religion is to be more than just habit or part of the socializing process by which we are integrated into society, we have to affirm it for ourselves, find the source of its life and repeat in our lives the spirit of the past. Only that way does the past live – for myself and for the other. Religion, therefore, is at the heart of culture, but it is also at the heart of what people affirm to be true in an absolute sense.

In today's world we are familiar with many religions. Hinduism and Islam can no longer be considered exotic forms of 'paganism', wearily awaiting the final missionary effort. The other, the stranger, may well be our next-door neighbour. In the West a once largely homogeneous culture is now remarkable more for a beneficent pluralism of religion than for any wholesale commitment to its traditional Christian roots. This raises the obvious question: What is religion, and more particularly what are *the religions*, for in a pluralist society? In approaching this problem I want to affirm two principles: openness to the other and faithfulness to one's own. The first needs little by way of apologia; the second is much more likely to get well-motivated liberal hackles rising. And yet, if the point I have just made is correct – that religions bring a wealth of traditional wisdom to focus on the question of truth – then it must follow that the two should be taken together. Dialogue and communication between religions does not just happen. It requires a very positive sensitivity to the nuances of faith and, above all, to claims to truth. Openness to the other entails respecting his or her sense of loyalty to tradition. Only the two together are likely to ensure a lasting harmony of religions.

Respect for Tradition

This study is intended as an exercise in Christian theology, an attempt to understand the phenomenon of religious pluralism. How am I as a Christian to understand my relationship with people of other faiths? The first task is to look at what is happening to the religions in today's world. Ours is an age of increasing rootlessness, with more and more people searching for meaning and identity anywhere but in their own tradition. In much of the post-Christian West the search is for new experiences and maybe even for a new religion. Elsewhere the challenges of modernity produce a different reaction. In almost all the major religions we may discern examples of a retreat into the safety of the past. Ancient cultures are beginning to turn in on themselves. Fundamentalist groups – from media-conscious Bible-belt evangelicals in the United States to the extreme nationalism of right wing Hindu organizations in India – are becoming more vocal and more influential. In the Middle East (but not just in the Middle East) violent fanatics are only too ready to invoke the sanction of religion for anti-social, not to say immoral, acts of petty tyranny and outright terrorism. We may blame pluralism for the break-up of what were once homogeneous and peacefully organized communities, and long for the days when order and stability kept communities intact, if not isolated from each other. But pluralism itself is not the problem. When people are under threat one answer is to retreat to the apparent security of a golden age when strangers knew their place and kept to themselves. Such nostalgia is dangerous and destructive. No society can survive, least of all in a world of rapidly increasing communications, by simply erecting the barriers of authoritarianism. When western technology and a ceaseless flow of petrodollars flood the Middle East, an ancient and still largely feudal society is convulsed by the challenge of a modern world which it is quite unprepared to face. When the children in a Gujerati village get access to television they not only see what is happening in Delhi and other parts of India but are exposed to American films and news from all over the world. One could list so many examples of the way in which 'the other' becomes known; expectations are raised, traditional values are questioned, and familiar ways of life are threatened. But the solution cannot be to ignore the new by proclaiming the old more vociferously, or the old will most certainly wither and die. Loyalty to the tradition and values of the past, the very life-blood of a community, has somehow got to be married with a willingness to integrate the stranger, in whatever form he or she may happen to appear.

These reflections are not prompted simply by contact with the Church in the Third World. When large numbers of Bangladeshis move into the East End of London, they may well be the latest in a long line of immigrant communities, following the Irish and the Jews. But the local people who have, perhaps, lived there for generations, very quickly find themselves in the minority; their perception of a once so familiar world is irrevocably changed. A theology of religions begins not with distant and exotic cultures but with experience of the stranger in our midst, with a reflection on the nature of human religiosity in all its many forms. This is where the sometimes painful attempt to live out the faithfulness-loyalty tension makes itself felt. It may be a cliché, but it still needs to be said that this is a task of our times, entailing a reflection both on the riches of the Christian tradition and on the insights which the other may bring to our encounter. In fact, of course, the other has always been there and Christian culture has usually coped with the problem by a mixture of theological apologetics, missionary zeal and, sometimes, pure aggression. The temptation is still to opt for some form of Christianity-centred absolutism: to regard the religion of the other as, at best, a pale reflection of my superior religion or, at worst, the work of the devil. Nowadays for a variety of reasons we are less sure. More recently a different approach has become popular: to relativize all religions, reducing them to a few common features and thus evacuating the specific mystery of each. Both positions ignore the true reality of the problem of the other. If the one errs on the side of 'loyalty', the other sells out to 'openness'. Can anything be saved from either position? Is there such a thing as a 'middle way', avoiding the extremes? Or do we have to look for something quite new?

There is no easy way out of this dilemma. It is no overstatement to say that our sense of Christian identity is in crisis. The old apologetics which put the other firmly in his or her place is no longer adequate to cope with the questions which the world puts to the Church, and which the Church, if it is to be faithful to its mission to preach the Good News, must put to the world. The fact is that theologians are dealing with a very complex problematic which cannot just be restricted to the hoary old question of the salvation of the non-believer. As long as we live in a Christianity-centred culture we are always going to be asking how 'they' fit into 'our' world. But in our present post-Christian culture and more especially in a Hindu, Muslim or Buddhist culture the positions are reversed: how does a Christian minority fit into a Hindu, Muslim or Buddhist world? In this situation what does it mean to be Christian?

Mission and Dialogue in Today's World

Christianity is, of course, a missionary religion. One might almost say that it is defined by its commitment to proclaim and build the Kingdom of God announced by Jesus Christ.[1] But a further and

more exact definition of that mission is a lot more difficult. Mission
to whom? For what? A review of missionary theology over the last
twenty years would recognize three significant developments:
liberation, inculturation and the meeting of faiths.[2] All three go
together. The problem of injustice, notably the disparity between
the wealth of the First and the grinding poverty of the Third World,
needs precious little comment. The gospel is all about God's concern
for the poor and the Kingdom will never be built without a prophetic
response to their cry for help. Secondly, that somewhat confusing
neologism 'inculturation': adaptation of the universal message of the
gospel has always been a missionary priority, if only so that the Word
of God may be heard in language which people can understand.[3] The
present call for inculturation goes much further, stressing that the
Church is not a monolithic, still less western or eurocentric, structure, but it is the presence of God's Spirit alive and active amongst
different peoples who are called not to lose but to develop their own
culture in the light of the gospel. And thirdly and perhaps most
significantly, the inter-religious encounter.[4] Sometimes Roman
Catholic theologians give the impression that this is a discovery of
Vatican II, when in fact Protestants have been wrestling with this
problem for years. The theology of religions, however, is constantly
under review: dialogue and mission, the relationship of dialogue and
evangelization, the nature of conversion, the very role of the
Church. Dialogue may have become part of the jargon of the
ecumenical age and can easily conjure up images of cosy parties of
eager like-minded groupies gathered to pore over their favourite
obsessions. The fact is that no word is so expressive of the Church's
self-understanding in today's world. Even if, as we shall see, the
meaning of the word needs to be clarified, it sums up a whole
movement, both within and outside the Church, towards a deeper
appreciation of the way God is speaking in today's world.

These developments are interdependent and one cannot attempt
to preach the gospel today without some reference to each of them.
The reflections in this book, however, are centred on the third, for it
is here that we touch on an area of crucial concern for a society which
has lost its specifically Christian identity and must as much redis-
cover its own cultural roots as learn to live with the other in a
multi-cultural world. What is at stake is not just our theology of
mission but, if mission is constitutive of the very nature of the
Church, our own self-understanding as Christian.[5] If we are to
recover that consciousness of what it means to be Christian and grow
in it, it is essential that we understand what our relationship to the

peoples of other faiths can and should be. Much is already happening in inter-religious cooperation. From the highest level, in the World Council of Churches and the Vatican Secretariat for non-Christians, to the local grass-roots in parishes and neighbourhood meetings, the apostolate of inter-faith dialogue is being seen as a major and exciting development in the life of the Church. Much progress, new initiatives; but no one who is seriously involved – whether as teacher or pastoral worker or just as a thinking member of the local congregation – can avoid for long the complex theological questions posed by the existence of sometimes very large communities of other faiths in our midst.

It is relatively easy to be 'open'. But there are other issues which the Christian has to face, notably the credibility of the Christian tradition in a pluralist society. Is there anything which makes the Christian different from the other? Does my openness to the other compromise my loyalty to my own tradition? As soon as we raise these immediate questions, all sorts of others rise to the surface: questions about salvation, about truth in religion and about the very nature of religion itself. And these are not just distant theological abstractions. If faith is to be mature and not a barely detribalized sense of belonging to the 'group', then it has to learn to relate to the other as other. This is not just a mission – something we do because we are sent. It is also a task of self-transformation. Any relationship established between two people must, eventually, change both partners. How far can, or should, such change go? As committed Christians we may well regard ourselves as agents for change in the other. Can we also allow that members of other faiths have as much of a role to play in our growth as we have in theirs? The experience of many people today is that a real human contact with the other can help us to know our own tradition better. Whether we expect it or not, the mission to the other becomes a mirror to ourselves.

Changing the Perspective

In the West we still have not grasped the force of this new situation. We still entertain a Christianity-centred version of the universe. But once one moves outside what used to be called Christendom the world of religions, and God's purposes, seem very different. In India, for instance, only 2.6% of the population are Christian. The vast majority are Hindu, but there is a sizeable minority which is Muslim, not to mention smaller communities of Sikhs, Jains, Buddhists, Jews and Parsis. The Christian Church is small but well-organized, dating back in its Syrian form to the early centuries of the Christian era. But it is identified with India's colonial past and is regarded by many Hindus with some suspicion as the agent of foreign domination. With some justification they see the Church's purpose as the conversion of the pagan, and that means the destruction of native culture and traditions. In fact conversions have been largely confined to low-caste and tribal groups but it is difficult for Christians to avoid giving the impression that they are only concerned to develop and maintain their own institutional structure. As in the countries of the West, the model of the Church which has prevailed until relatively recently, is that of the visible institution – not even the community but the building which houses the community.

As any Third World theologian will testify, missionary theology involves a lot more than merely translating European idioms and symbols into local equivalents. The theology of conquest has long given way to a theology of context. Theology in India, for instance, has already developed its own particular form and traditions, in dialogue with Indian culture.[6] This does not mean that it simply adapts to a different language; a truly contextual theology must differ from our traditional western conceptions in several respects. Christology, which in the West has always been expressed in the language of Greek philosophy and tries to show how Jesus the man can also be truly God, has to face a very different problem in India: the uniqueness or special status of Christ as the sole mediator amongst a whole variety of incarnations or *avatars*.[7] In the West we are concerned to make the symbolism of our sacramental and liturgical practice meaningful in a secularized environment; in the East theologians find themselves asking what is so specific or privileged about the Christian sacraments, devotions, prayer, pilgrimages, etc. when there is such a wide variety to choose from in other traditions. Above all, of course, the West has to operate in a largely post-Christian or dechristianized world. Our primary concern must be to make our faith meaningful to people who appear to have no time or place for religion. In the East religion is a fact, a real issue which cannot be ignored. The problem is not *whether* religion, nor is it even *which* religion. The question is how religions are related in a much greater purpose, how they can and do support people of faith who, Catholic or Protestant, Hindu or Muslim, are all alike afflicted by the evils of poverty, injustice and oppression which beset so much of the Third World. Who is the God, that Ultimate Mystery, to which all religions point? What do the different faiths have to say to each other?

9

Theologians East and West have to allow for this new perspective. As the Indian theologian, Michael Amaladoss, has put it recently, 'Under the impact of a positive experience of other religions, the centre of the framework is changing from the church to the kingdom. The change is making us look in a new way at Christ, at the church, at salvation and at mission'.[8] Theology is done from below upwards rather than proceeding deductively from given truths. His reflections begin with the suggestion that the process we are living through is a paradigm shift. A paradigm is 'a framework of meaning that makes sense of a body of data perceived as a system'. The language is inherited from the highly influential work of the philosopher of science Thomas Kuhn.[9] Kuhn's concern, of course, is with the way the scientist works. The popular notion is that the scientist simply gathers more and more data and therefore in some way manages to 'control' reality 'out there'. The operation is really much more complex. In the first place we have to recognize the extent of our own conditioning, the fact that we come to the data of experience with certain presuppositions. If we are to make any sort of progress in understanding we must first overcome the natural human tendency to make reality conform to expectations. Our choice of data is highly selective. Usually we go on straining the theory in order to make it accommodate as much data as possible. But there must come a time when some item of experience just refuses to 'fit'. At that point a paradigm shift is needed: a new theory which will cope more adequately with the 'facts' of experience. The application to theology is obvious. A new problematic, raised by the experience of dialogue, has to be integrated into the tradition. The old paradigm no longer provides satisfactory answers to the new questions which the Church itself is beginning to raise.

Amaladoss is not alone in applying Kuhn's insight to the theology of religions. Theologians as far apart in their fundamental orientations as Arthur F. Glasser and John Hick have made exactly the same point. The former, from an evangelical background, recognizes the inadequacy of the total discontinuity model of religious relationships.[10] Contact with the other in dialogue means that, at the very least, we have to accept all religions as separate traditions providing answers to ultimate questions; Christianity is not 'above' the action any more than any other religion. Theologians have to address themselves to the full richness and complexity of the scriptural tradition and find there a new or more developed model or paradigm which will enable the Church to define and express the gospel message more coherently. Hick goes much further.[11] His

'Copernican Revolution' in theology is perhaps the most radical of all attempts to come to terms with the new problematic. Again he begins with a positive experience of the other. Pluralism cannot be treated as a disagreeable fact to be explained away. It is the very stuff of theology. Both contemporary experience and the history of religion pose positive questions for the theologians. Why the other? What is God saying through the communities and traditions which are beginning to make an increasingly significant impression on our once safe and snugly insular Christian world?

The programme suggested by these questions is enormous. We are asked to change our traditional paradigm of Church-centred theology to something which, following Amaladoss, is Kingdom-based. Furthermore, the new problematic demands that we seek out those truths and values in other religions which are already making a positive contribution to the building of that Kingdom. At the very least this means that theologians and historians of religion should learn from each other; religious traditions may be very different but they also hold much in common. Secondly, we need to ask what precisely is the 'data' of theology in our modern pluralist world. Until fairly recently we would all admit to being perfectly content with a deductive paradigm for theology, based on an articulation of the ancient tradition. Now theologians often live in more than one culture. Their inheritance, not to say experience, includes different customs, traditions, literatures, myths and religious paradigms. An Indian theologian, for instance, may be just as familiar with the *Bhagavad Gita* as with some of the Christian classics. They are part of his culture and have become part of his world. But this experience affects all Christians, not just the professional theologian. Anyone who is in dialogue with modern culture soon finds that the Christian 'story' cannot be limited to its traditional Christian language or culture. And the more we dialogue with this world, the more Hinduism, Buddhism, Judaism and Islam become part of what it means to be Christian. Today we need a theology which will clarify the conceptual problems of inter-religious encounter as much as we need one which emerges from that encounter.

Theology of Religions

Over the last few years a number of fairly general surveys of the theology of religions have appeared. They summarize a vast amount of material from all sides of the Christian tradition and show remarkable agreement about the 'map' of the area. Alan Race, for instance, finds three 'patterns' of thought: the exclusivist, the inclusivist and the pluralist.[12] The first two are criticized as being inadequate to present-day needs, the third applauded and developed. Gavin D'Costa, on the other hand, makes a similar analysis but his Roman Catholic presuppositions dictate a different order: pluralism and exclusivism are dismissed; inclusivism defended.[13] Paul Knitter, in his critical survey of Christian attitudes, provides the most detailed guide to the theological scene.[14] With his – perhaps unique – knowledge of Protestant theologies of religion he manages a much more searching analysis of the 'exclusivists'; inclusivism he prefers to call the 'Catholic Model' while pluralism is entitled the 'Theocentric Model'. He follows Race's order but gives a more satisfactory defence of the pluralist position. Another version, much briefer but following almost exactly the same set of titles, is that of Raimundo Panikkar.[15] He speaks of exclusivism, inclusivism and what he calls parallelism: the thesis that all religions run parallel to meet only in the Ultimate, at the end of time. But he devotes most of his attention to a fourth model, interpenetration, which arises from the parallelist model while seeking to avoid the latter's implicit relativism.

It would be a mistake to see this sort of theological pluralism as a recent development. Theologians have been thinking seriously about the problem of the other for more than a hundred years and in that time no one theology of religions has emerged; today we find ourselves caught in what another survey calls a 'dialectical morass'.[16] Theology has become polarized between the positions of radical exclusivism and various forms of relativism. Let us not begin by assuming that there are 'right' and 'wrong' places on what is really a whole spectrum of opinions except, perhaps, at the extremes. Rather, we are dealing with different 'models' of theology which attempt to preserve some fundamental insights of the tradition. More importantly, they embody certain values without which no adequate theology of religions can be constructed. To make sense of the 'dialectical morass' we need to reflect very carefully on the origin of these ideas and the values they represent.

In the rest of this chapter my main intention is to analyse further the interaction of the two values of faithfulness and openness as they have affected the recent history of theology. My initial contention is that theologians are not responding to the same problem – or, at any rate, like Kuhn's scientist their presuppositions are such that they see the problem quite differently. Exclusivists take as their primary value faithfulness to the tradition. Such a position sees the problem of the other as largely his or her problem. How can members of other faiths be saved? Is there salvation outside the Church? The pluralist, on the other hand, finds such thinking inappropriate to today's world of religious pluralism and begins with a very different problem: what is the *theological* meaning of the other? Attention is focused on the significance of the religions as such. This is not a question of the Church losing its missionary nerve, joining the colonial withdrawal, as it were. The terms of the debate have changed. The grand eschatological vision, which saw the Church gradually but inexorably spreading its influence over the non-Christian world, is now no longer seen to fit the 'facts'. At a time when interest in other faiths is on the increase, when immigration has led to the presence of some large communities of other faiths in our western cities, when we think of the comparative failure of missionary effort and accept that wherever the Church has encountered a sophisticated or developed faith or philosophy it has made little progress, we have to ask the question: What is God saying through this situation? What is the Christian significance of religious pluralism in today's world?

This is the agenda: two sets of questions which I will refer to simply as the old and new problematics. The extent to which the inclusivist paradigm manages to bridge the gap as a genuine third way will occupy us in due course; I will argue that it does not and that our task is that of going 'beyond inclusivism' while still holding two sets of values together. And yet to distinguish two problematics only states the problem in a different form; it does not solve it. The strict exclusivist will insist that Christian theology should remain apologetic, seeking only to defend its own claims. The pluralist end of the spectrum takes the line that theological judgement by one tradition on another is anachronistic in today's world of many cultures and instant communication. Religions are already sharing so much; it is only a matter of time until all the present unnecessary barriers are broken down and 'sectarian' theology becomes a relic of the past. Neither position convinces since neither faces up to the problem with which I began: our relationship with the one who is other. It does not matter whether that other is a member of another faith, or is from the Third rather than the First World, black rather than white, female rather than male, this class or caste rather than that one; theology still has to answer the question which is raised by the stranger in our midst. That there is a gap between old and new problematics, between those who see the problem of religious pluralism as a 'salvation problem' and those who see it primarily as a 'truth problem', seems to go without saying.

Pluralism: the Origins of the New Problematic

Our first task is to indicate how theology has found itself polarized between the two ends of the spectrum. I shall begin with pluralism since it seems to me that this is rapidly becoming the prevalent fashion in modern theology. It is important briefly to consider its antecedents in that type of theology called liberal protestantism which emerged in the nineteenth century. Pluralism in theology takes us right back to the spirit of the Enlightenment, a spirit of rationalism and antagonism towards ecclesiastical authority and traditional religion. Up until that time Christianity held an unquestioned position not as the superior religion among many but as the embodiment of true religion, divinely revealed and sanctioned by an authoritative Church. With the Enlightenment comes the destruction of the concept of a classical culture, based on Christianity, valid for all time and all people. But what challenged this assumption of the superiority of Christianity was not so much the discovery of 'the other' – other religions had been known for centuries – as the discovery of the nature of the self as a knowing subject. As so often, the fundamental issues turn out to be philosophical before they are theological. The source of the revolution lies in the theory of knowledge. Kant's concentration on the conditions of possibility for human knowing led to the discovery that knowledge depends as much on the nature of the knower as it does on the object known. We impose our own conditions on experience; thus our traditional concepts of God depend on a human ability to project images and models, to make God in our own likeness. Knowing is not just a matter of passively accepting or experiencing what is 'out there'; we have an active role to play in the process. Thus, if knowledge in general must be considered in some sense to be dependent on, or relative to, the particular knower, then meaning and truth are relative to the society or historical perspective in which they are formulated. This fundamental shift in the theory of knowledge has had an enormous influence on all the sciences, notably anthropology and psychology, and, through them, on theology.

I shall take up this point in a later chapter. For our immediate purposes it is essential to take note of the rise of a new historicism. The danger of reading into other cultures and epochs the thought-forms of our own has always been there, as the history of theology makes plain. One of the positive results of the shift to the subject was that the social and historical sciences quickly drew attention to the context within which ideas and beliefs develop. Theology too,

14

anchored in an historical revelation, was forced to take note of research into the origins of that revelation. Thus towards the end of the century, with the progress being made in the scientific study of religious phenomena, enormous stress was laid on properly objective study: understanding all religions, including Christianity, in their correct cultural context. This, of course, had its own effect on the study of Christian origins; it suffices to mention in passing Strauss's work on the gospel tradition which increased scepticism about the possibility of grounding Christianity in a specific historical revelation. And as the traditional ways of studying Christianity found themselves open to challenge, so interest in other forms of religious experience grew by leaps and bounds. The texts and teachings of non-Christian religions had for centuries remained the preserve of a few eccentrics, but in the imperial age scholarly research into ancient learning and exotic cultures became a major growth industry, so that by the end of the nineteenth century the new discipline of Religious Studies, sometimes referred to as the History of Religions or Comparative Religion, had begun to emerge.

At the same time another current of thought can be detected which is an attempt to counter the scepticism encouraged by the turn to the subject —the Kantian 'Copernican Revolution'. This is the growth of religious idealism: the attempt to anchor religion in a particular intuitive sense or idea and thus to safeguard the autonomy of theology and free it from the strictures of historical method. Largely through the influence of Schleiermacher one gets a new theory of religion as a certain fundamental awareness of the divine which, *de facto,* is common to all the historical religions. Schleiermacher's grounding of religion in the *a priori* 'feeling of absolute dependence' opened up the possibility of understanding all religion in terms of inner experience. Christianity becomes one, albeit the highest, expression of this universal religious sense. Historicism and idealism are just a couple of the strands which go to make up the complex theological school known as liberal protestantism which, by the end of the nineteenth century, formed the dominant apologetic for Christian missionary activity. Add to all this the rise of evolutionary thinking associated with the names of Darwin and Huxley and we arrive at a fulfilment theory of the relationship of Christianity and other religions. Religions, like any other aspect of the human species, could be shown to be in process of development. How is Christianity the 'absolute' religion? It is simply the highest point yet achieved in the human movement towards the Absolute.

The most influential exponent of this type of theological pluralism

15

is the German liberal theologian, Ernst Troeltsch, who died in 1923. As a historian of religion Troeltsch sees religions as a series of separate complexes and more particularly sees Christianity as a historical phenomenon which must be set in its own context and not treated as a unique supernatural entity which owes nothing to the culture out of which it has been formed. At the same time, Troeltsch the Christian theologian is concerned to seek out elements of transcendent value in the multiformity of religious culture which can be evaluated in such a way as to show the absolute or unique status of Christianity. Troeltsch's theory of the relationship of religions is notoriously difficult to interpret. Nevertheless it is still a remarkable attempt to marry together the two sides of the liberal protestant inheritance. He finds in human subjectivity an innate orientation towards the Divine, an *a priori* religious sense, which, precisely because it is fully human, can only be realized in the firmly historical and social reality in which human beings exist – namely, the particular religious traditions of humankind. Thus all religions are relative, i.e. finite, expressions of the one inexpressible Absolute. But what about the traditional claims of Christianity to represent a unique revelation of that Absolute? This, of course, is the problem. At first Troeltsch seems content to see Christianity as the culmination of all religious endeavour. Later he realizes that this will not do and that the only way of distinguishing between religions is in terms of cultural appropriateness and personal commitment. In the end he can only manage to give Christianity a sort of provisional status. It is perfectly possible to envisage a religion which will supersede Christianity in terms of ultimate status. Thus God's revelation in the Old Testament and in Christ are only stages in a general and continuing revelation. And in this present time Christ is the means by which I, as a particular individual born and brought up in the Christian tradition, grasp something of the essence of the religious sense. But absolute validity can no more be claimed for my particular religious commitment than it can for that of any religion. It follows, therefore, that truth can only be truth *for me*, for my culture and my religion. Troeltsch comes up with a sort of 'relatively absolute' status for Christianity which looks suspiciously like a contradiction in terms.[17]

Much current thinking in the theology of religions takes its rise from Troeltsch's agenda. (Pluralism often finds itself shifting in the direction of relativism, and becoming as general and difficult to pin down as extreme exclusivism is dogmatic and impervious to argument. To some extent pluralism is saying no more than that religions are partial, incomplete and only one way of looking at a complex whole. In that case what Panikkar calls 'parallelism' would seem a more helpful term to use. But a more developed relativist version becomes a thesis about the way religion is linked to culture. Thus, says the relativist, religions are particular frameworks of belief and behaviour which have a certain *internal* coherence. One can therefore raise questions about the truth or falsity of individual assertions within the framework. What one cannot do is ask whether the framework *as a whole* is true or false. This is because a religion is by definition culture-relative; it can only be understood in relation to particular cultures and customs which are appropriate to particular people. Why are people Christian rather than Hindu, Muslim rather than Buddhist? The obvious answer is that they were born into that religion. Statistically this makes sense; a random sample of Thais or Sri Lankans would produce a vast majority of Buddhists whereas a group of Iranians or Pakistanis is more likely to be Muslim. But statistics are often a poor guide and, while one cannot ignore the obvious connection between culture and religion, it is just not the case that religious commitment is culture-dependent or culturally conditioned. If religions *were* identical with culture then the question of truth-claims might be a lot easier to solve. It is, however, all too easy to say that religions are only true for particular communities and have no truth-value outside that community; that religious commitment can, in practice, be reduced to a question of birth. If this were the case, then it would be only a short step to say that Hinduism is true for Indians, Christianity for Europeans, etc. Truth, in other words, is relative to culture.[18]

Many pluralists would accept the logic of this development and are careful to avoid the charge of relativism; but pluralism does not imply relativism any more than exclusivism demands a totally negative judgement on the religions. It would be quite wrong to assume that theologians are unaware of the other side of the argument, that the so-called exclusivist is irrevocably committed to one extreme and the pluralist to the other. A striking feature of contemporary theology is its ecumenical dimension; theologians operate both from the centre of their own tradition and at the fringes of others. It is enough to note for the moment that pluralists are conscious of the data of religious studies and the experience of dialogue. They make us wary of the assumption that each religious tradition is separate and self-sufficient, that it has no need to develop or change or to be enriched by outside influences. The self-sufficient status of theologies, not to mention religious traditions themselves, is denied by the evidence of history. Religions and the theologies to which they give rise are not static systems. As I shall hope to show, they all depend, and are based, on a complex relationship between ancient traditions and symbols, on the one hand, and an ever-changing set of social and material conditions of experience on the other.

The Reaction of Dialectical Theology

What, then, of the origins of the so-called exclusivist wing? Troeltsch's pluralism, if not exactly relativist, does raise a fundamental challenge to much traditional Christian thinking. If it is true that all religions including Christianity are culturally and historically conditioned, how are we to argue for the privileged status of the Christian revelation? The fundamental tenet of Christian faith is that in the incarnation of Jesus Christ the Absolute has taken a historical form in which is made present the definitive revelation of God. In which case does it not follow that God is known to us only insofar as he makes himself known? Liberal theology tended to see all religions as part of a cultural continuum, expressions of an *a priori* religious awareness of the Divine. The reaction was led by the dialectical theology associated with the name of Karl Barth.[19]

The emergence of the historical study of religions in the nineteenth century put all forms of knowing, including the religious, on the same level, thus making religion inseparable from culture. The dialectical theologians reinstated the authoritative position originally held by the Church but now expressed by the Word of God revealed in the Bible. Thus the position of a liberal theologian like Troeltsch seems to be that religion, of its very nature, gives partial and limited glimpses of an Eternal Truth. Truth is therefore something which grows gradually. We remain always pilgrims on a journey of faith towards an Infinite and Incomprehensible Mystery which cannot be encapsulated in the whole wealth of the religious traditions of the world, let alone in one. This all sounds very reasonable, but what sort of theology of religions results? Troeltsch looks for criteria by which to distinguish between religions and proposes relative human *values*; Christianity is the highest religion because it represents the highest point of human development. This, however, seems to beg the question: how does our finite humanity come to know that which is Unlimited and Absolute? To Troeltsch's agnosticism Barth replied with a massively articulate theology of the Word of God: we know God not because of

18

any innate capacity to understand God or to discern him in what are essentially human values, but simply because God has chosen to reveal himself to us. Through the miracle of faith we come to acknowledge the true nature of our existence – to know our sinfulness and radical distinction from God, on the one hand, and to experience the love and forgiveness which are revealed in the death and resurrection of Christ, on the other.

Now Barth did not set out to write a theology of religions as such. His importance from our point of view is that he gave expression to a very different type of theology from the fulfilment theories of the liberals. He stands, therefore, towards the other end of our theological spectrum: God's Truth is revealed in Christ, and only in Christ, the Word of God for all peoples and all religions. In the first place his theology should be seen very much as a reaction against theories of religion which made Christianity the highest evolution of some sort of universal religious consciousness. Barth attacks the relativism implicit in the liberals' concern for religious values. Such evolutionist thinking, especially after the disaster of the First World War, fails to take seriously the reality of evil and human sinfulness. Rather, says Barth, we must recognize the infinite qualitative distinction between God and humanity and return to the heart of the Reformation proclamation of the gospel, the Good News of God's salvation through faith, not works. 'Let God be God', is Barth's fundamental premise. God is the totally Other, standing in opposition to all that is human; Barth's main concern is to maintain the sovereignty of God and his freedom to act and to reveal himself. God is not to be constrained by any human activity. Hence the radical and unambiguous distinction which Barth makes between religion and revelation. All human religion, including Christianity as a historical phenomenon, comes under the judgement of God. Men, says Barth, thought they were talking about God when they were just talking about themselves at the top of their voices. God is not a human projection; so much of human religiosity makes God in our image and thus reduces him to our level. In a telling phrase Barth refers to religion as 'unbelief . . . a concern . . . the one great concern of godless man'. It is therefore God's revelation in Christ which relativizes religion, not the world of religions which relativizes revelation.[20]

This is a quite uncompromising Christ-centred (if not Christianity-centred) theology of religions. Together with as influential a figure as Hendrik Kraemer, Barth is usually taken to task, however, for his negative judgement on non-Christian traditions about which he admitted he knew nothing.[21] We may well ask whether this dialectical method of doing theology – setting the 'Yes' of God's revelation in tension with the 'No' of human ignorance and sin – really presents us with the language and the concepts to deal adequately with the problem. It is clear that there is an important insight here, and I shall want to argue later that a sort of dialectical structure is to be found in all religions. But Barth and even Kraemer are at best ambiguous about whether the religions are the source of general, let alone special, revelation. This takes us back to our problem about the knowledge of the Divine. We find that Barth takes it as axiomatic that knowledge of God comes only through God's revelation and that revelation is only in and through the Word of God. His theology is thoroughly christocentric.

As a biblically-based account of God's free and loving activity in which he reveals his salvific will for humankind through the Good News of the death and resurrection of Jesus Christ, Barth's theology reminds us of the demands of the old problematic. But how is that Good News to apply to people who have either never heard of Christ or, more awkwardly, having heard of him are quite content to remain practising their ancient traditional faith and feel no compulsion towards conversion? Barth's vision of the love of God revealing itself in the life of sinful human beings has at least one major weakness. It limits the mode of revelation of God's will to the proclamation of the gospel; implicitly it presents us with a model of a God who is known only through the preaching activity of his Church. But – we may well want to ask – cannot God be known in any other way? Are we correct in limiting the salvific activity of God to one particular mode or form? It may be that Barth does full justice to the Pauline and Reformation understanding of justification through faith alone, but is this the whole of the Christian tradition? Reformed theology wants to stress the discontinuity of faith: it is something totally new which breaks in and, as it were, overthrows human religiosity. The inclusivist Catholic tradition, on the other hand, with a broader sense of the sacramental, seeks always to maintain a certain continuity between Nature and Grace; God can be known through his effects, through the signs which he has left in the world, and thus through all that is truly human, even the searchings and strivings of human religion.

The Two Problematics

The above must suffice as an account of the two wings of the 'dialectical morass'. It is clear that what we are dealing with are not dull academic musings but some of the key issues in theology and the study of religion. Thus far all I want to emphasize is that theology must try to hold together the insights represented by Troeltsch and Barth. Both theologians would strongly have rejected the description of their theology as 'relativist' and 'exclusivist', and it seems to me to be essential to consider in more detail the agenda and the problems which their theological methods raise. In passing we have already raised some of the more obvious questions: the christological dilemma about the unique or normative status of Christ and, dependent on that, the place of the Church and the nature and purpose of Christian mission. There is, however, a more fundamental issue: how can one speak of 'knowing' God? Is Christ the only or the 'one way'? Are there other ways and, if so, how are they related to Christ? Dominating the whole controversy about religion and revelation is the question about continuity or discontinuity: are religions fundamentally continuous with each other, different manifestations of a universal human religiosity, some version of Schleiermacher's religious *a priori*? Or is Barth correct in positing a total discontinuity between 'religion' as *our* effort to reach God and 'revelation' as *God's* movement towards us in Christ? This in turn raises another issue: the nature of religion and human religiosity. Must it necessarily have the negative connotations which the Barthian tradition puts upon it? Such a fundamental premise seems to have prejudged what is really a philosophical question about the nature of religion and human knowing with a theological statement about the way that God is present in the world of religions. Theology, in Barthian terms, must be considered internal to one religion. The liberals question this: how much should theology be purely confessional – the articulation of one tradition – and how much should it be based on the data of religious experience generally? Troeltsch's dilemma, as we have seen, is how to get the balance right: on the one hand, there is the claim of Christianity to be, in some sense, the absolute religion which is true for all humankind, and on the other, the claims of the whole world of the great religious traditions to their own autonomy and right to judge Christianity as Christianity judges them.

The aim of this survey of the 'dialectical morass', as it has emerged in this century, has been to show something of the very different agendas which are being proposed for a theology of religions. I have spoken above of a 'spectrum' of opinions, but such a title does not get us all that far until we begin to examine the context within which

21

these theologies operate. It may be possible to bring the three paradigms together as theories or 'answers', but – to repeat – they are in fact based on very different questions or perceptions of the problem. All are united in their concern for truth. But whereas the liberal wing, following Troeltsch, think of religious truth in global terms – that truth is a function of the whole religious history of humankind – those who take Barth's dialectical line operate within a quite different framework. For them truth emerges from the articulation of the Christian tradition itself. Obviously we are faced with a crucial question here: the nature of the theological enterprise. A pluralist theology of religions starts from empiricist presuppositions. Truth-claims are to be adjudicated by observation between the religions. Confessional theology, on the other hand, is based on an authoritative tradition which – almost by definition – is considered the touchstone of truth by which all others are to be judged. The two ends of the spectrum see the nature and purpose of theology quite differently.

In this chapter I have tried to show where these different theologies are coming from; my object in the next three will be to explore in more detail the language, the logic and the presuppositions of the three paradigms, not with a view to developing a new spectrum, but in order to show how the old and the new problematics are related. This will, I hope, shift the emphasis away from the more traditional forms of Christianity-centred theology towards something more focused on the inter-faith dialogue itself in which the other has a more positive role to play.

Notes

1. cf. 'The "Established" Church as Mission: the Relation of the Church to the Modern World' by Roger D. Haight, *The Jurist* 39 (1979), pp. 4–39.
2. A bibliography to show this judgement to be less than superficial would necessarily be enormous. A series of articles which survey the field in some detail has recently been published in the 'Theological Trends' series of *The Way* by John Ball. He covers the three areas mentioned above: 'Incarnational Christianity', January 1985, pp. 54–61; 'Liberation Theology', April 1985, pp. 140–148; 'The World Religions', January 1986, pp. 53–60. The most authoritative guide to contemporary trends in missiology is the *International Review of Mission*. A Roman Catholic perspective is to be found in the publications of *Pro Mundi Vita*, an international information and research centre in Brussels.

3. For a masterly attempt to unravel the various strands of this problem see Robert J. Schreiter, *Constructing Local Theologies*, London: SCM 1985.

4. A select bibliography on the theology of religions is appended to this book. For a brief bibliography, with commentary, see Gavin D'Costa, '20th Century Christian Attitudes to Other Religions: a Bibliographical Guide', *Anvil*, vol. 4, no 2 (1987), pp. 175–185. To this should be added three collections of papers which reflect the debate as it has emerged in the United States: *The Myth of Christian Uniqueness*, edited by John Hick and Paul F. Knitter, New York: Orbis 1987; *Towards a Universal Theology of Religions*, edited by Leonard Swidler, New York: Orbis 1987; *Religious Pluralism*, edited by Leroy S. Rouner, Notre Dame, IN: University of Notre Dame Press 1984. Records of, and comments on, actual dialogue are to be found in various journals, such as the *Bulletin* of the Vatican Secretariat for Non-Christians, *Current Dialogue* from the WCC, *The Ecumenical Review* and *The Journal of Ecumenical Studies*. A recent, and welcome, addition which aims to cope specifically with the British scene is *Discernment*, published by the BCC.

5. The missionary crisis faced by the Church is summed up by Juan Luis Segundo in *The Liberation of Theology*, Dublin: Gill and Macmillan 1977, p. 213: 'If it is true that the number of those converted to Christian faith and practice has no direct relationship with the number of the saved, then why go out and convert people? Why have faith and the Church at all?'

6. Protestant theology in India has a long and distinguished history, boasting such names as M.M. Thomas, Paul Devanandan and Stanley Samartha. An excellent survey of the theology of all traditions and denominations in India is Robin Boyd's *An Introduction to Indian Christian Theology*, Madras: Christian Literature Society 1969. For a more systematic biblically-based theology see his *Khristadvaita, A Theology for India*, Madras: CLS 1977. Since the Second Vatican Council the lead in theological thinking in India has passed to the Roman Catholic Church. Here we are less indebted to a few influential individuals and creative studies, and much more to theological centres and colleges which support cooperative enterprises, such as the National Biblical Catechetical and Liturgical Centre (NBCLC) and Dharmaram College, both in Bangalore, the Vidyajyoti Institute in Delhi and the Jnanadeepa Vidyapeeth near Pune. Notable collections of essays, conference addresses and articles are *Research Seminar on non-Biblical Scriptures*, ed. D.S. Amaloparvadass, NBCLC 1974; *Theologizing in India*, ed. M. Amaladoss, T.K. John and G. Gispert-Sauch, Bangalore: Theological Publications 1981; *God's Word Amongst Men*, ed. G. Gispert-Sauch, Delhi: Vidyajyoti 1973.

7. In today's India many Hindus profess a great admiration for, if not faith in, Christ without ever seeing any need to convert exclusively to Christianity. Hans Staffner SJ in *The Significance of Jesus Christ in Asia*, Anand, India: Gujarat Sahitya Prakash 1985, has collected

23

together various examples of Hindu responses to Christ, including those 'to whom Christ's social teaching was a source of inspiration', those 'intensely committed to Christ but found it difficult to join in any of the existing churches', and those 'who claimed to remain Hindus'. Bede Griffiths, acarya-leader of the Saccidananda Ashram at Shantivanam, Tamil Nadu, and author of several books on Hindu-Christian dialogue (including *Return to the Centre*, London: Collins 1976 and *The Marriage of East and West*, London: Collins 1982; see also the biography of Griffiths by Kathryn Spink, *A Sense of the Sacred*, London: SPCK 1988) has remarked that India has not rejected Christ but it has rejected his European Church (cf. *The Tablet*, 13 February 1986).

8.   'Dialogue and Mission: Conflict or Convergence?', *International Review of Mission* 75 (1986), pp. 222–240.

9.   Thomas Kuhn, *The Structure of Scientific Revolutions*, 2nd ed., Chicago, IL: University of Chicago Press 1970.

10. 'A Paradigm Shift? Evangelicals and Interreligious Dialogue', in *Missiology* 9 (1981), pp. 393–408. Glasser shows how evangelicals are beginning to face the changing climate in inter-faith relations.

11. The key text is *God and the Universe of Faiths*, London: Macmillan 1973, but, as D'Costa points out in his *John Hick's Theology of Religions*, Washington, DC: University Press of America 1987, Hick's thought and ever-developing arguments need to be understood in the full context of his personal history.

12. Alan Race, *Christians and Religious Pluralism: Patterns in the Christian Theology of Religions*, London: SCM 1983.

13. Gavin D'Costa, *Theology and Religious Pluralism: The Challenge of Other Religions*, Oxford: Blackwells 1986.

14. Paul F. Knitter, *No Other Name?: A Critical Survey of Christian Attitudes Toward the World Religions*. London: SCM 1985.

15. Raimundo Panikkar, *The Intra-Religious Dialogue*, New York: Paulist Press 1978.

16. cf. Harold Coward, *Pluralism, Challenge to World Religions*, New York: Orbis 1985, p. 25. The particular value of Coward's book is that, however briefly, he manages to give some account of how *all* religions, not just Christianity, recognize and deal with the problem of the other.

17. Troeltsch's 'early' position is to be found in *The Absoluteness of Christianity and the History of Religions*, London: SCM 1972. His 'later' position is best represented by the posthumous essay, 'The Place of Christianity among the World Religions', originally published in *Christian Thought: Its History and Application*, London 1923, and available in the collection *Christianity and Other Religions*, edited by John Hick and Brian Hebblethwaite, London: Fount 1980. A full bibliography of Troeltsch's works is to be found in *Ernst Troeltsch and the Future of Theology*, edited by John Powell Clayton, Cambridge: Cambridge University Press 1976.

18. An excellent account of the various issues at stake in this area is 'Theology and Cultural Relativism: What is the Problem?' by Sarah

Coakley in *Neue Zeitschrift für Theologie und Religionsphilosophie* 21 (1979), pp. 223–243.
19. J. Aagaard, in 'Revelation and Religion', *Studia Theologica* 1960, pp. 148–85, suggests that the liberal theology to which Barth reacted was concerned primarily with religious values and understood religion as 'the highest peak of the life of the human spirit' (p. 155). Christianity as the most developed expression of this life is simply the fulfilment of all other religions.
20. *Church Dogmatics*, 1/2, pp. 280–361.
21. Race sees Barth's theology as 'the most extreme form of the exclusivist theory' (op. cit., pp. 11–17) and Knitter makes him the prime representative of what he calls the 'conservative evangelical model' (op. cit. pp. 80–87). Race refers to Barth's oft-quoted and much misunderstood conversation with D.T. Niles in which Barth justifies his assertion that Hinduism is 'unbelief' on purely *a priori* grounds; cf. D'Costa, *Theology and Religious Pluralism*, p. 52.

2 RELIGIONS AND THE WORD OF GOD

For all their usefulness in summarizing theological opinion about the relationship of religions, our surveys have the singular disadvantage of presuming that all theologians are asking the same questions. Even as perceptive an account as that of Peter Schineller, with its diagrammatic summary, tends inevitably to gloss over the problem.[1] To an extent the spectrum idea is helpful. At one end stand the exclusivists for whom the absolute status of the Christian revelation must be maintained against the false claims of other religions; at the other are the radical relativists for whom there is no such thing as absolute truth in religion: all religions are equally valid paths to the *summum bonum*, however that is to be formulated. All the issues are here, but how are we to judge between these positions? All have very different views of the nature and relative importance of the key concepts – religion, revelation, church, salvation, mission – not to mention the place of Christ or ways of deciding between a variety of different truth-claims. I make no apologies in what follows, therefore, for probing beyond the popular images set up by the paradigms and discerning what sort of agenda different theologians are running.

In the last chapter we looked at the origins of the dialectical morass; in this one I want to examine the notion that the so-called exclusivists have nothing to offer to a theology of religions. What is exclusivism anyway? How does it contribute to the current debate? And where does it differ from its inclusivist sister? That there is such a way of thinking as exclusivism among Christians is obviously – and sadly – still the case. It is true that there are fundamentalist sects which seem content to condemn non-Christians to hell-fire for the singular crime of being ignorant of Christ. And not only fundamentalists but more mainstream evangelicals are constantly harping on the millions who have never heard the gospel and are therefore *ex hypothesi* beyond the bounds of eternal salvation. Nor should we be too slick in our dimissal of exclusivism as part of the extremist fringe. Sometimes it appears closer to home. Until fairly recently traditional Catholic theology has tended to be exclusivist, distinguishing between those within and those outside the Church, which is defined in rigidly institutional, not to say political, terms.

To consider this last point in detail would take us far afield into the history of Christian missions and a very different theology of religious pluralism, in which our ancestors confronted a world neatly divided into Christians and pagans and infidels.[2] But there is no point in wasting time on empty polemics; our whole understanding of the Church – and the relationship of the churches – has changed with the coming of the ecumenical age.[3]

It is not, however, the near total lack of ecumenical vision which raises difficulties with such conservative and exclusivist theologies of religions. Many evangelists set themselves a major problem with the salvation of the non-believer. In emphasizing the need for some empirical historical contact with the Word of God they make it difficult to build any sort of bridge between Jesus Christ and the great world religions. But again we must ask: what sort of a model of theology does this betray?[4] The stress is very squarely on the articulation of the Word of God, the proclamation that Jesus is Lord. Mission means bringing people's attention to the Word, for that is the only way they can encounter the Lord Jesus Christ who is the one source of truth and salvation. A brief reflection on the thinking behind this concept is instructive. If God is revealed exclusively through his Word, it is obvious that one must face the problem of how that Word is to be heard. Hence the high energy, high tech, high efficiency, evangelical movements, mainly based in the USA, which seek to propagandize the Third World with their own particular brand of God-culture. Their zeal is impressive, their motivation questionable. A highly selective use of biblical texts makes for a total distortion of the true nature of Christian mission. One example will suffice. Most evangelists begin from a literal interpretation of Jesus' great commission at the end of Matthew's Gospel: 'Go and make disciples of all nations, baptizing them in the name of the Father and of the Son and of the Holy Spirit' (28.19–20). Obedience is the fundamental virtue. The command is to 'make disciples', who are modelled on the evangelist himself, fully regenerated in the Spirit, and responsible and committed members of the Body of Christ, the Church.[5] But should the Gospel be interpreted in this way? Can it be interpreted literally? Most exegetes would make the Great Commission dependent on the Great Commandment – which, on any reading of the Gospel, must be considered prior. The command to love God above all things and one's neighbour as oneself must be seen against the whole context of God's revelation of himself to his people. Evangelical theology need not be fundamentalist, but it still begs the question: what is the relationship between the Word which is Truth and Life and the words of the gospel in which, as Christians believe, the revelation of God himself is conveyed? How do we set about interpreting what is, after all, a formula of words before it is *the* Word? More is implied in the science of theology than reading the Scriptures more loudly. Theology is first and foremost a science of interpretation, and problems raised by the interpretation of Scripture are the biggest objection to exclusivist thinking. Nor is this just a peculiarly Protestant problem. While it is raised in an acute form in all schools of Protestant theology which pay special attention to biblical theology, Roman Catholics cannot afford to be complacent; the recovery of a sense of Scripture as the root of all theology has perhaps been the greatest revolution in the thinking of the Roman Catholic Church since Vatican II.

We shall have more to say about this key issue in due course. Meanwhile let us concentrate on the connotations of the word 'exclusivism'. It implies a narrow elitism, a religion of the privileged initiates, which in some shape or form has been the order of the day for centuries (and in some obscurantist corners still is). However it does not follow that the term 'exclusivism' is appropriate to cover all forms of Protestantism. Such a title gives the impression that the main concern of the theologian is to defend an ecclesiocentric universe (i.e. identifying Christ with the visible Church) against the false claims of other visible institutions, the religions. Allowances must certainly be made for the highly regrettable Christian chauvinism of the not so distant past, but as a reading of contemporary mainstream Catholic and Protestant theology it will not do. The task of theology, both Catholic and Protestant, is certainly to work from within a tradition. But the object need not be narrowly apologetic or polemical. In fact all the signs are that the mainstream of what I have referred to as a confessional theology of religions is concerned simply to work out the implications of the Mystery of Christ in a very new situation – the world of many religions and of none. That there are more and less adequate versions of this type of theology is obvious, but in itself unremarkable. My contention is that the title 'exclusivism' is misleading. It suggests that theologians are only concerned for who is and who is not to be excluded from the company of the elect. But to speak of Barth – and perhaps even of Kraemer – as exclusivists, and therefore by implication somehow to be opposed to Rahner and the Catholic tradition who are seen as fundamentally inclusivists, seems to be somewhat question-begging to say the least. It is not that Barth *excludes* all non-Christians *a priori* from the possibility of salvation and that Rahner by a Jesuitical sleight of hand

28

known as the 'Anonymous Christian' argument manages to *include* them. Rather both are fundamentally universalist in their answer to the old problematic, the salvation of the non-Christian. Each posits the salvation of the non-Christian; they differ in their explanations of *how* it is possible.

The fundamental task of the confessional theologian is the articulation of the Christian tradition as something which is in some way true for all people. Certainly the answers are very different and some theological premises seem almost inevitably to give an unhelpfully elitist tinge to their soteriology. But this should not obscure the fact that the various ways of doing confessional theology are to be distinguished in degree rather than in type. We have already mentioned the influential names of Karl Barth and Karl Rahner. It is obviously true that they belong to quite distinct theological traditions and have different interests. But the 'exclusivism' and 'inclusivism' associated with them are similar at least to the extent that they conceive of the *purpose* of theology in the same way. Thus it seems to me to make sense in the first place to concentrate on what holds Protestant and Catholic theologians together rather than on what divides them. For all their differences, my contention is that they are united at least in their concern to extend, rather than minimize, the mystery of God's activity in Christ. If this is the case, then it must follow that the distinction beteen these two paradigms is false. With due exception made for the extremes, what are often called exclusivism and inclusivism are not separate positions but versions of the same *universalist* premise – different sides of the same coin, as it were. The difference between them depends on how they see that salvation being extended to those outside the visible Church and therefore on the values of the religions as such.

Barth's Universalism

A positive reading of Barth on the religions does seem to go against much current theological opinion which identifies Barthianism with the worst kind of Christian arrogance. His is usually taken to be a negative attitude, rejecting all religious traditions other than the Christian as totally false. The problem is that he is too easily taken to be the spokesman for evangelical Protestantism as a whole, which, given the vastness of his output, is hardly surprising. His is a thoroughly christocentric theology which tends to put all others in the shade: but to make him *the* example of the Reformed theology of religions suggests a fundamental confusion. That Barth can be used to back a certain *a priori* exclusivist position *vis-à-vis* the religions is clear. It has been done. But it all depends on which Barth one reads. Like Troeltsch, Barth changed his approach over a long and active life. The early Barth is negative. Here his main concern is with a particular interpretation of religion; he never intended to write a theology of religions, and indeed never till the end of his life did he consider the religions as a theological problem.[6] In the later Barth, we get a totally different emphasis on the nature of redeemed humanity. Here is a universalism which does deal very positively with the old, if not the new, problematic.

This account of Barth's implicit theology of religions needs to be spelled out in more detail. What is this vision of a redeemed humanity? In what way can it be said to include those outside the explicitly Christian fold? I have already given a summary of his interpretation of human religiosity with its celebrated distinction between Religion and Revelation. The two are opposed quite radically; God reveals himself uniquely in Jesus Christ, thus consigning all natural theology and, by implication, all religions to the category of 'unbelief', mere human striving for the Divine. So strongly is this put that we seem irrevocably condemned to an exclusivist version of Christianity. Is there any way across the divide? Certainly we must admit that a lot of Barth's language, not to say his whole personal orientation, is unsympathetic, but we must also take note both of his overall style and method and of the context of the earlier volumes.

This latter point is made with some clarity by Moltmann.[7] Barth, he reminds us, was setting up his dialectical theology at a time when the 'bourgeois Christian world' was declining. The alternatives we face, religion as human self-assertion or faith as a response to God's self-revelation, were keenly felt by Barth. He levelled his attack not against the world religions but against what he sees as the real enemies of biblical faith: superstition and self-righteousness. It is therefore a mistake to see his criticism of religion as directed against the Hindu or the Muslim. Barth sets out to write a theology of religion, not religions in the plural. Secondly we should note that he writes rhetorically rather than systematically, piling argument on argument, with the express purpose of allowing the Word of God to unfold itself. His is a theology of proclamation, rather than a point by point analysis. What emerges is dialectical theology in which the emphasis is seen to shift from the negative, the 'No' of God's judgement, to the positive 'Yes' of divine election. To take one particular statement in isolation risks distorting the whole. Each part responds to a particular situation. The polemics of *Romans* and the early volumes of the *Church Dogmatics* are not to be taken as normative of Barth's theology as a whole; rather they should be set dialectically against the more visionary account of Christian anthropology which we find in the later writings. Here he moves away from a strongly christocentric bias and seems much more ready to emphasize the role of the Holy Spirit in the work of salvation.

Barth allows that Christ died for all people, not just for Christians; indeed he is bound to say this, for anything less would be to put limits to the salvific power of God. But the truly universalist nature of his soteriology comes in his treatment of divine election. Jesus Christ is both God who elects and Man who is elected. Through Christ humanity is somehow involved in the divine self-election. What is revealed in the incarnation is a sort of reciprocal movement: God 'elects himself' through the person of his son and in his son he elects the whole of humankind.[8] It is this prior activity of God's grace, revealed in Christ, which changes the human situation. For Barth, Jesus is the chosen one whose election makes for a real and objective change in the very nature of the humanity he represents. But Jesus is more than an example of redeemed humanity: he *is* humanity. And that means that, at least in principle, there can be no real distinction between Christian and non-Christian. The difference lies at the level of explicit knowledge of what God has revealed of himself in Christ. Christians are not *ipso facto* the community of the redeemed set apart from those outside the fold. They are the ones who know in faith what this mystery of God's love is accomplishing in the world. The distinction is between faith and unbelief – the correlates of revelation and religion – and between the faithless, whether Christian or no, and the unbelieving.

The question of whether explicit knowledge of God is possible outside the revelation in Jesus Christ raises, of course, other problems about the value of the religions as such, which we will have to consider in due course. But as far as the old problematic is concerned, Barth is far from negative. He operates within an eschatological perspective. What is necessary for salvation has already been accomplished in Christ; its fullness is something which necessarily we await in the future. The individual stands in a potential relationship of faith to the Word which only needs time to be made quite explicit. The non-Christian is saved in exactly the same way as the Christian – through the grace of God, not through the works of religion. To that extent it seems safe to say that there is no problem over the salvation of the individual, even if we have to say that the

31

individual is saved despite his religion rather than because of it. What, then, of the religions themselves? As we have already noted, the basic thesis of the early Barth is that human religion is to be transformed by the revelation of God in Christ. Here Barth introduces the term *Aufhebung* with its deliberately ambiguous or perhaps dialectical meaning, of 'abolition' and 'elevation'.[9] In the first place Barth is criticizing all human self-assertion, especially in Christianity itself which, all too easily, can ignore or overlook the central affirmation that Christ has come for the reconciliation of the whole world. He is not, therefore, entering into a polemic against the religions as such. He wants to affirm that religion can be considered 'true' once it has been elevated by grace – just as any human sinner can be justified by grace. In the first part of the *Dogmatics* he shows how it is possible to speak of Christianity as 'true' religion – once it is 'elevated' by the grace of God to a life of obedience to the Word. However, in Volume Four the perspective has changed from the sovereignty of God to the *humanity* of Christ. The whole movement seems to be the other way, spelling out the implications of our 'horizontal' relationship with the Father. What is revealed in Christ is the truth about our *redeemed* nature; Christ as the one who exists for everyone else becomes, as it were, the mirror who reflects the truth of what they are to become in imitation of him.[10]

The fact that this revelation comes about only through Christ does not, in Barth's terms, make for an exclusivist insistence on the historical form which that revelation has taken in Christianity. Precisely because the Word is the centre and the limit of that revelation, 'other words' may be true insofar as they reflect the fullness of the Word. Barth admits that in a world of sin and secularism it is impossible to articulate 'the truth of the one Word of God, Jesus Christ Himself' through any form of human words – whether in the Bible or Church or outside. The assurance that that revelation is given comes not through any human experience of sincerity or piety but through the relationship of faith established by God himself in Jesus Christ, the Word of God. But the possibility cannot be discounted that the Word *is* spoken outside. If there are 'other words', 'they are true words only as they refer back to their origin in the one Word, i.e., as the one true Word, Jesus Christ himself, declares Himself in them'.[11] A theologian of religion will find Barth infuriatingly coy here. He never actually refers to 'other religions' or 'other faiths' since for him there is and can only be one revelation from which all others take their rise; but the implication that 'other words' can mean 'non-Christian religions' is there. He quickly changes from this unwonted reticence to his more normal rhetorical style as he goes on to speak of the criteria by which the signs of the one true light may be tested. Later he does speak explicitly of the non-Christian as existing 'in the world which God created good as the external basis of the covenant and therefore for this salvation, and which He has reconciled in Jesus Christ in fulfilment of this covenant and in realisations [sic] of the election in which he, too, is elect. He, too, is reconciled to God. Jesus Christ died for him. And he rose again for him'.[12] It is true that the non-Christian is not yet caught up explicitly in the life of the Spirit, yet the promise of the Spirit has already been made for him and applies to him; it is harnessed, ready, and when the time comes no rebellion, sin or ignorance will be able to resist the power of the Spirit. Thus it is possible for an essentially human religion like Christianity to be 'sanctified' by the presence within it of the Holy Spirit. And while this only applies to Christianity as being the locus of the revelatory Word of God, it is still possible to understand all human religiosity as being eventually taken up into, or fulfilled by, the Holy Spirit. 'In this sense', says Barth, 'Jesus Christ is the hope even of these non-Christians'.[13]

So what of Barth's judgement on the religions as such? We note, first of all, that there is no exclusivist divide set between Christianity and the other religions. In historical Christianity, as 'true' religion, God's revelation is incarnated and takes shape: it is at the same time 'abolished' and 'elevated'. But precisely because it is religion, Christianity must be related to all other religions; there can be no absolute distinction of kind between them. And therefore it is possible to talk about God's revelation 'elevating' the world of non-Christian religion as well. It is true that Barth does not develop an explicit position vis-à-vis the world of non-Christian religion, but he does speak of the cosmos as a whole, using Calvin's terminology, as the theatrum gloriae Dei, and is prepared to accept that that world does reflect the light of the one true light, however corrupt humanity may be.[14] The world of religions, for all that it manifests a state of ignorance and superstition, stands in a real relationship to Christ – even if one needs to describe it in terms of a sort of potential which has still to be actually realized.

To sum up, then: Barth's point is that what God has done in Christ is *for all*, for those who confess and accept that relationship *and* for those who live unspiritual or sinful lives, in whom the work of transformation has still to be accomplished. His theology of religions is set in thoroughly eschatological terms, looking forward to the *parousia* when the definitive revelation of God's glory will be made. Meanwhile all we have are signs of the mystery which is Christ, the religions which are both reflections of the light of revelation and potential recipients of the promise of the Spirit. The negative judgement on the religions in Volume One finds a new context in Volume Four: the dialectic has shifted and the fulfilment theme been brought to the fore. But the relationship between religion and revelation remains dialectical, for that is the way the mystery of God's being is seen to unfold, elevating humankind to that vision of God's glory, which is the end and purpose of all religions. It may sound like another version of the liberal protestant theology of fulfilment, but what is being proposed here is really quite different. For the liberals fulfilment means some sort of evolution into the one absolute religion, to be identified with Christianity. In Barthian terms it has the sense of 'elevation', the state of gradual purification in which religion is exalted beyond itself by the action of God. Meanwhile the coming reign of God which Jesus announced is already growing; the world is already being transformed through the action of the Spirit.[15]

Shifting the Perspective: the Religions Themselves

Now my main concern has been to avoid the mistake of taking Barth – and the early Barth at that – as representative of evangelical exclusivism. There is a positive aspect to religion: it is not the searching and self-assertiveness of sinful humanity, but represents the human response to God's unveiling of himself in Christ. If we take the religious history of humankind seriously we recognize that God has been and is at work through his Spirit, preparing for the final revelation which will only be completed at the end of time. Such a perspective can be developed fruitfully in a much more openly universalist direction. At the same time a purely Barthian approach to the religions presents some major conceptual difficulties. I have already mentioned above one objection to Barth's evangelical theology. In concentrating so much on a model of salvation as enlightenment, in which the revelation of the truth about humankind must necessarily go hand in hand with a recognition of the free gift of God's mercy, Barth sets himself a very real problem about how the salvation of the non-Christian is actually accomplished. How can anyone be saved by the grace of God offered in Christ without actually *knowing* the truth proclaimed in the gospel? What can be said in Barth's defence is simply to repeat: he is not intending to write a theology of religions. Like most evangelicals he is quite prepared to leave the question of the salvation of the non-Christian to God himself. For Barth such questions are of little or no significance for an avowedly kerygmatic theology. The task of the theologian is not to produce a system of apologetics but to respond to *the* fact which differentiates the Christian from all other religions: faith in the 'philanthropic God Himself', the one who is revealed in the death and resurrection of Jesus Christ. 'Theology itself is a word, a human response; yet what makes it theology is not its own word or response but the Word which it hears and to which it responds. Theology stands and falls with the Word of God, for the Word of God precedes all theological words by creating, arousing, and challenging them'.[16] If this is true then it is small wonder that the 'problem of other religions' makes little impression on the pages of the *Church Dogmatics*. What we have is a highly Christ-centred and, indeed, Spirit-centred eschatological vision.

As a theology of the Word of God it clearly has a strongly missiological slant, but it does not necessarily follow that the fundamental perspective is 'exclusivist'. The problem surely lies elsewhere. I have tried to show that for Barth the world of the religions is the sphere of operation of the Spirit and, because that Spirit is already at work, there can be no absolute discontinuity between Christ and the non-Christian. But where is the link between the Word and the 'other words'? Barth cannot find much room for the values of the non-Christian religions as such; they are significant only insofar as they reflect the single truth that is Christ. And they cannot be considered salvific *in their own right*. This is the weakness which prompts the exclusivist tag. Can it be remedied by recourse to a more open and sympathetic account of the religions? Certainly this is what we might expect from Hendrik Kraemer, the celebrated Dutch missiologist and historian of religion.[17]

Kraemer stands in much the same Reformed tradition as Karl Barth and more often than not is put into the same 'exclusivist' bracket.[18] And it is only fair to admit that most Protestant mis-siology has still not found a way out of Kraemer's highly evangelical 'biblical realism' enunciated with such power at the famous Tam-baram ecumenical conference in 1938. As a theologian Kraemer lacks Barth's profundity but, unlike Barth, he speaks from real experience: he spent years in the field. He is wary of the dangers of praising and criticizing other faiths from an uncritical *a priori* standpoint. His attempt to wrestle with the implications of the old problematic is nothing if not instructive as an account of the encounter between evangelical theology and the religions.

Kraemer takes up a point made earlier by Troeltsch, that religions are *totalities* which consist of particular apprehensions of the whole of existence.[19] A religion is an indivisible unity; every aspect, practice, or dogma has to be related to the whole. What we should avoid is the all too frequent tendency to abstract bits from what is really a single and indivisible entity and reduce religious traditions to a few common elements. To do that is to take the religions less than seriously. Thus Kraemer is particularly critical of the liberal attempt to produce essences and common elements on the basis of perceived similarities. These can only be at best superficial and at worst positively misleading; they cannot provide any basis for assessing the truth-claims of particular religious doctrines or beliefs. Such beliefs can only be understood in their proper cultural, historical and – perhaps – geographical context. All these factors are important in the formation and growth of particular traditions. Thus Kraemer as the missionary strategist is clear that the Gospel message must be presented in forms appropriate to local cultures. His main point, however, is that what claims to be a universal message must find ways of making itself intelligible to all people; it cannot remain isolated within a Christian, or western, cultural form. Proper appreciation of non-Christian religious culture is an essential preparation for missionary activity: the proclamation of the Good News to all peoples. Thus for all that he resembles the pluralists in his reading of the wider religious scene, as a theologian he claims that it is only the grace of God revealed in Christ which can judge between the religions.

In several weighty and highly influential tomes Kraemer's 'biblical realism' spells out his reformed theology of mission. I have already drawn attention to the neo-orthodox perspective and pointed out that it was born of a reaction to liberal protestant theology which saw all religions as historically and culturally conditioned structures which could be set in some sort of continuum. In other words Christianity is not essentially different from any other religion.[20] But dialectical theology holds that the revelation in Christ is above all the religions, including Christianity, even though *de facto* that revelation is made through the historical forms of the Christian tradition. According to Kraemer the Bible confronts the 'bad news' of human sinfulness and self-seeking with the 'good news' of God's love for humankind revealed in Christ. Only God can reveal God; only God himself can bridge the infinite qualitative distinction between God and humanity. Our task is not to seek and strive to know God – that is the work of godless religions – but to accept our sinfulness and to open ourselves to the possibility of God's self-revelation which alone can save us. This is what God has done in Christ and only in Christ. We are saved by a gratuitous act of God's love, and by that alone.

Clearly there are important insights here about the nature of Christianity and, indeed, about the nature of human religiosity in general. Kraemer underlines the reality of evil in the world and the limitations of the human condition which simply cannot raise itself to God by some latter-day Pelagian 'will-to-power'. Kraemer's constant recourse to 'biblical realism' is indeed to show that once one has recognized the reality of evil in oneself, the idea of 'self-salvation' becomes ridiculous. One is thrown back to an act of faith in God, the only source of salvation. Secondly, like Barth, Kraemer seeks to maintain the 'privileged' status of Christianity as the locus of that salvation. Where the liberals posit a basic continuity between religions, dialectical theology insists on a radical discontinuity. In Christ, God has made a radical intervention in human history which puts all other insights or attempts to come to terms with the Divine in question. If God is God, this 'scandal of particularlity' is perfectly possible, even if it makes no 'logical' sense.[21] Evangelical theologians may have a point when they object to any attempt to reduce the historical Jesus of Nazareth to some sort of 'archetype' or exemplary model for human living. The cross of Christ is, in many ways, the ultimate question-mark which is put to all human efforts to accommodate or unite religions together.

This is the challenge which dialectical theology makes to the pluralists. It is all too easy, however, to cast Kraemer as the villain in the plot, the dogmatic exclusivist opposed to relativizing liberals. As already pointed out he is, for a start, just as aware as the pluralists of the complexities of the different world religions and the difficulties involved in their interpretation; the fundamental premises on which Kraemer operates may be those of dialectical theology, but he brings to the debate the perspective of the historian of religion and the practical missionary. For all his 'biblical realism' he is very critical of many of his fellow evangelicals and even of Barth. In the work which made such an impact at Tambaram, *The Christian Message in a Non-Christian World*, Kraemer emphasized the principle of discontinuity. In the Christian faith God reveals himself; non-Christian religions are the record of human striving and attempts to grasp the Divine. There can be no points of contact between the two and a theology of fulfilment is patently absurd. In *Religion and the Christian Faith*, published in 1956, the polemics have abated somewhat. Kraemer is less concerned to knock Hocking's liberal idealism on the head. Instead he turns his attention to the wider theological issues and the implications of a tradition which includes the Johannine Logos as well as the Pauline theology of justification by faith. He is clearly uneasy with Barth 'in spite of fundamental agreement'.[22] Kraemer applauds Barth's attack on all forms of relativism; Barth's insistence on the sovereignty of the biblical revelation is exactly right. The problem is that he is not biblical enough: 'He has the same passionate theological sincerity as the Reformers, but runs the risk, as they did, of reproducing a curtailed Paul'.[23] Kraemer seems more aware of the scriptural warrant for some sort of general revelation in non-Christian religions. God does speak to all people and it is impossible to ignore the signs of that revelation wherever people are seeking genuinely to know the Divine. Kraemer continues to stress that the revelation is made in Christ, but the character of the response – in all empirical religions – is dialectical: it contains elements of acceptance and rejection. Human sinfulness distorts the revelation; thus God speaks but more often than not hearing is defective. Even in the earlier book Kraemer had attacked the idea that revelation could be conceived in 'an intellectualist way . . . as an extraordinary form of epistemology'; faith in biblical terms is a continual struggle: 'God works in man and shines through him. The religious and moral life of man is man's achievement, but also God's wrestling with him; it manifests a receptivity to God but at the same time an inexcusable disobedience and blindness to God'.[24] In the 'later Kraemer' we find no less emphasis on this theology of a God who wrestles with sinful men and women, nor is there any question of a continuity being established from the non-Christian religions to Christianity. However he quite explicitly sets out to correct the impression, created by the first book, that the religions are 'purely human products'. Moreover he wants to show that *in all religions* there is a dialectical response to what God is trying to reveal of himself.[25]

This development between the two books is a matter of emphasis, of course, but insofar as it leads to a more positive assessment of the status of the non-Christian it is significant. Kraemer as a historian cannot but take into account the complex data of the various religious responses to revelation in formulating his theology; in other words he knows the religious scene well and can argue *a posteriori* on the basis of 'the facts'. But as a theologian he also argues from first principles, *a priori*, and formulates this theology in strongly biblical terms. Without resorting to too much oversimplification, it seems fair to say that he gives us a theology of a righteous God struggling to reveal himself to a sinful humanity. In the later book Kraemer still speaks of the religions as separate totalities which have to be interpreted on their own terms. He rejects any attempt to build a theology on common elements or similarities. The problem is not how to relate the different religions together by some comparative method, still less to separate out the 'good' elements from the 'bad', but to show how the universal message which is Christianity can be expressed in a different language or cultural framework.

Kraemer seems to accept that all religions, like Christianity, share the same dialectical structure; the 'Yes' is inseparable from the 'No'. One can, no doubt, argue at great length about the adequacy of his missionary strategy, but that is not the immediate point at issue here. For Kraemer himself it is enough to show that the missionary must *begin* from the position that God does work in all forms of human religiosity, even though there may not be agreement amongst the religions over how this might happen. As far as the Christian theologian is concerned this account of human religion as dialectical in structure is faithful both to the data provided by the world of religions and to Christian theology itself. This is not to assume that all religions are therefore continuous with one particular form, namely Christianity, which can be said to 'fulfil' the others. Kraemer may accept a common starting point, without which missionary activity is impossible, but he sees no need to posit a common goal *a priori*. That there may be such a common goal is not for him controversial, but it cannot be defined in the present. He therefore proceeds, like Barth, to proclaim a mystery which remains in the hands of God and is not to be predetermined by human agreement about the nature of religion or the relationship of religious traditions.

Does Kraemer produce a more generous estimate of the religions as vehicles of a 'general' revelation which is somehow continuous with the 'special' revelation given in Christ? Religions exist as all-inclusive systems and theories of life which are inseparable from, and can only be interpreted within, particular cultural forms, but this does not condemn them as mere 'human achievements', examples of our struggle to know God which are negated by God's infinite condescension to us. Like Barth Kraemer wants to avoid any natural theology arguments for knowledge of God. However, general revelation properly defined and understood is *not* the same as natural theology. Kraemer prefers to speak of general revelation not as a philosophically grounded knowledge of God, but as a genuinely divine disclosure of the gracious God through the medium of the created world. This, he thinks, is all part of what is to be found in the biblical evidence: the revelation of a God who struggles with sinful humankind. There is thus plenty of evidence in the Bible for human idolatry and sinfulness. At the same time we are given hints of a genuine acceptance of God, 'but never in the sense of an autonomous faculty or achievement of man; always as evoked and wrought by God'.[26] The eternal Logos was certainly rejected, yet God goes on revealing himself uninterruptedly with both discernible and indiscernible effects. 'It is', says Kraemer, 'a perpetual dialectic'.[27]

Ultimately, however, Kraemer has difficulty in following this programme through consistently. He is quite prepared to admit some form of real encounter with God in creation but 'to think systematically in terms of "continuity" as to the relation of the Christian faith to the non-Christian religions is self-defeating and self-contradictory'.[28] He turns out to be more ambiguous than dialectical. And yet he leaves us with an important insight about the nature of religion and the manner of God's encounter with all humankind – the 'perpetual dialectic'. If one form of historical empirical religion, namely Christianity, is dialectical through and through in structure, is there any reason why other religions may not be the same?

What are the roots of this ambiguity? The implication of Kraemer's – and Barth's – theology is that 'other words' may indeed be speaking of *the Word* since that Word, almost by definition, is addressed to humanity *as a whole*. And, if the interpretation given above is correct, the strength of 'biblical realism' is that it speaks cogently of the incarnate Word of God as the *Word for all peoples*. But how is this possible? Is Kraemer's theology capable of addressing this problem? Sometimes one feels that Kraemer has managed to back himself into a corner which does indeed deserve the title exclusivist. His rigid revelation-religion dichotomy only begs the question of how, in practice, one can ever separate the two. Not even Christianity, as Barth constantly repeats, is 'pure' revelation. The problem for an absolutist creed, claiming universal value, is that it must make some distinction between the essence or core of the revelation it proclaims and the cultural forms in which it has traditionally been expressed. In other words the Christian message, which has been expressed in language suitable for a largely European context for centuries, must take on different forms appropriate to particular cultures. There are at least two major problems here. The first is historical. All religions change over the centuries and a monolithic notion of a particular religion is inappropriate to our understanding of the relationship between religion and culture. Kraemer knows this, and wants to give due weight to the relativity of religious culture, but his theology is so bound up with biblical categories and symbolism that he finds it impossible to speak of the mystery of Christ except in Christianity-centred – and therefore eurocentric – terms.

The second problem is more theological and arises from Kraemer's fundamental missiological concern. He does not seem to accept that a truly dialectical theology of religions must have certain implications for missionary strategy and our theology of salvation. If Kraemer is to be faithful to his dialectical premise – that God is *already* struggling with sinful humanity, that the Spirit is *already* at work in the non-Christian world – then he must find some way of recognizing and describing such signs. This he is unable to do, nor does it seem to be important. For Kraemer the missionary strategy of inculturation seems only to be a matter of clothing the Christian message in a different language and therefore making it more acceptable in a non-European context. But this, despite Kraemer's first-hand knowledge of the wider religious scene, only makes for a negative judgement on all religions. Do they contain anything of value for salvation? According to his dialectical assessment the answer ought to be 'Yes'; but the answer from Kraemer the missionary must be 'No'. Kraemer finds himself in an impasse, on the one hand wanting to proclaim Christ as 'the Way', normative for all, on the other not wanting to drive a complete wedge between those who have explicitly acknowledged that revelation and those who have not. However, if revelation is regarded as the *sine qua non* of salvation then it becomes very difficult to see how this is possible.

The Place of the Word

I began this chapter by suggesting that all three paradigms have different perceptions of the problems of religious pluralism. Barth and Kraemer present us with a Word-centred universe. Their version of the old problematic is not so much 'how is the non-Christian saved?' but 'what is the place of the Word in that salvation?' There is no great difficulty, even in a Barthian framework, in working within an eschatological vision. God saves in his own way and in his own time, because the definitive revelation of his will has already been made known in Jesus Christ. But what is the relevance of the Word to this grand vision? How is the mission of the Church to be understood in a pluralist age? If, as both Barth and Kraemer admit, God's Spirit is already at work within the religions, making them 'other words', there can be no place for exclusivism. This is clearly all to the good, but it does not follow that the only alternative is pluralism. Other options still need to be examined. Meanwhile the Barth-Kraemer approach reminds us of the positive points which dialectical theology can make to a theology of religions. A pluralism which reduces all religions to a few common denominators runs the risk of erecting itself into a new dogmatism. The integrity of religious commitment demands that difference as well as similarity be taken seriously. To that extent Kraemer's prophetic voice still rings true. Protestant theology has always sought to protect the sovereignty of the Word and the insight which sets human religiosity in dialectical tension with God's revelation of himself is surely a most useful insight for understanding the continuity between the Word and the 'other words'.[29] The specific character of the Word is well-protected by a theology which is aware of the need to safeguard its own identity in a world of indifferentism. We shall return to this point in Part Two.

The problem is that we are still stuck with a theology of religion rather than religions. Are the terms of this theology capable of sustaining a genuine acceptance of the religions on their terms rather than on ours without which dialogue is likely to be totally one-sided? To take this step is, I would suggest, to bring about a major shift of perspective.

Notes

1. J. Peter Schineller, 'Christ and Church: A Spectrum of Views', *Theological Studies* 37 (1976), pp. 545–566. Schineller is right that the positions he distinguishes depend on very different views of the place of Christ and Church in the theological scheme. 'Logically', he says, 'you cannot hold two of them' (p. 547), but he has to admit that theologians are likely to find themselves shifting towards neighbouring positions.

2. An account of traditional Christian exclusivism, looked at from a very British perspective, is contained in Kenneth Cracknell's *Towards a New Relationship, Christians and Peoples of Other Faiths*, London: Epworth 1986, chapter 1.

3. cf. the evidence for the growing inter-Christian dialogue contained in

the symposium *Christ's Lordship and Religious Pluralism,* ed. Gerald H. Anderson and Thomas F. Stransky, New York: Orbis 1981, especially the contribution by Pietro Rossano, at that time secretary of the Vatican Secretariat for non-Christians: 'Christ's Lordship and Religious Pluralism in Roman Catholic Perspective', pp. 96–110, notable for both its scriptural and ecclesial perspectives.

4. A highly articulate example of evangelical theology is *Christianity and World Religions* by Norman Anderson, Leicester: I V P new edn 1984. Anderson is right that speculation about 'the ultimate salvation of others' should not be allowed to compromise the sovereign graciousness of God (p. 32ff). But the primary evangelical concern is always for mission; hence: 'Our duty is to obey and be his witnesses . . . our message is a call to radical repentance . . .' (p. 169).

5. See, for example, C. Peter Wagner, 'Let's sharpen the cutting edge', *Global Church Growth,* 23 (1986), pp. 9–12. 'I see obedience to the Master as a starting-point for formulating the attitude to mission strategy. The Great Commission is a clear commandment. We are to go into the world, preach the Gospel to every creature . . . As servants we need have no doubt as to the will of the Master.'

6. J.A. Veitch, 'Revelation and Religion in the Theology of Karl Barth', *Scottish Journal of Theology,* 24(1971), pp. 1–22, suggests that Barth intended to devote his attention to this problem after completing Volume Five of the *Dogmatics* when he 'would probably have recognised other religions as occupying a place in the dialectic between Revelation and Religion which is synonymous with religiosity' (pp. 20f.).

7. J. Moltmann, *The Church in the Power of the Spirit,* London: SCM 1977, p. 154.

8. *Church Dogmatics (CD)* IV, 1, pp. 564ff.

9. *CD* I, 2, pp. 280ff.

10. *CD* IV, 2, pp. 24ff.

11. *CD* IV, 3, p. 123.

12. *CD* IV, 3, p. 355.

13. *CD* IV, 3, p. 356.

14. *CD* IV, 3, p. 137. cf. J.A. Veitch, art. cit., p. 18.

15. cf. *CD,* IV, 3, p. 354. According to Philip J. Rosato, *The Spirit as Word,* Edinburgh: T. & T. Clark 1981, Barth 'the reputed christologian is also, or even primarily, Barth the genuine pneumatologian' (prologue, p. vi). In the unfinished *CD* his pneumatology remains 'anthropologically wanting' (p. 189), but, as Rosato suggests, 'theology must be pneumatology if the equipoise between Christ and the Christian is to be kept intact' (p. 181). Rowan Williams, 'Barth on the Triune God', in *Karl Barth – Studies in his Theological Method,* ed. S.W. Sykes, Oxford: Oxford University Press 1979, pp. 147–193, says that the role of the Spirit, even in the later part of the *Dogmatics,* presents a difficulty which can be resolved by developing what Barth has to say about the resurrection (*CD,* IV, 1, pp. 283–357), representing 'God's freedom to be Spirit' (p. 182).

16. *Evangelical Theology*, London: Collins, Fontana ed. 1965, pp. 20–21.
17. Hendrik Kraemer (1888–1965) is first and foremost an orientalist whose personal experience of life in the Dutch missions of Indonesia in the twenties and early thirties colours all his theological work. He was the dominant figure at the International Mission Conference at Tambaram, near Madras, in 1938. His contribution to that debate was published as *The Christian Message in a Non-Christian World*, London: Edinburgh House Press 1938. The best of his later work is to be found in *Religion and the Christian Faith*, London: Lutterworth 1956.
18. As for instance by Knitter, op. cit. p. 82, and D'Costa, *Theology* pp. 52–79, who nevertheless notes that in understanding Kraemer's theology one of the main factors to keep in mind is his 'practical, scholarly and experiential contact with the major world religions' (p. 54). The relation between Kraemer and Barth is discussed by Origen Vasantha Jathanna in *The Decisiveness of the Christ-Event and the Universality of Christianity in a World of Religious Plurality: Studies in the Intercultural History of Christianity*, Berne: Lang 1981, pp. 484–492. Jathanna notes that Kraemer never subscribed to 'the Barthian theology as a system' but always struggled to take seriously both his own 'biblical realism' and the phenomenology of religions.
19. *Christian Message*, p. 136, where Kraemer speaks of the need to develop what he calls a 'totalitarian' approach to religions. He is not using the word in any political sense. Rather 'one does not know what the real force, value and function of the idea of God or of redemption . . . or of anything else is, if one does not primarily take into account what is the fundamental existential apprehension of the totality of life which dominates this whole religion . . .'
20. For Kraemer the roots of the 'western crisis' are to be found in 'the spirit and attitude of relativism' which pervades and distorts so much of Christian theology, ibid. pp. 6–17.
21. Kraemer is clearly unhappy with attempts simply to evacuate the problem of particularity by subordinating 'special' to 'general revelation' in the manner of Enlightenment rationalism. He is critical of the model of God as the 'Pedagogue' which 'wholly misconceives the peculiar character of revelation', ibid., p. 117.
22. *Religion and the Christian Faith*, p. 192.
23. ibid. p. 193.
24. *Christian Message*, p. 73, p. 126.
25. *Religion*, pp. 321ff.
26. ibid. p. 341.
27. loc. cit.
28. ibid. p. 351.
29. Rowan Williams, 'Trinity and Revelation', *Modern Theology* 2, 3 (1986), pp. 197–212, considers the problem of the authority of religious language. We use the language of revelation 'to give some ground for the sense in our religious and theological language that the initiative does not ultimately lie with us; before we speak, we are addressed or called' (p. 198).

3 INCLUDING THE RELIGIONS

this is my concl

In the last chapter I came to the conclusion that Barth and Kraemer propose a certain universalism. Their theory of religion allows for the eschatological fulfilment of God's purposes disclosed in Jesus Christ; God's revelation is for all. When we turn to the 'inclusivist' side of the universalist coin we find that salvation, revelation and mission form the agenda here as well. The answers are different, but only because of the different relative weight given to these issues. In Reformed theology, for instance, the proclamation of the Word is the sole sacrament of encounter with God. Catholic theology has a much more developed sense of the sacramental and therefore a different conception of the way God reveals himself. The problem presented by the other is less a problem about the effective proclamation of the Word and much more about the identity of the Church as the locus of God's sacramental activity. And the more Catholics become aware of the Church as a communion of people, a social reality, the more the identity of other social realities, the actual religions, becomes problematic. This is not to say, however, that Catholic and Protestant approaches are contradictory once they are set in context as emphasizing important insights of the whole Christian tradition. To pick up the point emphasized earlier, these two types of approach differ more in degree than in kind. As confessional theology they aim to articulate the beliefs of the Christian community. Thus their intentions are the same, while they differ, and differ quite profoundly, with respect to the scope of the theological principles involved.

In this chapter I want to take further this discussion about the nature of the confessional theology of religions. The object is not, however, to set 'Catholic' over against (or even alongside) 'Protestant' theology. Insofar as it is necessary always to consider the context within which any theology arises, we must first ask whether there is in the Catholic tradition a recognizable form of theology of religion, be it called 'inclusivist' or whatever. Why is it different from any other? What sort of questions are Catholics asking? And why? But secondly, in our pursuit of the emerging 'new problematic' I want to suggest that 'inclusivism' represents not so much an alternative theology as a significant shift of perspective: the recognition of the other not just as an individual but as a person who shares in a collective religious identity.

The Catholic Inheritance

We may begin by considering where Catholics find themselves with regard to the complex 'dialectical morass' which we discussed earlier. What have Catholics inherited from this debate and how have they reacted? Vatican II, as Knitter says, is something of a watershed, not just putting the problem of religious pluralism and dialogue on the Catholic map but also going some way towards underlining the crucial issues in any theology of religions. In terms of theology the major contribution has come from Karl Rahner and his 'Anonymous Christianity' theory. But however much he may have been responsible for formulating the theology of Vatican II, Rahner did not conjure his ideas out of nothing. It is not as if the Catholic Church suddenly caught up with the ecumenical debate when Pope John XXIII threw open the Vatican windows. The recent flowering of ecumenical activity is as much the result of years of patient theological pondering as it is a response to the 'signs of the times'. Vatican II was in many ways the culmination of years of gradual change in theological perceptions.[1] Churches, theologies and even religions are no longer seen to be mutually exclusive. In the theology of religions in particular Catholics and Protestants have learnt from each other to overcome their traditional isolationism. And just as more recent Protestant theology has moved away from the rather harsh and unnuanced judgements of the early Barth and Kraemer, so we can discern a similar movement within Catholic ranks.[2] The debate which surrounds the Anonymous Christian is part of this development – a debate which still ruffles the feathers of normally placid Catholic ecclesiastics.

Catholic theology is, of course, heir to a venerable patristic and scholastic tradition. The Fathers of the Church, the Apologists in particular, had their own problems with the pagan philosophers who represented the Other in the early centuries of the Church's life. Some of the concepts which they proposed for understanding the relationship of Christianity and pagan culture are still valid. Writing in the post-war years the French Jesuit theologian, Jean Daniélou, had recourse to the patristic concept of 'divine pedagogy'.[3] The tradition of the Church, following the witness of Scripture, is that God has revealed himself to all peoples through his providence in the world. God leads all people – the 'pagans of the Old Testament' as much as members of other faiths – to knowledge of, and participation in, his interior life. Taking as his basic principle the axiom that there is no salvation except through faith in Christ, Daniélou is faced with the old problem of the salvation of those for whom there has never been any possibility of explicit knowledge of Christ. What does one say of those who have died before Christ? His answer is couched in terms of the gradual revelation of God's purposes to humankind through the history of salvation. The Bible is a record of that history which is all of a piece leading up to the definitive revelation in Christ. Thus we begin not with the Mosaic but the Cosmic Covenant, symbolized by the rainbow, the sign of 'the everlasting Covenant that was made between God and every living soul' (Genesis 9.16). The stages in the history of salvation unfold: cosmic religion consists of a response to God's revelation of himself in the world and his call to recognize the demands of conscience; in the Jewish religion the holiness and faithfulness of God are manifested; in Christianity the mystery of the Trinity – the Father giving himself to the Son in the Spirit of love – is revealed. That to which all religions are pointing becomes known explicitly in Christ.

This salvation history approach seems at first sight very different from what we have already noted in Barth. Yet the problem they address is the same. Daniélou shows his appreciation of Barth by taking up the revelation-religion dichotomy; thus the religions are human realities, 'man's search for God', while Christianity is divine, 'God's search for man'.[4] But this cannot be an absolute divide. Daniélou is as much opposed to the Pelagianism implied in the concept of 'natural religion' as Barth, but he does not want to go so far as to deny a fallen humanity all possibility of knowledge of God. The salvation history approach noted above presumes that the saints of the Old Testament and those who by extension can be associated with them – the Greek philosophers, the Buddhist and Hindu sages – are saved without actually knowing it. They participate in the single mystery of Christ retrospectively, as it were. But what sense does it make to speak of knowing something *implicitly*? Daniélou refers us to the act of faith. Following Aquinas he notes that the substance of faith is always and everywhere the same and consists of belief in Christ, whether the fullness of that faith is apprehended or not. This is because the object of faith is the God who in his providence continues to reveal himself to all those who sincerely seek him. The fact that the fullness of this faith in Christ may only be unfolded over a long period does not alter the fact that that fulness is implied in every act of faith. Daniélou's point seems to be that the fundamental distinction is not between revelation and religion as such but between those who belong to the world of grace and those who belong to the world of sin – those, that is, who have deliberately chosen to exclude themselves from the realm of God's providence. Rather, it is perfectly possible to speak of a Cosmic Covenant which includes the faithful of all pre-Christian religions as participating in one single and, by definition, supernatural mystery.

Here he does part company with the early Barth. There is the same eschatological vision founded on faith in God's election of humankind in Christ. But while for Barth this hope in the future is essentially an expression of the tragic rupture between God and the sinner which can only be fully overcome at the end of time, for Daniélou the mystery of creation and redemption is continuous. God has never ceased to manifest himself: fully in Jesus Christ, but before that to Abraham and Moses through intervening in history, and before that to the nations represented by persons like Abel and Noah. Such a cosmic revelation was most certainly obscure, and we must always remain agnostic as to how many gave their adherence to it. Nonetheless it points to the very purpose of revelation: the redemptive activity of God in the world.

The religions are, therefore, a *preparatio evangelica* – a preparation for the fullness of revelation contained in the Good News of what God has done in Christ. This typically Catholic strategy with its hunmanist overtones seems in marked contrast to the spirit of the old adage *extra ecclesiam nulla salus*.[5] In fact it allows for a reinterpretation by simply broadening our understanding of Church. The patristic theme of the *ecclesia ab Abel* can be invoked to include all 'holy pagans' who like Abel express in their lives the supernatural quality of faith in the provident God who alone can save.[6] As with Barth, though in a somewhat different way, the salvation of the non-Christian ceases to be a problem. Various versions of the thesis are possible. Hans Urs von Balthasar takes much the same sort of line as Daniélou, though he does seem rather more susceptible to the charge of exclusivism. For him God's outpouring of his Spirit in the Incarnation is the sole expression of God's being. Christ is the 'form' who represents all that God is; for Christ to be anything less than the fullness of God's revelation would make God less than God. Which is not to say that our perception of the 'splendour of the Lord' in Christ is perfect or exclusive to Christians. Von Balthasar finds no more difficulty than Daniélou in extending the sphere of grace to those outside the bounds of the visible Church. 'If men humbly seek their God, this grace can be well received and lived by non-Christians.

The missionary Church has found many traces of Christ's grace among many peoples'.[7] As long as we work with a concept of faith as an assent to revealed truths we reach an impasse, for who can assent to what has not been revealed and proclaimed? The scriptural evidence and the patristic tradition, however, emphasize that the primary object of faith is not truth in the abstract but a person, the God who saves us in Christ. Faith is, therefore, not to be equated with knowledge as representing simply intellectual assent, but the movement of the whole person towards his final salvation in Jesus Christ. Understood in this way, the boundary between explicit and implicit faith in Christ is no longer clear. And it therefore follows that missionary strategy must aim at building up all that is good in the religions, that the fulfilment which is found in Christ may gradually become explicit through conversion and true commitment.

The religions are, therefore, provisional, a 'pedagogy' to bring non-Christians to Christ.[8] But they are essentially continuous with Christianity. The Catholic answer to the old problematic is more positive than the Protestant, though both face similar conceptual problems; it is, for instance, just as difficult to conceive of fulfilment through the Church as through the Word. To do this, post-Vatican II Catholicism has developed an ecclesiology which is less concerned for the definition and organization of those 'within' and much more aware of its relationship with and mission to those 'without'.[9] This has been achieved largely by breaking down the distinction between the two. Once it is accepted that salvation is not the privilege of belonging to the group, but the gift of sharing in the divine activity, our model of Church must also change. Today we are less concerned for institutional models and more aware of the Church as community, the pilgrim people of God. But we also have to live with a tension, that between the Church as the present manifestation of the mystery of Christ and the full reality of that mystery as something dynamic, being acted out in the whole of human existence. And the more we are prepared to accept that the revelation of God's love which is made in Christ is also the sum and goal of history, the more difficult it becomes to say where the limits of the Church may be. The problem of the other is no longer that of overcoming apparent discontinuity; rather, we are forced to recognize that he or she may actually be a lot closer to the end of the pilgrimage than we are. Thus contemporary Catholic theology is much exercised by the problem of the identity of the Church and by the nature of mission which is so much a constitutive element of the Church. At the same time as it is giving a whole new dimension to the old problematic, we may also notice glimmerings of the new.[10]

Vatican II and the Values of the Religions

Anyone looking at the Second Vatican Council's Declaration on the Relationship of the Church to non-Christian Religions, *Nostra Aetate*, today is likely to be a trifle disappointed.[11] Here we find what appear to be rather brief, bland perspectives on the world of the great religions. Nothing remarkable is said. What *is* remarkable is that anything is said at all. The history of the document is a worthy object of study.[12] Originally there were no plans to issue a special statement on the religions. It all started because John XXIII wanted to heal the wounds of anti-Semitism by developing a more positive theology of Christian-Jewish relations. Political considerations dictated that nothing should be said which might appear to have a pro-Israel, and therefore anti-Arab, bias. Hence the document was expanded to include Islam and then completely redrafted to make reference to all the great world religions.

The basic perspective is that of the history of salvation noted above. The familiar theology of the relation between the people of the Old Covenant and the new people of God sets the scene, as it were; it has simply been expanded to include all people. The Church therefore is a sign of the coming reconciliation of all in Christ. Taking up a very Pauline theme the Council suggests that the Jews, continuing in God's favour, will be redeemed, if only at the end of time. A useful image to describe the central perspective is that of concentric circles. God's saving design extends to all; religions such as Hinduism, Buddhism and 'other religions to be found everywhere' are glimpses or partial expressions of the truth which is revealed through the Church in Christ. Attention is given primarily to what people hold in common and what promotes fellowship between them; there is only the one God who is the goal of all human striving and the answer to all our questions. Thus the Church 'rejects nothing which is true and holy in these religions'; as Christians we are called upon to witness to Christ the way, the truth and the life but also to encourage the real religious values which are to be found in other religions, to promote their spiritual good and to bring the best out in them.

How new is all this? The practical acceptance of the values inherent in non-Christian religions is certainly new. The Council makes it very clear that ancient prejudices must be rejected and emphasizes a new vision of God's fatherly care for all peoples, whatever their particular religious allegiance. As a pastoral programme it is of immense significance and demands careful meditation and thought. As theology it could be argued that it is simply a reaffirmation of the ancient perspective outlined by Daniélou: it is found in the Wisdom literature of the Old Testament, the universalism of Paul in Ephesians and Colossians – all things created in Christ and for Christ – and Luke's theology of the Holy Spirit in Acts. Can it be taken further? The document provides a few pointers. Two principles have to be held together. On the one hand salvation is in Christ and Christ is 'the truth'; on the other we must give full weight to the conviction that there may be elements of what is 'true and holy' in all religions. The document goes no further than this in attempting to describe such elements; but such a positive affirmation is itself a major development. The emphasis is on promoting a programme of action rather than defining the agenda of theological debate.

This is not to say that there is no such thing as a typically Catholic approach to the theology of religions. But Vatican II is perhaps more notable for its powerful incarnational spirituality and the rich imagery of its theology of the Church than for the clarity of its theology of mission.[13] Thus it is only right to draw attention to various tensions which have arisen: between different models of the Church, between a realized and a futurist eschatology, and between the claim of dialogue and more traditional forms of proclamation of the gospel message. Catholic theology of religions has found itself caught up in the same problematic, being heir to a complex debate in the wider Christian world and trying to come to terms with its own tradition. Critical surveys of this development have, as we have already noted, been done. My aim at this stage is more limited: to note questions rather than answers, and typical trends rather than dogmatic positions. If I now attend to that most Catholic of all theologians, Karl Rahner, it is not with a view to exhaustive analysis, which is quite beyond the scope of this study. Rahner's famous 'Anonymous Christianity' thesis was first proposed in 1961 and thus antedates the Council.[14] Catholic theology may have moved on but the questions Rahner raises are still relevant. My own intention is to focus on some of these issues and, particularly, to note the emphasis he puts on the religions themselves as possible vehicles of salvation. In so doing we will also have to pick up the key point of contention between explicit and implicit knowledge of God. Both points lead us to ask not just about the values of the religions as such but about the very nature of human religiosity.

Rahner and the Anonymous Christian

Rahner is an articulate exponent of the Roman Catholic biblical and scholastic tradition, but he is clearly much more and it is impossible to understand his approach without some reference to his philosophy of religion. The familiar language of Anonymous Christianity must be set against the background of the controversial use of a particularly rich philosophical tradition reaching from Aquinas through to Maréchal and Heidegger. Rahner wants to argue for a sort of Kantian *a priori* condition of possibility for having any knowledge of the Infinite: namely the transcendental openness to Being as such. For him all human religiosity is expressive of this fundamental awareness of, or openness to, the Divine. From this premise he builds his theory of the supernatural-existential: grace is not an extrinsic addition to human nature, but definitive of our nature as persons who in all our human acts of knowing and loving are orientated towards the Infinite Mystery. Every time we reach out beyond ourselves to the True and the Good we are experiencing and responding to grace; we are therefore in some sense knowing God even if such a knowledge must be described as 'unreflexive' or 'unthematic', implicit rather than explicit. Thus, Rahner bases his theology of religions on the biblical doctrine of God's universal will to save, and continues in the Catholic tradition of the continuity of Nature and Grace. At the same time, it seems clear that he finds in all religions a certain fundamental religious sense, an experience of the Divine which is the heart of all true human religiosity.

Not that Rahner is content with a vague 'common essence' or fundamental experience of holy mystery which all religions can be said to share. Human religiosity exists in particular forms – the actual societies in which human beings live. In Rahner's view the doctrine of God's will to save does not confront disembodied spirits or an abstract idea of humankind, but human persons who belong to particular societies and share a particular history and culture. The relevance of this principle to his thesis is obvious: full weight must be given to the historical religions as vehicles of grace not just because humanity is naturally orientated towards a divine destiny, but because *as a matter of fact* that orientation finds its expression in the only way possible for a human being, namely *in society*. If the great historical religions are where human beings are, then that is where God's grace must be made available to them. Thus Rahner argues not just for the Anonymous Christian but for Anonymous Christianity: an institution or what he calls a 'possibly lawful religion' rather than just a collection of right-minded individuals. This move represents something of a shift of perspective and has been the subject of more than a little controversy.[15]

Religion can be valid and lawful if it represents God's salvific action, his revelation made through the incarnation of Jesus Christ. That immediately seems to rule out the possibility of any religion other than Christianity being 'valid and lawful'. However, as a matter of fact, Christianity has not always been the way to reach salvation. Christianity had a historical starting point; it may be the 'absolute religion' but it reveals a God who acts in time. Rahner's point is that just as salvation comes – *if* it comes – to Christians *in history*, so it must come to all people. But if we are talking about God's grace being revealed in and through the temporal process of human history, then one must also accept that the point at which the historical reality of the Christian revelation becomes an *obligation effective* in the actual existence of a non-Christian community cannot be determined in advance. In other words, we cannot rule out the possibility that God's grace is not already at work within a non-Christian religion in the same way that God's grace may be said to have been present in the historical community of the Old Testament long before the definitive revelation made in Christ. Thus, just as Christianity itself is a social reality instituted through a particular response to historical revelation, so *in due time* non-Christian religions will open themselves to the demands of this absolute religion. A 'lawful religion', therefore, is one which in some sense approximates to the paradigm set by Christianity or, more precisely, to the mystery of God's self-revelation in Christ. Rahner's point is that *if* supernatural virtues of faith and love exist in a non-Christian religion they may be said to be there in virtue of God's gift of himself in Christ. Until the moment when the gospel really enters into the historical situation of an individual, a non-Christian religion does not merely contain elements of natural knowledge of God but also contains supernatural elements arising out of grace which is a 'gratuitous gift on account of Christ'.[16]

Rahner wants to bring together two fundamental axioms: the biblically-based doctrine of the universal will-of-God-to-save and the specifically Christian article of faith that there is no salvation *apart from Christ*; but he is saying more than just that it is possible for non-Christians to be saved. Rather he emphasizes that non-Christian religions can be *lawful* even though they obviously contain elements of sin and superstition. It does not follow, of course, that all religions are lawful in all their elements nor that every religion is lawful, but one must at least admit the *possibility* that there are grace-filled elements outside the Christian revelation which exist in virtue of (and not despite) their historical and social structure. Non-Christians may be saved – if they are saved – like Christians through their historical religious practice and not through some sort of *Deus ex machina* from outside which nullifies the values inherent in that particular religion. It therefore follows that the right-minded Hindu is saved through the practice of his Hindu tradition insofar as it represents spiritual and moral principles through which Christ is in some sense present.

This is to say that Christianity confronts such a non-Christian not just as an individual but as a member of a tradition which is already orientated towards its fulfilment in Christ. If the other has accepted 'the immeasurableness of his finite existence as opening out into infinity'[17] such a person has already been given revelation in the true sense before being affected by missionary preaching. For Rahner the Anonymous Christian is someone who has already been touched by the mystery of God's love which is present explicitly in Christianity; if someone is on his or her way to salvation without actually being touched by the preaching of the gospel then the grace of that salvation is there *in virtue of Christ*, for there is no other salvation. What, then, of explicit confession of Christ? This is not rendered obsolete but must be seen as a higher stage in the development of a Christianity which is already present wherever the grace of Christ is seen to be operative. Rahner's argument is simply that Christianity means 'taking possession of the mystery of man with absolute optimism',[18] the explicit working-out of what is already present elsewhere. But it is a function of that optimism to recognize that even in today's world of pluralism and scepticism there may exist forms of living which, while not being formally Christian, may in fact grasp Christianity more genuinely than many of its more explicit forms which can so often be empty and 'used as the means of escape from the mystery instead of openly facing up to it'.[19] The fundamental truth about God and humanity which is revealed through Christianity is continuous with whatever is not deliberately antipathetic to it. Thus when I look to the future and the possibility that cultures may not be explicitly Christian I know that 'ultimately it cannot trouble me. Why not? Because I see everywhere a *nameless Christianity*, and because I do not see my own explicit Christianity as one opinion *among* others which contradict it'.[20] Explicit Christianity need not see itself in some sort of competition with other religions, always anxious to keep one jump ahead, as it were;

Christianity is more adequately described as the heart or fulfilment of true religion everywhere.

How is Christianity more than 'one opinion' among many? Rahner stresses that Christianity retains a qualitative distinction from all other religions not because it somehow exists apart from or above history but because it has most deeply penetrated that history and therefore fulfils the deepest aspirations of all human religiosity. This notion of *fulfilment* puts Rahner's theology solidly in the Catholic mainstream. Christianity is the universal message which does not deny or refute other outlooks on life but gathers up and preserves all the genuine affirmations of humanity. To be a Christian is to recognize in one's explicit confession of Christ that one is the *avant-garde*, the sign of what Christ is actually accomplishing in the world.[21] Thus Rahner tries to steer a middle way between the extremes of exclusivism and indifferentism. On the one hand he proposes a universalist vision couched in the evolutionary language of salvation history. On the other, he wants to maintain the absolute status of Christianity as the religion which cannot accept any others as of equal right. The tension is not easily maintained.

The problem with all universalist visions, however, is that they appear to reduce the significance of all particular expressions. What value does Christian faith really have? The fact that others do not confess the fullness of that faith does not in itself mean that God's Spirit is not already at work or that God is not recognized outside the bounds of the visible Church. Indeed the signs are already there. But in that case what is the Church for? Is Rahner doing any more than providing comfort for members of a shrinking Church, the sense that everyone is *really* a Christian anyway and that we need not worry about the falling numbers in the pews? We should note that when, in the article quote above, Rahner uses the term Anonymous Christian for the first time, he is not concerned with a theology of religions as such but with the problem of Christian identity in a world of indifference and formal rejection of explicit Christian faith.[22] When the Christian is surrounded by a world of pluralism and unbelief, says Rahner, why be a Christian at all? How does the Christian accept the signs of God's grace amongst other religions without his own explicit acceptance and profession of faith seeming irrelevant? These are the sort of questions from which Rahner's theology of religions arises. Unlike Barth, who begins with a problem about human religion in the abstract, Rahner addresses the contemporary reality of the religions themselves. The existence of so many non-Christians in our midst and the comparative failure of missionary effort issue a direct challenge to the Church and its claims to preach Christ as the way for all, as the one and only valid revelation of the living God. What sense does it make to say that the salvation of God in Christ is mediated to the entire world and all religious cultures through the Church?

Rahner and his Critics

Although focusing on the major issues Rahner lays himself open to criticism from all sides.[23] On the one hand he is accused of taking the religions too seriously and on the other of not taking them seriously enough. Thus some would say that once the particularity of Christianity has been reduced to a common essence shared with all religions – and indeed with all people of good will – the true challenge of the gospel preaching and the richness of the Christian tradition may be completely lost. A rather different perspective suggests that he does not go far enough and remains basically an old-fashioned Catholic dogmatist. Thus it is said that the terms he uses are offensive to members of other faiths, disclosing a paternalism which insists on defining them in terms of what they are not, rather than accepting them fully as what they themselves profess to be. The non-Christian is, to put it rather crudely, a Christian 'in disguise', a Christian in all but name. Strangely then, Rahner is taken to task *both* for promoting a sense of complacency within the Church *and* for seeking to maintain an attitude of simple ecclesiastical imperialism without.

In this situation it becomes imperative to be clear about Rahner's intentions. How does he view the problem of the other? He makes it clear that his position is always that of the dogmatic theologian, interpreting the tradition *a priori* as he sees it; there is no need, therefore, to take into account the data of an extremely complex non-Christian religious world. He is, on the other hand, quite prepared to challenge the empirical sciences of religion to proceed to 'discover historically and concretely in the individual religions what the systematic theologian thinks he can find there at least partially and imperfectly'.[24] Just how much scope he actually leaves the historians of religion by working out a very specific theological *a priori* is a moot point; can they build on the theological position which Rahner presents? Leaving that to one side for the moment, let us simply note Rahner's answer to those who accuse him of some sort of theological imperialism: they mistake the status of the thesis. It is not intended as part of a new missionary strategy nor is it meant to impress non-Christians with a sense of their newly discovered dignity. The theory is part of Christian dogmatic theology, providing an answer to a particular question which is central to the meaningful articulation of Christianity in today's world. It is addressed not to the Hindu or Buddhist but to the Christian whose self-understanding is challenged by the existence of the Hindu or Buddhist.

Rahner's main concern is with the old problematic: how is one to avoid setting up a complete discontinuity between Christianity and other religions? As a dogmatic theologian he must allow for the possible salvation of the non-Christian, as of any righteous individual. And very few theologians would have any problems with Rahner's universalist premise. The debate – to repeat – is about the means. Basically there are two possibilities: Rahner's existentialist model and the eschatological model favoured by Barth and Kraemer. Evangelical theology prefers to leave the question open: God has his own ways. Rahner wants to be more specific and, following Catholic tradition, invokes a high Christology which makes the particular revelation in Christ one example of what is – or, rather, may be – happening in all historical religions. As an answer to the problem of the salvation of the Hindu and the Buddhist Rahner's must be deemed a more satisfactory theory than the individualistic eschatological versions of most mainstream protestant theology. He wants to give full value to the religions themselves. But, say Rahner's more conservative critics, how different is this from the liberal protestant approach which we discussed earlier? It is clear that, in Rahner's theology, there is no difference between the way God saves Christians and the way he saves non-Christians. Rahner's God has 'no favourites'. If he saves Christians where they are – in company with each other, a social institution – then he saves non-Christians where they are, as members of other socio-religious institutions. The God of the incarnation is at work through his Spirit in the world which he created and is in process of redeeming.[25]

It may then be objected: why Church? It it not reasonable to ask what difference it makes for someone to confess the Christian faith, to be baptized, to become a formal Christian? If the Anonymous Christian is a Christian in all but name anyway, why worry about explicit conversion? Rahner's missiology is far from the indifferentism of which he is accused; neither is it obvious that he totally disregards the prophetic role which Christian faith must play in a theology of religion.[26] In my version of the 'spectrum' of opinions I have suggested that Rahner is, in fact, closer to Barth than to

Troeltsch; 'exclusivist' and 'inclusivist' are both christocentric. Rahner clearly acknowledges the new problematic but his main concern is to produce a more acceptable answer to the old. Thus for the moment let us focus on his more liberal critics and ask what weaknesses they find. To caricature somewhat: they wonder whether this theology of fulfilment or continuity means any more than that all non-Christian religions are making a relatively bad job of what Christianity does perfectly. Christianity is erected *a priori* as the 'universal message' which gathers up and thus preserves everything else; all the religions can be set in some sort of a continuum. Does it not follow that the others are simply poor versions of Christianity? Rahner's 'old-fashioned triumphalism' makes this the inescapable conclusion, with the result that we fail to see other religions as having any real value *in themselves*. The only aim of dialogue is, then, to show the inadequacy of the other tradition while remaining confident that I am, if not in possession of the truth already, then at least a good deal closer to it than the non-Christian. Dialogue becomes a more subtle form of conversion.

How does Rahner answer this objection? He would argue that to see non-Christian religions simply as inadequate versions of the absolute religion which is incarnated in Christianity misses the point. *All* religions – not just Christianity – are characterized by socio-historical structures which *de facto* are the means by which the Spirit operates in the world. His thesis proposes Anonymous Christianity not just the Anonymous Christian. This takes us back to the question of the 'lawfulness' of a religion. As we have noted, Rahner insists not that non-Christians can be saved *in spite* of their religious practice but *through* it. The life of grace cannot be reduced to a sort of internal, individual experience of revelation alone, which abstracts a person from his history and traditional religion. The situation of many religions today is no different from that of the people of the Old Testament: salvation is mediated through traditional religious forms. Rahner's critics object that he simply makes Christianity the basic model which includes all the others. Does Rahner allow a pluralism of religions? In one sense, yes: there are, in practice, a number of different ways to salvation. As long as human beings go on experiencing the life of grace they do so in human society. But he will still insist that salvation is always through the grace of God made manifest in Christ. The mystery of Christ is the mystery at the heart of all religions. One can have a pluralism of forms of institutional religion which are all included within one and the same mystery.

Does this work? Can Rahner marry this sacramental or incarnational approach with the fulfilment model mentioned earlier? He has to admit that non-Christian religions can only have a qualified validity. He allows only the *possible* lawfulness of non-Christian religions, up to that moment when there occurs an encounter with the historical phenomenon of Christianity which, once understood, becomes the necessary means to salvation for that particular individual. Acceptance of the truth about himself and his fundamental orientation towards God which he finds to be fully revealed in Christianity will necessarily entail conversion. The Church then becomes the authoritative source of God's revelation, the locus of lawful religion. Rahner fully accepts the possibility that such an appreciation of Christ and Christianity may still entail rejection; every person remains free. But just how culpable any individual may be is not for the Christian to judge. Meanwhile, until such time as that genuine conversion is effected, a non-Christian religion *may be* lawful; that is to say it may be a means of mediating salvation. However, it is still only partial and provisional, *a preparatio evangelica*, awaiting its fulfilment in Christ and the Church.

Religions and Dialogue

Rahner's intentions are plain, but the objections remain. Perhaps the strongest criticism is that he fails to address the problem of the other or to take seriously contemporary experience of dialogue and inter-religious encounter. In a pluralist world such a totally Christianity-centred theology may be considered somewhat limited. For all that Rahner speaks of the historical and social realities of the religions, they remain wholly abstract systems of belief. Dialogue is a one-sided affair; the religions may be accepted as lawful but there is no incentive to get to know them, still less to learn from them. It may be true that the thesis is a response to a problem of Christian theology, but the fact remains that theory has an effect on practice; if terminology fails to express a reality exactly it is bound to condition attitudes and, perhaps, fail to encourage the sort of sensitivity which is essential if true dialogue with non-Christians is to take place. No one would want to take the language of Anonymous Christianity into dialogue so why use it at all? And it might also be argued that, while a fulfilment theory may initially draw religions closer together and encourage the partners in dialogue to look for common ideas and values, the reality is often much more difficult and such high expectations are easily disappointed. Thus in theory righteous non-Christians are Anonymous Christians because they follow the same path as the explicit Christian; they enjoy the same status as any graced human being who meets and is, however gradually, transformed by the Spirit of Christ. If Rahner is correct, one would expect to find signs of an explicit movement towards Christ. In practice it is difficult to see this actually happening; non-Christians are very often quite content to remain within their own tradition.

Despite the fact that his Anonymous Christianity thesis is scattered over innumerable articles and essays and nowhere receives a systematic treatment, Rahner seems thoroughly consistent within his own stated principles. Whatever objections may be raised, it remains an impressive achievement – one of the few really positive attempts to articulate for Christians the problem of their relationship to the other great religious traditions. Clearly Rahner has made a crucially important contribution to the inter-religious debate. In presenting us with a fully worked-out theology of Vatican II he has redefined the terms of the old problematic. No longer can we be content with the rather guarded agnosticism which grudgingly admitted 'holy pagans' to the Kingdom but granted no redemptive significance to their religious traditions. To that extent this thesis avoids the absolutism of Barth and Kraemer which finds it difficult to give value to traditions other than Christianity. And he presents us with an important alternative to the fulfilment theory of Daniélou by allowing for the sacramental presence of the Holy Spirit within the religions. Yet, for all that it neatly solves the problem of the salvation of the non-Christian, it does precious little to enhance inter-religious understanding. Other religions are readily assumed into one all-embracing Christian creed. That this is not Rahner's intention does not take away from the unfortunately patronizing tone of the thesis. And the fact that so many theologians find something distinctly unsatisfactory about such a theory, especially those working amongst large Hindu, Muslim or Buddhist majorities, ought to give us pause for thought. Rahner's perception of the problem as internal to the traditional Christian problem of salvation hardly addresses itself to the contemporary scene. To speak of the other being saved through his or her own tradition does very little to promote genuinely reciprocal dialogue unless great efforts are also made to stress and approve the values of that tradition for their own sake. Rahner specifically asks us to do this, to discover the 'shape of grace' at work within the other, but he makes no contribution himself. This is inevitable since he has no first-hand knowledge of religions other than Christianity.

Thus we can say, from the point of view of the old problematic, that some version of the thesis is clearly necessary if one is not to drive a wedge between Christianity as traditionally understood and the other great religions of the world. Yet at a time when knowledge of, and genuine respect for, these religions is increasing, it is becoming more and more difficult to justify a theology which depends so heavily on the *a priori* dogmatic categories assumed by Rahner. This is not to say that there are no dogmatic principles to be maintained, or that problems like the salvation of the non-Christian or the nature of Christian mission are not problems. But is such an 'internal' theology sufficient? Does it not have implications externally? The suspicion remains that a theory originally invoked to explain the salvation of the non-Christian in a world which is rapidly becoming less rather than more Christian, in the end produces a theology of the relationship of religions which fails to engage the sort of questions which that world is putting to the Church.

I started this chapter by referring to the emergence of a Catholic approach to the theology of religions. I wanted to stress that it is unhelpful, to say the least, to draw distinctions between Catholics and Protestants by suggesting that the former, operating out of a rather more broadly-based tradition, have simply added another string to the theological bow. Such distinctions between Catholic and Protestant approaches to theology in general, and to the theology of religions in particular, are not so easy to make these days. There are many Catholics like Daniélou and von Balthasar who seem more at home in Knitter's 'mainline protestant model' than in the Roman Catholic approach typified by Rahner.[27] That said, there is some point in the distinction; a theology which tries to be true to Reformation principles is going to have a different conception of salvation and mission from one with strong allegiance to a Natural Theology tradition. What I have tried to argue is that 'exclusivism' and 'inclusivism' do not represent different theologies of religions which can be identified with conservative evangelicalism on the one hand and Roman Catholicism on the other, but are different facets of a single universalism. Perhaps we can call them two styles of approach, the one reminding us of the prophetic call to conversion, the other seeking to hold all the signs of God's grace together in a single vision. In very different ways both try to be faithful to the biblical doctrine of the universal love of God. We may agree that there is a very definite shift of perspective from the one to the other, from the individual to the religions themselves. Each has particular insights to offer in building a theology of salvation and mission – still a very necessary task.

Once we pass beyond the old problematic, however, we have to ask whether either is equal to the task demanded of today's situation. The new problematic, which we must now examine in detail, moves the conversation away from 'internal' dogmatic theology to engage a totally different theological perspective. Once we accept that the other can be saved through the practice and belief of his or her tradition we must attend carefully to the detail of that tradition and resist the temptation to find there a scaled-down version of ours.

Notes

1. cf. Arnulf Camps, *Partners in Dialogue: Christianity and Other World Religions*, New York: Orbis 1983, especially pp. 81ff.

2. A useful summary of Roman Catholic thinking since Vatican II is contained in Paul Knitter's aptly titled 'Catholic Theology at a Cross-roads', *Concilium* 183 (1986), ed. Hans Küng and J. Moltmann. Since Vatican II theological reflection on the problem of the relationship of the Church to peoples of other faiths has been carried on at a number of different levels. The *Bulletin* of the Vatican Secretariat for non-Christians, while aiming to be ecumenical in scope, makes for a useful Roman Catholic journal of record of inter-faith activity. Issue 34–35 (1977) contains a useful, if dated, bibliography.

3. Daniélou's early work *The Advent of Salvation*, New York 1962, originally published in English as *Advent* in 1950, presents us with a beguiling definition of Christianity as 'the eternal youth of the world' (p. 18). Religions such as Judaism and Buddhism, which comes before Christ are not so much false as *old*, survivals of ancient civilizations. Such anomalies as Islam are 'regressions'. 'They have abandoned certain aspects of Christianity, as if things were going too fast for them, to get back to that idea of pedagogy' (ibid.).

4. *Le Mystère du salut des nations*, Paris 1948, pp. 17–18.

5. The origins of the celebrated Roman Catholic dictum, 'outside the Church no salvation', are mentioned briefly by Knitter, op. cit. pp. 122–123 and Race, op. cit. p. 10. See also D'Costa, *John Hick's Theology*, pp. 73–82. Hans Küng considers the declarations on free-dom of religion and belief of Vatican II 'an epoch-making reversal of the attitude to those outside the "holy Roman Church" ' in *On Being a Christian*, London: Collins 1977, p. 97. It should be noted that there are various instances well before the Council of the Church officially condemning a narrowly exclusivist interpretation. cf., for instance, the condemnation by Alexander VI of Jansenius' proposition that pagans, Jews, heretics and the like are in no way under the influence of Christ (DS 2305); Pius IX's teaching that those invincibly ignorant of Christianity can gain eternal salvation (DS 2866); and – the most celebrated recent case – the condemnation by Pius XII of the American Jesuit, Leonard Feeney, who held that all non-Catholics were

excluded from eternal salvation (D S 3866).

6. cf. *Holy Pagans of the Old Testament*, London: Longman 1957, pp. 29–41.

7. Hans Urs von Balthasar, 'Catholicism and the Religions', *Communio*, 5 (1978), pp. 6–14.

8. A valuable attempt to combine this ancient patristic theme with the modern perspective is to be found in the work of the Indian theologian Chrys Saldanha, *Divine Pedagogy: A Patristic View of Non-Christian Religions*, Biblioteca di Scienze Religiose 57, Rome: L A S 1984. Saldanha focuses on Justin, Irenaeus and Clement of Alexandria. The concept of pedagogy when used by the Fathers served to 'bring out the preparatory character of Greek philosophy as well as the transcendent nature of Christianity' (p. 153). The task of maintaining a balance between the two remains just as difficult today as in the early Church.

9. cf., for example, the highly influential work of Avery Dulles, particularly *Models of the Church*, New York: Doubleday 1974, and *The Catholicity of the Church*, Oxford: Oxford University Press, where Dulles comments that 'Catholicism is irrevocably bound to affirm that the fullness of grace and truth came into the world through Jesus Christ, and is disposed to find elements of truth and goodness in religions that have developed without benefit of exposure to Judaism and Christianity' (p. 63).

10. This is particularly apparent in the recent phenomenon of Liberation Theology which is as much about the liberation of theology from its traditional 'classical' concerns as it is concerned for the liberation of oppressed groups and classes. cf. John Ball, art cit., *The Way*, April 1985, for a general survey, and: G. Gutierrez, *A Theology of Liberation*, New York: Orbis 1973; J.L. Segundo, *The Liberation of Theology*, New York: Orbis 1975; Leonardo Boff, *Jesus Christ, Liberator*, New York: Orbis 1978.

11. *The Documents of Vatican I I* , with commentary and notes, ed. Walter M. Abbott, London: Chapman 1966. cf. the *Declaration on the Relationship of the Church to non-Christian Religions*, (*Nostra Aetate* [*N A*]), pp. 660–668. Also available in *Christianity and Other Religions*, ed. Hick and Hebblethwaite, pp. 80–86.

12. An account of the genesis and development of the conciliar texts is to be found in *Commentary on the Documents of Vatican I I*, ed. Herbert Vorgrimler, London: Burns and Oates/Herder 1967. cf. particularly vol. I I I, pp. 1–151, for the history of *N A* .

13. Although *N A* is the single most important document of the Council on other faiths, the topic is touched on, explicitly and implicitly, elsewhere. A fuller account would have to include at least the following: *Dogmatic Constitution on the Church (Lumen Gentium)*, esp. 13 and 16; *Pastoral Constitution on the Church in the Modern World (Gaudium et Spes)*, 92; *Decree on Missionary Activity (Ad Gentes)*, 9, 11, 15, 18; *Decree on Priestly Formation (Optatam Totius)*, 16; finally, as background to our theme, the *Decree on Religious Freedom (Dignitatis Humanae)*, has a particular significance.

14. A useful bibliography of Rahner's work available in English has been compiled by C.J. Pedley, *Heythrop Journal*, 1984, pp. 320–360. The major article which develops Rahner's thinking on Anonymous Christianity is 'Christianity and the non-Christian Religions', *Theological Investigations (TI)* 5, pp. 115–134. Other articles which repeat and amplify these ideas include: 'Thoughts on the Possibility of Belief Today', *TI* 5, pp. 3–22; 'Anonymous Christians', *TI* 6, pp. 390–398; 'Anonymous Christianity and the Missionary Task of the Church', *TI*, pp. 161–178; 'Anonymous and Explicit Faith', *TI* 16; pp. 52–59; 'The One Christ and the Universality of Salvation', *TI* 16, pp. 199–224; 'On the Importance of Non-Christian Religions for Salvation', *TI* 18, pp. 288–295; 'Church, Churches and Religions', *TI* 10, pp. 30–49; 'Jesus Christ and the Non-Christian Religions', *TI* 17, pp. 39–50. cf. also Rahner's major work: *Foundations of Christian Faith*, London: Darton, Longman & Todd 1978.
15. Rahner makes this point against Henri de Lubac in *TI* 12, pp. 162f. and expounds his concept of a 'lawful religion' in *TI*, 5, p. 121ff., arguing that 'by the fact that in practice man as he really is can live his proffered relationship to God only in society, man must have had the right and indeed the duty to live this relationship to God within the religious and social realities offered to him in his particular historical situation' (p. 131). cf. the comment in Dulles, *The Catholicity of the Church*, p. 63, that post-Vatican II thinking accepts the mediation of divine grace through the *social institutions* of the religions.
16. *TI* 5, p. 121.
17. *TI* 5, p. 131.
18. *TI* 5, 'Thoughts on the Possibility of Faith Today', pp. 3–22.
19. ibid., p. 8.
20. ibid., p. 9.
21. *TI* 5, p. 131.
22. *TI* 5, esp. p. 9. cf. Peter Hebblethwaite, 'The Status of "Anonymous Christians" ', *Heythrop Journal*, 1977, pp. 47–55.
23. The objections to Rahner's thesis have been admirably summarized by Gavid D'Costa in 'Karl Rahner's Anonymous Christian – A Reappraisal', *Modern Theology*, 1; 2(1985), pp. 131–148. An example of a recent 'liberal' critic would be Alan Race, *Christianity and Religious Pluralism*, London: SCM 1985, pp. 45–62; while the trenchant criticisms of H. van Straelen, *The Catholic Encounter with World Religions*, London: Burns and Oates 1965, pp. 95ff., echo the more conservative reaction to Rahner represented by Henri de Lubac and Hans Urs von Balthasar.
24. *TI* 18, pp. 288ff.; cf also *TI* 5, p. 122; *TI* 17, pp. 39ff.
25. Central to Rahner's argument here is his understanding of grace. Having established that the right-minded non-Christian already stands within the ambit of God's sanctifying grace, Rahner shows that *all* grace is continuous and requires *of its very nature* to be made explicit. Grace, as the gift of God himself, is always seeking ways to make itself present. Rahner speaks of the 'incarnatorial dynamism inherent in

grace' which wills to extend itself into all dimensions of life and make itself explicit both historically and socially. Thus grace naturally seeks objectification in the social structure of our existence: within non-Christian traditions and then within the Church which is their fulfilment. *TI* 12, pp. 161ff.; *TI* 16, pp. 52–59.

26. For Rahner mission is definitive of the Church as the embodiment and sign of God's grace present to the world. The purpose of mission is to improve the situation in which salvation can be achieved; once we are consciously aware of who we are the likelihood that we will arrive at our fulfilment is greater than if we merely possess and fulfil that humanity at an unconscious level. Such supernatural virtues as are present in other faiths cannot remain unfulfilled; our very nature as human beings demands that they become historical and categorical. As Rahner says, 'love strives for what is greater . . . it is precisely this striving which constitutes that love which is an absolute duty', *TI* 12, p. 178.

27. The underlying areas of disagreement between Rahner and von Balthasar, so marked in *Cordula oder der Erntsfall*, Einsiedeln, 1966, are illuminatingly analysed by Rowan Williams in his essay, 'Balthasar and Rahner', in *The Analogy of Beauty*, ed. John Riches, Edinburgh: T. & T. Clark 1986.

4 THE NEW PROBLEMATIC

The concept of theology with which we in the West are most familiar
– if not necessarily comfortable – conjures up the picture of cloistered academics seeking out more and more contorted formulae to
defend an ancient tradition from the challenges of modernism. If we
think like that, so much the worse for the study of theology. It is true
that most theologians have to do their work in the study rather than
in the bazaar. But none can afford to ignore what John XXIII called
the 'signs of the times'. These represent not secular annoyances to be
kept clear of the eternal and sacred science but the very stuff of
theology. Where do we hear the Word of God in today's world?
Theology has to learn to accommodate itself both to history – its own
and that of the 'outside' world – and to the beliefs, aspirations and
concerns of all men and women of good will. Thus a concept of
theology which seeks only to defend the Word runs the risk of
ignoring where that Word may be speaking. As the liberation theology
movements constantly remind us, to do theology today means letting
them both reinterpret each other. Pluralism itself is not a threat to
theology, any more than poverty and injustice are; each can be an
incentive to probe the ancient tradition more deeply. The problem is
not pluralism but indifferentism: the notion that all religions are much
the same anyway and that all are equally truthful or equally valid ways
of salvation. Once we accept such a premise theology ceases to exist
and religion soon loses its inner vitality and power to support.

In a theology of religions an adequate understanding of the nature
of religion is obviously crucial – and we shall have the opportunity to
consider this in more detail later. As yet we are still considering
different approaches to the problem of the other. Once theologians
have accepted that the Word may be articulated to, and even
through, the other they can no longer be content with a largely
'internal' model of theology. This is the new agenda: can theologians
marry Christian integrity with an openness to the 'signs of the times'
manifested in other religions? The paradigm known popularly as
pluralism is an attractive option, but it covers a number of
approaches and raises its own questions – not least about the nature
of theology itself.[1]

In this chapter I want to consider the emergence of this different understanding of the scope and method of theology. It will entail three main points of discussion. First, I want briefly to take up where we left off in the opening chapter about the origins and nature of the pluralist end of the theological spectrum. What we are observing in much current theology of religions is a shift from a christocentric to a theocentric version of the universe: the privileged position of Christianity as the only way is to be rejected, and other religions must be accepted as equally valid paths to the one God. This position has its roots deep in the history of theological debate and has been most notably articulated by Troeltsch. In the context of the missiological debate, it has been argued persuasively by the influential American philosopher, William Ernest Hocking. Secondly, I want to look at the work of Wilfred Cantwell Smith, a historian of religion who has been deeply concerned to bridge the gap between religious studies as science and religion as it is actually practised. His approach tries to include theology and theological claims within the purview of religious studies. Here we will consider what sort of theology must result once one begins to assimilate and react to the data of the world of religions. Thirdly, we shift gear slightly and look at the work of the British theologian and philosopher of religion, John Hick, whose theology has been revolutionized by his encounter with the world of religious pluralism.

A World of Many Religions

Our concern here is with a second and much more radical shift of perspective. The problem of 'otherness' is seen no longer in terms of the salvation of the individual or even the values of the other tradition. Pluralist theologians look first at the world of many religions and only then at the position of Christianity. They are less concerned with Christian mission than with asking what Christians have to learn from the other. This, of course, is a highly complex, not to say emotive, area. But in looking at the issues raised by the pluralist model it should be emphasized that there is room for a good deal of nuance, that pluralists have important insights to offer and that, however much they may seem to challenge the traditional version of Christian theology, they cannot be rejected out of hand. I hope that what may emerge from the discussion are some of the crucial issues: the nature of human religiosity, its instantiation in 'the religions' and, as noted above, the task and scope of theology in the face of the world of religious pluralism.

I have already outlined the origins of the pluralist approach to theology of religions with particular reference to Troeltsch. However, it was Hocking as much as any particular individual who provoked Kraemer's 'biblical realism' reaction and thus managed to polarize Protestant missionary thinking. Although neither a missionary theologian nor an historian of religion, Hocking questioned the traditional conception of evangelization, which for him is associated with a model of mission as the aggressive extension of Church frontiers.[2] Much wider issues are at stake. Religion is an essential element in the development of a sound world civilization and any theology which suggests a radical discontinuity between religions and a revelation particular to one tradition must be rejected. At the same time a syncretistic merging of traditions in a single world faith risks losing that vision which is particular to each religion. Rather, suggests Hocking, by deepening the particular insight in the light of the broader vision which all religions share one can look forward to a growing convergence and a common enlightenment. Hocking's theology revolves round two postulates: that religion must be *universal*, because it arises from a universal human craving for absolute truth which is valid for all peoples, and that religion must be *particular* because it can only exist in a human community to which it has to be communicated. The two coexist in a sort of tension through the person of the mystic who is the link between the religious ideal and the community. Some religions emphasize the particular over the universal. Judaism, Hinduism and Confucianism, for instance, can be classed very generally as 'local' religions in the sense that they can only be understood by reference to the particular conditions of the communities in which they emerged. Buddhism, Christianity and Islam, by contrast, began essentially as reforms of what were originally seen as religious aberrations. Their historical founders all called on people to recognize the universal element which was in danger of being ignored or forgotten. The former, says Hocking, are not missionary; the latter, with their universal message, are. The latter want to make exclusivist claims for their own creed over any other. And, once seen in historical terms, this move is quite comprehensible. But all religions contain elements of the universal *and* the particular. Hocking prefers to relate religions together by means of an Hegelian idealist philosophy of the steady emergence of Spirit in the history of religion. The dialectic between the particular and the universal gradually works itself out. No religion can consider itself absolutely true. Rather, from the 'partially false' a tendency can always be discerned towards a 'truer position'.[3]

Despite what appears as a somewhat naive optimism in the ability of religions to improve themselves, Hocking is trying to hold together two points. There is not just a semi-mystical idealist vision of religion as the common quest of humanity but also a realization that the 'common essence' can only be approached through the separate existing traditions. But that is precisely the problem for all pluralists: they want to work from the *real*, that is to say existing, traditions and not some ideal essence, yet they are also concerned to avoid any value-judgement which might be interpreted as exalting one religion above another. In fact the single world religion which Hocking envisages turns out to be a reconceived Christianity – not, in Hocking's case, because of some inbuilt Christian chauvinism, but because the symbolism of Christianity may well turn out, in his opinion, to be the best expression of a world faith. This makes Hocking, like so many pluralist theologians, a pragmatist. But no more than Troeltsch is he a strict relativist. The problem for the theocentric theologian lies elsewhere. What role should theology be playing in the inter-religious encounter? Integrative and strictly non-judgmental by seeking out common elements and essences? Or analytic and critical, devoted to 'second order' issues of method?

As we have already noted with regard to Troeltsch, we find that there are really two items on the agenda, represented by the academic disciplines of theology and the history or phenomenology of religions. What is the relationship between them? The study of religion can and, according to many scholars, *must* be treated strictly as a science to be set alongside other legitimate aspects of human study. Historians of religion have to 'bracket off' their own religious commitment if a correctly objective methodology of study is to be achieved. But within the discipline itself a sometimes heated debate has gone on between those who want to promote a scientific study of the empirical phenomena of religion which prescinds from questions of truth and value altogether and those who insist that such questions are part and parcel of the study of religion. For the latter theology must be considered another aspect of the properly scientific study of religions.[4]

Theology and the Study of Religion

Perhaps the strongest advocate of this integrated study of religious culture is the celebrated Canadian Islamic scholar Wilfred Cantwell Smith.[5] Although primarily a historian of religion rather than a theologian, Cantwell Smith takes very seriously the reality of the transcendent, a proper appreciation of which he takes to be essential to an adequate science of religion. The proper object of the history of religion is humanity in its transcendent dimension, and he talks somewhat portentously of comparative religion as the 'disciplined self-consciousness of man's variegated and developing religious life'.[6] What is called for by the new pluralism is a reassessment of traditional theological categories and their replacement by a theology which aims to contribute to the general understanding of human existence in today's world. It is not, therefore, that one aims at developing a specifically Christian theology of religions but a Christian theology which takes into account the data and questions raised by other faiths. For Cantwell Smith the crucial questions are those which arise from the very existence of other faiths, not from the particular apologetic concerns of one faith. 'We explain the fact that the Milky Way is there by the doctrine of creation, but how do we explain the fact that the *Bhagavad Gita* is there?'[7] Traditional Christian theology has tended to be very deliberately centred on the defence of Christian truth-claims against all others. Cantwell Smith finds such a theology arrogant and inappropriate to a new situation.

Cantwell Smith is critical of rigid methodologies. In fact he is suspicious of any approach to religious studies which emphasizes the role of the student as observer rather than participant. For him the history of religions is an enterprise which involves the whole of human culture. It cannot be fenced off as a separate type of study with its own special method, but the same can also be said for theology. If the study of religion should manifest a concern for the development of humanity as a whole, how much more should the science we call theology. 'All theology,' he said, 'is self-theology, and yet it must exclude no-one'.[8] In other words theology is autobiographical yet world-orientated; the theologian must start from his own history but he soon finds that that history cannot be separated from the history of the other.

As a historian of religion perhaps Cantwell Smith's most important contribution is a redefinition of religion. Religions must not be separated from their living and growing context in the lives of people; they have always been in a process of flux and change and still are. He objects to the sort of academic abstractions which turn religious traditions into separate and rather static entities – a proposal which inevitably gives rise to the idea of religions as competing ideologies. He sees religions as cumulative traditions which preserve the faith-experience of persons and therefore of historical communities. What holds them together is not so much a common ground or essence as a historically conditioned structure of faith. As a Christian who is deeply conscious of the relativity of religious belief Cantwell Smith is concerned to see the history of Christianity as one particular strand in the complex web of human history. His proposal is for a theology which aspires to be part of a general movement towards the truth.[9] Therefore the only way to understand religions is 'from the inside', as it were, that is to say through actual contact and dialogue. He thinks that what is being prepared is the ground on which people can actively work out the areas of common concern. Gradually they can recognize the differences between them and the unique contribution which each can make to a common enterprise. These two notions, of cultural relativity and the 'global' or universal conception of theology, have been taken up by Hick.

Copernican versus Ptolemaic theology

What happens when theology tries to accommodate itself to other religions? Anybody seriously concerned with the contemporary religious scene must sympathize with, or at least understand, the position taken up by Troeltsch and Hocking. But does it follow that we must be prepared to question the finality or definitive status of Christianity? This seems to be the major implication of a 'global' theology. Is it inevitable? To some extent Hick and those who follow a pluralist line are the successors of liberal protestantism and are very much concerned with the problems of historicism and cultural relativism which were raised but never answered by Troeltsch. Hick himself began in the mainstream of institutional Anglicanism but was later converted to a strongly evangelical faith in which he found his own personal commitment.[10] In many ways he still seems to be attached to this personalist piety and emphasizes the importance of the personal act of faith, though he is no longer prepared to insist on exactly the same sort of commitment as the norm of faith for everyone. Jesus Christ is still the way for those explicitly committed to him, but it no longer makes sense to speak of him as the sole Saviour *for all*. Hick's writing makes it clear that he is much exercised by the inadequacy of traditional christocentric theology, especially as regards the problem of salvation. But he also draws our attention to what I have called the new problematic: the increase in the number of non-Christians in the world, the growing presence of immigrant communities and the comparative failure of missionary effort. He adds further considerations, above all the fact that religious affiliation is usually determined by geography or local culture. As we noted earlier, if I had been born in South-East Asia I would very likely have become a Buddhist and not a Christian. 'Can we be so entirely confident that to have been born in our particular part of the world carries with it the privilege of knowing the full religious truth, whereas to be born elsewhere involves the likelihood of having only partial and inferior truth?'[11] According to Hick, these factors, taken together, demand a radical shift in the way we do theology of religions.

Claims to uniqueness or normativeness on the part of Christianity, or any religion, are simply an inappropriate response to the problems raised by the pluralism of modern religious culture. Are not non-Christian traditions equally valid – each tradition expressive of a particular movement of faith or experience of divine revelation? The global pattern, established in the 'golden age' of religious creativity, from around 800 BC until the period of expansion of Islam after the death of the prophet Muhammad, has remained 'fairly stable' ever since. Change and expansion has been minimal. Hick, therefore, moves toward a radical rethinking of the theology of religions. It is based on a single presupposition, that the great world religions are all responses to an experience of Ultimate Reality. As far as it goes, such a premise is essential to any theology of religions, even though we might want to strike a sceptical note and add with Barth and Kraemer that all historical-empirical religions, including Christianity, are in need of reform and some sort of fulfilment. But Hick goes further, speaking in Troeltschian terms of the world religions as culture-specific totalities. Each religion is a particular system which, strictly speaking, can only be understood within its own tradition. Following Cantwell Smith, he rejects the Western preoccupation with religions as mutually exclusive ideological systems and therefore asks us to make no *a priori* judgement about the normative status of one tradition over against others. The idea of mission as an attempt to convert the non-Christian to the Christian way is simply misconceived. It might well be objected that Hick already betrays here a particular theological, not to say philosophical, stance – shifting quite deliberately from a christocentric to a thoroughly theocentric version of theology. We might want to ask whether it is possible to approach a religious tradition without any presuppositions in the hope of being totally objective and value-free. Putting that to one side for the moment, we must first let Hick speak for himself. In his celebrated 'Copernican Revolution' in theology he outlines a new approach to the problem of religious pluralism.[12]

Hick attacks traditional soteriology for being basically exclusivist, requiring an explicit knowledge of, or faith in, Jesus Christ for salvation. He quotes with disapproval fundamentalist statements about the damnation of those who have never heard of Christ and then himself goes on rather to damn with faint praise theologians who try to free Christianity from elitism by developing inclusivist theories of the salvation of the non-Christian. Traditional Roman Catholic concepts like implicit faith and baptism of desire, along with the ecclesiology of Vatican II and Rahner's theory of the Anonymous Christian, are tipped onto the theological scrapheap. For Hick they fail to get to the root of the problem, which, he thinks, can be addressed only by a total paradigm shift, a complete re-orientation of one's theology. Using the language of astronomy, Hick likens all such traditional confessional theology to the Ptolemaic map of an earth-centred universe. In theology Christianity is seen as the centre of the universe of faiths with all the other religions revolving around it and being graded in value according to their distance from the centre. Such theories as the Anonymous Christian are not so much a redrawing of the map of the universe, more another 'epicycle' – an attempt to accommodate growing knowledge of other faiths by drawing a more complicated, but still thoroughly Christianity-centred map. Sooner or later, says Hick, we have to face the fact that more is needed than another version of the old; we have to find a new paradigm, a shift from a Christianity-centred or Jesus-centred model of the universe of faiths, 'to the realisation that it is *God* who is at the centre, and that all the religions of mankind, including our own, serve and revolve around him'.[13] Hence the *Copernican* model: all religions relative not to a static Christianity but to God or, as Hick puts it in order to accommodate non-theistic religions like Buddhism, the Real.

This thoroughly theocentric position has a lot to recommend it in an age of religious pluralism, but it has also aroused considerable debate and not a little confusion. Over the years Hick has shifted his ground on a number of points but sees no reason to alter the central thesis. The argument, as we have noted, is basically cumulative. Although his fundamental objection to traditional 'exclusivist' theology centres on the problem of salvation he recognizes that christocentric theologies do have answers, even if they are of the nature of 'epicycles' to the original scheme and clearly are not to Hick's personal taste. There are, however, other more important issues at stake. For Hick the phenomenological and historical questions already mentioned are properly *theological* problems and the endless corrections and adjustments of traditional 'Ptolemaic' theology cannot answer them.

Moreover the same fruitless and self-defeating game is played by other religions too. Christianity has developed its own form of inclusivism. Hick asks: cannot the other religions do the same? Different communities learn to appraise their relationship with ultimate reality through the language, symbols and practices of a traditional way of faith. Each religion is perceived from within, says Hick, 'as "the way, the truth and the life" and judges alternatives in its light. And so we have the familiar world-wide situation of people being formed by a particular vision, which functions as the standard by which they judge all others'.[14] Hick points out that claims to superiority or some normative status can be, and are, made from within any religious tradition. Every religion, not just Christianity, claims to judge others. When we find that all religions see themselves as the standard – the sun around which the others rotate – we must begin to doubt the claim of Christianity alone to be privileged. What we see is simply a final vestige of the old imperialism. Christianity, to continue Hick's imagery, is just one of many planets, all relative to the single Absolute.

Doing Global Theology

What are we to make of Hick's Copernican theology? There is no need to repeat here the sometimes heated debate which he has provoked. As before it is more important to identify the problems as he sees them. What questions is Hick putting to traditional theology? On one fundamental premise he is surely right. Competition between what are fundamentally cooperative enterprises must be rejected. Religious chauvinism, the worst kind of exclusivism, is the enemy of true dialogue; it is clearly important to work for a more positive acceptance of the scriptures, beliefs and practices of other faiths. Hick is very forceful about the need to develop real tolerance between religions if unnecessary barriers are to be broken down and what he sees as a 'global ecumenism' to grow. But at what point does moral tolerance – that total acceptance of the other as a human being with rights like mine and traditions which are often very different – involve an ideological tolerance, a refusal to judge a person's beliefs precisely because they are the beliefs of *another*? Does this not represent a drift into relativism? Is there not a distinction between the two? Does the one demand or imply the other? Like Troeltsch Hick seems to think that religion can only be truth *for me*. If religious truth is always what is true for this or that particular person it makes no sense to speak of it as 'better' or 'superior'. Thus in shifting radically in the direction of the new problematic Hick can ask whether Christ is *in any way* the way to salvation for the non-Christian. Are not other faiths equally valid, each tradition being relative to the cultural form in which it is expressed?

This question is clearly of crucial importance to the viability of a global theology and needs to be considered further. One sometimes gets the impression from Hick that the first requirement in doing theology is, as some of his critics have put it, 'being nice to people'.[15] He is, however, making a perfectly serious theological point and we need to dwell on it briefly. One does not have to live in Northern Ireland or Punjab to know the power which religion has to arouse anger and violence. Such intolerance is obviously to be deplored. What Hick presumes, however, is that religion is to be identified with ideology and that ideology inevitably leads to a certain type of behaviour. The dialogal concept of religion put forward by Cantwell Smith denies this.[16] Dialogue is an exchange between persons and only secondarily an argument over opinions. One can accept the person without necessarily approving of his ideas. Panikkar argues the point in a rather sophisticated manner by proposing the thesis that 'the tolerance you have is directly proportional to the myth you live and inversely proportional to the ideology you follow'.[17] He means that we often make the mistake of relating to each other simply at the level of explicit ideology which we both recognize and not at the level of myth or story, the accepted horizon of our existence which we so often take for granted. The two have got to intersect; dialogue is about finding something to share in our respective life stories, our common condition as searching human beings. If we can learn to share an ideal we may be able to tolerate differences in ideas. 'Communion in the same myth is what makes tolerance possible'.[18]

The problem, of course, is that one cannot just cut off myth from ideology. They can be distinguished but not separated. The cultural values encapsulated in a person's myth speak of what is true; if they did not people would not believe in them. Here Hick seems rather to fudge the issue. He sees questions of truth as secondary to the common search for religious values – precisely the objection made to liberal protestantism by the neo-orthodox theologians. Indeed Hick seems to take a thoroughly pragmatic line about questions of religious truth. All religions 'exhibit a common structure, which is soteriological in the broad sense that it offers a transition from a radically unsatisfactory state to a limitlessly better one'.[19] But while we may be able to 'grade religions' according to various criteria, it is impossible on purely *a priori* theological grounds to judge between them. All we can go by is the effect religions have in people's everyday lives as they seek the way to salvation, as they move from 'self-centredness' to 'Reality-centredness', to use Hick's jargon. It may be possible *in principle* to judge which religion is the 'right' or 'true' way but all this means is that it can be done eschatologically, at the end of time. At that point Christianity may turn out to be the best way but there is no way we can know it now. In this sense Hick is being deliberately anti-relativist, even if somewhat agnostic.

Hick wants to have it both ways; indeed he needs to have it both ways. First he wants to hold that all religions are culturally specific totalities which cannot be judged on the basis of *one particular* religious tradition. This he thinks is essential if one is to be true to the enormous diversity of religious traditions. At the same time he does not want to let his avowed pluralism lead him into a total relativism, saying that religions are basically incomparable. But where in that case is the basis of comparison? This is Hick's difficulty. In theory, the different religions are reflections of the one Divine Reality, as the planets reflect the light of the sun. In practice, it is impossible to distinguish between them. The problem with a theocentric universe is that it begs the question of how one encounters or knows God in the first place. Hick, as a philosopher of religion, seems happy enough with a rather vague concept of God, what he calls – invoking Kantian terminology – the *noumenal* Real that grounds the particular *phenomenon*. But again the problem (which is faced in different ways by all religions) is precisely how to speak of this Ultimate Real if all we can apprehend is the particular imagery or symbolism of particular traditions. Religions may recognize that the language they use is relative, partial or inadequate, a matter largely of symbol and metaphor, but that does not stop them using that language or claiming that it does have some specific cognitive status. Hick would accept this; language (e.g. of the incarnation) may be mythological in form but it can still have an ontological status. But can one expect to 'demythologize' the language and still retain the real sense? While the historian of religions in Hick wants to give full weight to the phenomena of religious pluralism, the pluralist theologian or philosopher of religion is still stuck in the liberal protestant mode looking for the common ground of all religion. Hick posits a theocentric universe with a concept of God, or the Real, which is not specific to one religious culture. Here, I think, he parts company with Cantwell Smith for whom religious concepts and ideas are always culture-specific however much they may be in the process of flux and growth together. Hick, on the other hand, thinks one can speak of some sort of a common experience of God which is not culture-specific. He wants to say that we can only really know God by some sort of genuine religious experience, not through reasoning or inference. This basic soteriological experience, moving, as he puts it from self-centredness to reality-centredness, is the ground common to all religions.

Where does this idea come from? Again, how does one *know* the Ultimate? As a philosopher Hick may be able to produce a version of the Ultimate Reality as the *a priori* condition of possibility of human knowing, existence etc., but beyond that God has always got to be *somebody's* God. In fact, as has been pointed out, Hick's argument implicitly admits as much.[20] He takes his initial stand on a soteriological axiom: the universal will of God to save. But this, of course, is a Christian axiom. It is through entering into that religious tradition which is formed round the death and resurrection of Christ that the Christian understands something of what God is like. This is not to deny that the Buddhist may not have an equally valid insight into the Real through his participation in the on-going historical tradition which began with the Buddha's enlightenment. In fact Hick would accept that such diverse visions are complementary rather than contradictory. But the point is that each religion arises from specific cultural contexts which enable people to speak of God, or the Real, or Brahman, or Allah, or the Satguru, in the first place. To talk about the Divine at the heart of all religions entails immersing oneself in the cultural totality of a religious tradition. One cannot separate the particular tradition from the Reality to which it points. When Hick tries to do this, whether by looking for a common religious experience or for adequate common philosophical language, he inevitably ends up with an experience which is vague and a concept of God which is, to say the least, rather empty.

What is religion?

Hick's theocentric map makes for a Christology which many Christians would fail to recognize. There are many mediators. Jesus is just one of them. His way is valid as a system of morals which enlighten us and teach us how to find God, but it is illegitimate to think of him as a unique or normative figure for any except those who explicitly commit themselves to lead the specifically Christian way.[21] There is, perhaps, a prior issue: not so much what Hick's proposal must do to traditional Christology but what version he presents of religion – *any* religion. To speak of many mediators or a pluralism of religious experience does not make Hick a relativist, for he does not want to assert dogmatically that all religions are *determined* by culture or that they can *only* be understood as expressions of particular cultures.[22] He makes the important point that religions are the products of culture and that they need to be understood in relation to that culture. But he is clearly seeking for some criterion by which the truth-claims of religion can be judged. I have already drawn attention to the principle of eschatological verification above; at the end of time we may know which religion is true. Meanwhile we are left with various pragmatic considerations – how much a religion 'helps' one on the way to salvation. Hick does accept that a description of the world of religions as a series of pure relativisms will not do. All religions claim in some sense to be privileged, absolute or normative for all people. His point, however, is that the theological dogmatism which can so easily arise from these claims must be overcome; he wants ideological as well as moral tolerance. But it may be that he is missing a fundamental point here about the nature of religion itself. Picking up Smith's point about human religiosity always being found in particular historical forms or 'incarnations', it seems that what we are dealing with is a set of competing absolutisms, each of which claims to be privileged and, in some sense, to be judging the others. To give a truly objective account of this world means accepting the claims to some sort of finality or exclusiveness on the part of all religions.

Hick uses the celebrated Buddhist parable of the elephant and the blind men.[23] His stated position is that no one is privileged; all the blind men identify one particular part as the whole. To use the Kantian terminology again, each grasps only a phenomenal part of the noumenal whole which is behind all of them. The whole is therefore the sum total of the parts and yet much more; we can only learn about the whole by listening, as it were, to the various contributions of so many very limited viewpoints. In other words, various partial accounts of 'the Real' contribute to a 'global theology'. As far as it goes the parable is helpful. Hick uses it explicitly to explain the relationship between the great religious traditions and to show that our knowledge of the Divine comes from the particular data of religious experience as presented in the history of religion. What his interpretation ignores is that *each* interpreter, Hick himself included, claims that his version is privileged. In other words each perspective seeks to interpret the *whole*. His point about inclusivism – that it can be operated from within any religion – is exactly right.

But that does not destroy the case for christocentric theology.

Here, I would suggest, we have to note a crucial difference between the theologian and the philosopher.[24] The latter has to look at the whole data of religious experience, from the various traditions. Hick as a philosopher works *a posteriori*; he wants to construct a global theology of religions, one which is not built from within a particular tradition but which develops *in* and *through* dialogue. The theologian of any religious tradition, however, begins quite consciously from an *a priori* position, developing a theology *for* dialogue – that is to say, looking at the principles which are to be maintained if Christian integrity is not to be compromised. The blind men in the parable are theologians, not philosophers; they all claim not that their insight into the truth is inadequate and needs to be supplemented by the others (though they may well admit this) but that *in some sense* it is definitive for all or constitutive of the truth for all. Hick wants to be both; as a self-confessed ecumenical theologian he is actually proposing a different model or way of doing theology. This, as we have already noted, is a perfectly feasible project, but it would be disingenuous to suggest that it differs from traditional theology by attempting to be more 'open', 'objective' or lacking in *a priori* presuppositions. Such a theology does have certain preconceived ideas about the nature of religion and, more obviously, about the nature of truth.

What is Hick's understanding of the relationship of religions? All the great religions are continuous with each other; the knowledge of the Ultimate which can be gained through Christianity is no different *in kind* from that found in any other religion. Religion, therefore, exhibits common features, beliefs, practices, structures etc. The religious history of humankind is interdependent, not exclusive or monolithic. Furthermore we may expect religions to move more closely together as they learn from each other and become less culturally isolated. Meanwhile theology should be seeking to isolate and articulate further those items of common experience which give an insight into Ultimate Truth. The assumption is, however, that truth is independent of particular traditions and somehow common to all. We may agree with Hick that there is one Ultimate or Reality which all religions are seeking to describe but truth – even Ultimate Truth – does not exist independent of statements about truth. Hick's version of global theology raises the problem of how one is to translate from one tradition into another. If he is to be successfully non-relativist he must provide an answer to this question. To put what is really the same question somewhat differently, how is one to separate the 'general' or 'common' from the 'particular' or 'special'? Or, using Hick's image, how does one get from the particular 'planet' to the central 'sun'? To change the metaphor, Hick speaks as if all religions have a common core which is clothed in different sets of beliefs. What we have to do is strip away the outer layers to reveal the 'bare necessities' underneath. But can one remove the outer garments of a religion without radically altering its fundamental faith-structure? Would Buddhism without *anatmavada* or a Buddha cult continue to be Buddhism? Would Hinduism without temple worship, *sannyasa* or the myriad *bhakti* cults continue to be Hinduism? It may be true that all particular beliefs are different expressions of one and the same religious truth, but does that truth exist apart from its incarnation in the particular belief?

Truth and Dialogue

What *is* the essence of Christianity? Can it be determined from without and, if so, how? On Buddhist principles, or Hindu, or humanist? My point is that, in the end, religions have got to be self-determining and self-interpreting. Therefore Christianity will interpret Christianity to itself, likewise Buddhism. And each will, quite legitimately, make its own judgement on the values inherent in the other. This need not lead – as Hick seems to think – to intolerance and persecution, provided a spirit of genuine esteem and acceptance of the person is maintained. Nor need it result in the sort of cultural isolationism which Hick rightly deplores. But if dialogue is not to degenerate into a cosy exchange of vague imponderables, concentrating on the bland and uncontroversial, it must be prepared to accept *all* aspects of a religion, including many which may well make us feel uncomfortable and distinctly puzzled. More than that: we must recognize that all religions have certain truth-claims which are a significant part of the tradition; to ignore them is to take the religion less than seriously. One can and must enter dialogue with all the best intentions, without preconceived ideas about the other, without a sense of superiority, without bias or prejudice, but one person's 'bias' may be another's most dearly held beliefs. Admittedly the recognition of the difference is one of the most difficult problems in dialogue; let us just note for the moment that there must come a point when one acknowledges those fundamental convictions which cannot just be bracketed off and eradicated from the encounter. Not only is this psychologically impossible, it is also dishonest to pretend to a lack of conviction, and is no mark of respect to our partner in dialogue. All too easily in the interests of harmony we take for 'bias' what a particular tradition has always held as central, such as the divinity of Christ. We may well want to ask, as a result of our dialogue, what the divinity of Christ may mean in a Buddhist or Hindu context, but that is rather a different matter. Dialogue comes to an end as soon as we cut short the pursuit of the mystery of faith at the heart of the different traditions.

On this assessment, Hick's programme seems, if not relativist, then inevitably reductionist. In Cantwell Smith's version of global theology, however, the data of theology is the universal history of humankind, 'a theology of *homo religiosus*'. Smith is not here proposing a rather sophisticated syncretism, with each tradition contributing certain elements to a single whole. Rather he is underlining the need for theologians to revise their understanding of *Heilsgeschichte*, not focusing on separate communities of faith but recognizing that their individual histories have always been part of a single world history, and are increasingly so today. Thus to think of God's activity in the world as simply limited to one tradition is a total impoverishment of the rich diversity of human religious history. Nor is it an accurate account of the history of Christianity which has developed under the influence of, and been changed by, the existence of other religions over the centuries. Cantwell Smith therefore rejects a theology of religions which operates simply from within one tradition; it is quite inadequate for appreciating and assessing the faith of members of other religions. But he would also reject Hick's model which seeks to operate outside *all* particular traditions and demands they give up claims to a uniqueness which sets them apart. In principle it is certainly possible to work out a global theology on the basis of Hick's Copernican Revolution, with religious phenomena being graded and assessed according to the extent that they hinder or promote the single religious aim of salvation. Such an extrapolation of particular phenomena, however, goes counter to Cantwell Smith's much more intuitive approach which puts religious persons and their faith at the centre of the universe of faiths and sees religions as in a state of continual interaction and flux. His proposal is less radical but much more difficult to achieve: a type of theology which arises from within all the faiths, and is applicable to all the faiths. Can he manage both? Is it possible for theologians to remain faithfully anchored within their own traditions *and* incorporate the data of other faiths?

It is not surprising that one who eschews all attempts at 'grand

theory' has not tried to write such a theology.[25] Cantwell Smith
remains a grand prophet with a grand vision of the future of theology
in a pluralist world. And, as with any prophet, his thought is
sometimes diffuse and infuriatingly imprecise. However, his intentions are clear. He is not trying to relativize the Christian faith, nor is
he proposing any sort of syncretism. He is simply asking us to
rethink our way of doing theology in a multi-faith world. Such a
theology should be 'global' in the sense that it should take into
account the data of other faiths and seek to incorporate their insights
into an organized and articulate whole. This does not necessarily
mean that we ignore the Christian tradition or feel we have to reduce
it to those elements alone which may be said to cohere with the data
of other faiths. It means that we must accept that Christianity is itself
a historical event, that is to say that it has emerged in history and
developed and been changed within history. The Christian tradition
in our present age is not the same as that tradition one hundred or
even fifty years ago. Hence the need to set theological traditions
within their own historical context and to recognize that theology too
is particular and contextual. This much emerges from our understanding not just of the nature of history but of the way in which
theology has reacted to the received tradition. Theology answers the
questions which particular historical circumstances put to it. But in
so doing, that theology also changes the tradition itself. Theology
reacts back on the tradition, as it were, and thus the tradition never
remains static and fixed but is always there to be challenged and
reinterpreted by what is new – by a particular context.

Theology in a world of religious pluralism

This is a rather different version of 'global theology' from that
proposed by Hick's evolutionary model. The latter, not without
some foundation, seems at times to be an invitation to syncretism.
There is another possibility. Today we might want to argue that the
data of world religions have become a part of the Christian tradition
not in the sense that Christians must accept a new revelation, nor
simply because they are a 'problem' or a challenge to theology as
traditionally conceived, but because religious pluralism is part of
that context within which Christianity exists and with which theologians must work if they are to articulate that tradition meaningful-
ly in present circumstances. What we are looking at is not a straight
choice between a purely internal, confessional theology and Hick's
theocentric model which refuses to judge between traditions on *a*

priori grounds, but one which arises from the very process of inter-religious dialogue itself. Today's Christianity as a historical religion is different from what it was because the cultural and religious world of Hindus, Buddhists and Muslims is inescapably a part of the present-day experience of Christians. In this sense Cantwell Smith's call to work 'towards a world theology' cannot be ignored even if it does raise enormous conceptual problems.

I started this chapter with a caricature of traditional Christian theology. Cantwell Smith, with his demand for an answer to questions like 'Why the *Bhagavad Gita*?', is outlining the new problematic and demanding a new approach to theology. No longer can we be content to relativize the world religions in the light of Christian faith; such an interpretation ends up as a projection of Christianity on to the other. Almost all Christian theologies which are still dealing with the old problematic – using the language of 'natural' and 'supernatural', 'implicit' and 'explicit', 'provisional' and 'perfect', etc. – see the relationship of religions in terms of fulfilment. They produce an interpretation of the other in the light of Christian faith. This is certainly not illegitimate if we are content with a purely 'internal' theology of religions. But how far does such a theology enable us to deal with the new problematic? If we want to argue in terms of a theology of fulfilment, then we must also admit that it is possible for another religion – Hinduism, for example – to interpret Christianity in *its* light. Hinduism as the all-encompassing religion is the absolute and Christianity is reduced to the relative: precisely the argument that neo-Vedanta uses. Hick, who draws our attention to this point, considers it fatal to traditional 'internal' theology; for him it makes no sense for all religions to claim to be in exclusive possession of the whole truth. Might it not be, however, that this singular phenomenon is saying something important about the nature of religion, that what a person holds to be true must in some sense be universally valid for all people? If this is the case – and I believe it to be central to the new problematic – is there another way to go 'beyond inclusivism', some version, perhaps, of Cantwell Smith's global or dialogal theology?

Notes

1. The title 'pluralism' suffers from a certain vagueness. None of the surveys manages a definition beyond the general assumption that pluralist theologians see all religions as different ways to the one truth.

As Ursula King asks in her review of Race, *Heythrop Journal* 27 (1986), pp. 452–454, 'how can "pluralism" be a response to "religious pluralism"?' David Tracy speaks 'more accurately' of 'a pluralistic attitude' which is 'an attitude I fundamentally trust. But whenever any affirmation of pluralism, including my own, past and present, becomes simply a passive response to more and more possibilities, none of which shall ever be practised, then pluralism demands suspicion' (*Plurality and Ambiguity*, London: SCM 1988, p. 90).

2. Unlike Kraemer's magisterial *Christian Message*, *Rethinking Missions: A Laymen's Inquiry After 100 Years*, New York and London: Harper 1932, is in substance the work of a committee. Described by Eric Sharpe in *Faith Meets Faith*, London: SCM 1977, p. 82 as 'one of the more celebrated liberal Christian manifestos of this century', the book was inspired by Hocking's philosophical idealism. Hocking's theory of religion and his vision of a harmony of religions is expressed in *Living Religions and a World Faith*, London: Allen and Unwin 1940.

3. *Living Religions*, pp. 31–36.

4. That there has been a long-running debate between theologians and historians of religion over the relative status of their disciplines is well-known. Some of the major figures and issues which have been the cause of controversy are chronicled in such works as Guilford Dudley's *Religion on Trial*, Philadelphia: Temple University Press 1977 and Eric Sharpe's *Comparative Religion*, London: Duckworth 1975. The present more favourable climate of opinion is noted in *Contemporary Approaches to the Study of Religion*, ed. Frank Whaling, Paris – The Hague: Mouton 1984; cf. particularly the contribution by Ursula King, 'Historical and Phenomenological Approaches', which draws attention to growing dissatisfaction with 'reductionist models' of religious studies. Theologians such as Tillich and Pannenberg see the need for a new kind of critical theology which can bridge the gap between Christian systematics and the history of religions. In this regard note C.J. Bleeker, 'Comparing the Religio-Historical and the Theological Method', *Numen* 18 (1971), pp. 9–29; Richard H. Drummond, 'Christian Theology and the History of Religions', *JES* 12 (1975), pp. 389–405, and Charles Davis, 'Theology and Religious Studies,' *Scottish Journal of Religious Studies* 2 (1981), pp. 11–20.

5. A bibliography of the writings of Wilfred Cantwell Smith can be found in *The World's Religious Traditions: essays in his honour*, ed. Frank Whaling, Edinburgh: T & T Clark 1984, pp. 273–286.

6. *Religious Diversity: Essays by Wilfred Cantwell Smith*, ed. Willard G. Oxtoby, New York: Harper and Row 1976, p. 155.

7. From 'The Christian in a Religiously Plural World', an essay published in *Religious Diversity* and reprinted in *Christianity and Other Religions*, ed. J. Hick and P. Hebblethwaite, pp. 87–107.

8. *Towards a World Theology*, London: Macmillan 1980, p. 124.

9. This is the programme enunciated in idealist terms by Hocking, *Living Religions*, pp. 139ff., in terms of a 'reconceived' yet nonetheless dominant Christianity. Cantwell Smith in *The Faith of Other Men*,

New York: Harper, new ed. 1972, speaks of the need to build a 'world community' if humankind is to survive at all; in 'Theology and the World's Religious History' in *Toward a Universal Theology of Religion*, ed. Leonard Swidler, New York: Orbis, 1987, pp. 51–72), he presses the thesis that 'at least so far as the human is concerned (as over against objects and things), a study of history brings us closer to the truth than does science' (p. 69).

10. cf. *God and the Universe of Faiths*, p. 120f. For a full account of the development of John Hick's Copernican Revolution see D'Costa, *John Hick's Theology of Religions*, pp. 5–16.

11. cf. *God and the Universe of Faiths*, p. 132.

12. ibid., pp. 120–132. cf. *God has Many Names*, London: Macmillan, 1980.

13. *God and the Universe of Faiths*, p. 131.

14. 'On Grading Religions', *Religious Studies* 17 (1981), p. 455.

15. cf. 'On Grading Religions, Seeking Truth and Being Nice to People – a Reply to Professor Hick', by Paul Griffiths and Delmas Lewis, *Religious Studies* 19 (1983), pp. 75–80, an article provoked by Hick's 'On Grading Religions'. Hick replies in 'On Conflicting Religious Truth-Claims', *Religious Studies* 19 (1983), pp. 485–491.

16. cf. *The Meaning and End of Religion*, New York: Macmillan 1962, London: SPCK 1978 and particularly the essay 'A Human View of Truth' in *Truth and Dialogue*, ed. John Hick, London: Sheldon 1974, pp. 20–44. 'Truth and falsity are often felt in modern times to be properties or functions of statements or propositions; whereas the present proposal is that much is to be gained by seeing them rather, or anyway by seeing them also, and primarily, as properties or functions of persons' (p. 20).

17. R. Panikkar, *Myth, Faith and Hermeneutics*, New York: Paulist 1979, pp. 20ff.

18. ibid., p. 32.

19. cf. 'On Grading Religions', p. 452.

20. D'Costa, *Theology and Religious Pluralism*, p. 45, argues that 'in the final "eschatological analysis" a theistic God reappears at the *end* of the universe of faiths, once more pushing Hick back into the Ptolemaic camp from which he is trying to escape'.

21. *God and the Universe of Faiths*, pp. 163–179. Hick's point is not that the Christian response to God's revelation in Christ is illegitimate but that an insistence on the *exclusiveness* of this revelation is illegitimate. Hence a move to reinterpret the traditional language of Christology in mythological terms. 'That *God* has been encountered through Jesus is communicated mythologically by saying that he was God the Son incarnate. The myth is thus an appropriate and valid expression of the experience' (p. 172). Cf. 'Jesus and the World Religions' in *The Myth of God Incarnate*, London: SCM 1977, pp. 167–187. D'Costa, *John Hick's Theology*, pp. 119ff., discusses the christological implications. On the adequacy of such a mythological interpretation see J.J. Lipner, 'Christians and the Uniqueness of Christ', *Scottish Journal of Theology*

28 (1975), pp. 359–368 and 'Does Copernicus Help? Reflections for a Christian Theology of Religions', *Religious Studies* 13 (1977), pp. 243–258. The meaning and place of 'myth' in a theology of religions will occupy us in the next chapter.

22. Not that he is always safe from the charge of relativism. Thus in 'On Grading Religions' he makes the point that 'spiritual allegiance' arises from the 'genetic and environmental relativity of religious perception and commitment', art. cit., p. 456. He finds it disturbing that 'one's basic religious vision . . . has been largely selected by factors entirely beyond one's control'. Thus to claim a normative status for one's own tradition 'may merely be to be behaving, predictably, in accordance with the conditioning of one's upbringing' (p. 456). Roger Trigg, 'Religion and the Threat of Relativism', *Religious Studies* 19 (1983), pp. 297–310, admits that Hick 'does not appear to be relativist, since he is saying that different religions are reflecting the *same* Reality', but in his move towards the adoption of mythological and deliberately anti-realist language to describe central Christian doctrines are contained 'the seeds of relativism . . . The Christian conceptual scheme which identifies Jesus with God is to be seen as precisely that. It is one conceptual scheme amongst many, articulating the way that reality is for us. Different schemes may express things differently' (p. 301).

23. cf. *God and the Universe of Faiths*, p. 140.

24. cf. Lipner, 'Does Copernicus Help?': 'Religions regard a revelative event of some sort as the source and mainstay of their understanding of the Absolute, philosophers as philosophers do not; and while a religion may be perfectly justified in trying philosophically to substantiate this understanding, the primacy of its revelative experience remains unchallenged' (pp. 252–253). Keith Ward, *Images of Eternity*, London: Darton, Longman & Todd 1987, has shown how such a revelatory structure or 'iconic vision' is at the heart of all religious visions of reality. The historian of religion, Harold Coward, in his insightful *Sacred Word and Sacred Text: Scripture in World Religions*, New York: Orbis 1988, has demonstrated the formative power contained in traditional sacred scripture, both oral and written.

25. Cantwell Smith notes that 'I waited till my mid-sixties to publish my first work with the word "theology" in the title' ('Theology and the World's Religious History', p. 54). His contention that 'the true historian of religion and the authentic theologian are in the final analysis identical' and that 'a true understanding of the history of religion, and theology, converge' (p. 55) leaves open the question of how we measure truth and authenticity. Frank Whaling's judicious comments (in his *Christian Theology and World Religions, A Global Approach*, Basingstoke: Marshall Pickering 1986, on the possibility of a theology based on Cantwell Smith's 'universal theory of world religions' should be noted. Global theology 'finds its authentic place within an integral Religious Studies rather than within Christian theology. As such it can influence Christian theology but it does so from within a different area of concern' (p. 111).

Part Two

RELIGIONS IN DIALOGUE

But let me tell you, that to approach the stranger
Is to invite the unexpected, release a new force,
Or let the genie out of the bottle.
It is to start a train of events
Beyond your control . . .

    T.S. Eliot, *The Cocktail Party*, act 1, scene 1.

5 RELIGIONS AND RELIGIOSITY

So far my reflections have been limited to various theological approaches to the other. A complicated spectrum of opinion can be roughly divided into two major theories. The Hick and Cantwell Smith version, addressing itself to the new problematic, is thoroughly theocentric, while Rahner and Kraemer, for all their differences, are at least united in emphasizing the old, salvation, problematic. They seek to maintain a more traditional christocentric model of theology. Cantwell Smith and Hick think in terms of a theology which emerges directly from the inter-religious encounter; Rahner and Kraemer want a theology which prepares for that encounter. It is the same with their understanding of the nature and value of human religiosity, as we have seen. Hence a distinction can be made between a theology *of* dialogue and a theology *for* dialogue. The difference between the two approaches should by now be clear; the theocentric view seeks to establish the unity of religions from within the data of all religions, while the christocentric is based on the data of one religion, namely the Christian.

It is on the particular claims of Christianity that the two approaches differ most markedly. Christocentric theologians are understandably suspicious of the relativism implicit in the theocentric approach. Hence the move to produce ever more sophisticated 'epicycles' to their original salvation and mission-oriented theory. But they can scarcely avoid for very long the force of the new problematic: why other religions? What does their very existence have to teach us? Vatican II produced not just visionary meditations on the place of the Church in the modern world. It accepted diversity, pluralism and the freedom of all people to worship according to the dictates of conscience. In this situation mission becomes a complex task, though no less a part of what it means to be Christian. A concern for truth and the building of God's Kingdom must go hand in hand with an attitude of respect and openness to the other. Can a christocentric theology cope? Can commitment to truth revealed in one tradition allow that truth may also be revealed in another?

The pluralist theology, on the other hand, raises the sort of problems outlined in the last chapter, notably the philosophical problem of religious language – how does talk about God refer? – and the more theological problem of responding adequately to the demands of the Christian tradition: how to avoid exclusivism without opting for relativism? We may recognize with the pluralists that religions are genuine attempts to come to terms with the human relationship with the Divine but, as Hick admits, we still need some criteria by which they are to be graded, some sort of basis for the comparative exercise which necessarily precedes any sort of 'global' theology.[1] However, as I have argued above, pluralist approaches risk begging the question of how we come to know the Divine at all. Whatever the positive points of Hick's argument, the empiricist notion of religious truth which is implicit in the theocentric approach is fundamentally flawed. In seeking to overcome the relativist's dilemma by searching out the common elements and experiences in all religions, the pluralist gently slides over the fact that there are no human experiences which are not mediated through particular cultural forms.[2] If all religious experience is contextual, what is the basis of comparison?

I have already noted various aspects of the christocentric and theocentric theologies which are important pillars in building a theology of religions: the pluralist demand for openness and tolerance; the imperative to listen to the other through dialogue; the Barthian reminder of the prophetic or revelative nature of Christianity; the Catholic emphasis, exemplified by Rahner, on the continuity of Nature and Grace and the significance of the religions as social realities; and the point which emerges from both Rahner and Barth that, correctly conceived, Christian universalism issues in a theology of the Holy Spirit. The second part of this book is an attempt to outline a theology of inter-religious relationships, based on a dialectical resolution of the two problematics. I want to begin by picking up the point just mentioned: the search for common elements or essences. If, as I believe, this causes more problems than it solves, is there any alternative? In this chapter I want to examine the nature of human religiosity with a view to finding the structure, rather than the essence, common to all religious traditions. This demands a prior consideration of what our theologians consider essential to Christianity.

The essence of Christianity

Most Christian theologians would agree that Christ is the essence of Christianity. The theocentric approach questions this. Sometimes one gets the impression that Hick deals with the christological question by avoiding it altogether.[3] Be that as it may, the great merit of his approach is that he lets his experience of other religions challenge his traditional christocentric theology. He demands a radical paradigm shift and in his Copernican Revolution he gets one. But it is one thing to recognize the new problematic and quite another to solve it. By placing God at the centre of the universe of faiths and relegating Christ to the periphery he attempts a scheme which allows for harmony *between* religions at the risk of a radical rewriting of Christianity. It is doubtful if such a method is likely to achieve harmony *within* the religions. Hick rejects any particular item or aspect of one religion as the touchstone of truth within another. Thus when he seeks for a universal or common essence which transcends all religions he finds it in the search for salvation. Christ's is but one way. The idea of incarnation is a mythical story used to speak of the extraordinary closeness of the man Jesus to God; he becomes, as it were, the paradigm for all committed in faith to his way, but not normative for all people everywhere. The most one can say is that the way to God proposed and lived by Christ is the best current example. Hence an inevitably reductionist Christology.

That may be considered one side of the problem – keeping faith with the tradition. Rahner, representing the most satisfactory version of the old problematic, highlights the other. He puts Christ at the centre of his theology, describing him as the 'absolute Saviour', but how is such an opinion to retain a real openness to the other? Coming from a very different angle, Rahner sees christology as necessarily *prior* to soteriology, as the very condition of possibility of salvation.[4] The position to which he is committed stresses a soteriology which emerges from christology, from what God has done in Jesus Christ, not the other way round. But, however satisfactory an account of mainstream Christianity this may be, the language, if not the underpinning anthropology, tends to subsume all religions within the Christian dispensation. Despite his account of the 'lawful religion' – that is to say, his insistence that, if non-Christians are saved, they are saved in the particular historical and social situation in which they exist – we are still left with a model of salvation as *constituted* by the grace of God in Christ. If Hick produces a soteriological 'common essence' of all religions, then Rahner comes up with a christological version. He fully acknowledges the extent to which his christocentric theology of religions dominates his understanding of the shape of human religiosity. Indeed this is the heart of the Anonymous Christianity thesis: that all religions reflect the 'shape of grace' revealed in Christianity. Thus Christ is the perfect expression of redeemed humanity, the goal to which all are drawn, whether they are explicitly conscious of God drawing them or not. Rahner's is a high christology which makes it possible to talk in terms of Christ fulfilling the world of religions. Jesus is identified with the Christ of God, but the Christ is more than Jesus; the Christ is the Logos which is spoken by God in some way in all religions and which therefore fulfils all religious aspirations. Thus all religions can be said to be formed according to the paradigm set by Christ. In which case, what values do the religions have in themselves? Rahner has shown that it is possible to speak of the mystery of Christ which is revealed explicitly in Christianity as being present in other religions. But how does one avoid giving the impression that these other religions are 'really' Christian in all but name?

The sort of answer we give to this last question is going to depend very much on what we think constitutes religion. Both Hick and Rahner produce their own versions of an essence common to all religions but neither asks what constitutes a religion or what the function of a religion within a society or culture is. If Christ is the 'centre' or 'essence' of Christianity we still have to enquire into the nature of this essence. Is it the same in all religions, or different, and how? I hesitate to add to the bewildering variety of definitions of religion, and I certainly do not want to make the mistake of reducing all human religiosity to a few common denominators. Cantwell Smith has warned us of such dangers. If his programme is saying anything of value it is that a theology of religions must emerge from praxis and the experience of people in a multi-cultural world. This is the heart of his attempt to redefine the way we use the word religion; he wants to avoid all talk of 'essences' and, instead, develop the notion of 'cumulative traditions'. What different traditions have in common is the attitude of *faith*, that which expresses a person's sense of relationship with the Divine. 'The primary locus of religiousness,' he says, 'is persons, not things'.[5] The phenomena of religious history are of only secondary importance. The problem is that we have reified 'religion' and identified it with abstract creeds, rituals and codes. Christian theology for Smith is not the articulation of the essence of the tradition but the study of the life of persons who in a world of pluralist religious culture become aware of, and react to, not just one symbol system, one expression of faith, but a whole series. He thus draws our attention to the limitations of the 'classical' model of theology. Here he has surely discerned a most important development. Much more attention these days is being paid to the real values inherent in other religions. Only fairly recently have theologians begun to appreciate the true nature of Cantwell Smith's vision of religious history: ancient and sophisticated traditions which have sustained and continue to sustain communities and civilizations without – apparently – any help from Christianity to save them from their supposed sin and superstition. To that extent Rahner's existentialism is a useful lesson: he gives full weight to the religions in their social-historical forms. And, whatever the drawbacks of Hick's pluralist model, he does draw attention to the enormous diversity of religions and to the fact that no religion, not even Christianity, can claim exclusive rights to truth. Each is a product and expression of a particular human culture.

It is not, however, that easy to avoid talk of separate, if interdependent, 'religions', as Smith demands. He is right that religions are not to be treated as systems or ideologies which can all be reduced to lowest common denominators. But creeds, codes and rituals are significant not only in the formation of the actual traditions but in the development and daily lives of the people who believe and practise them; the life of faith takes on particular forms which *de facto* are different. In what follows I want to suggest that definitions of religiosity tend to determine theories of the relationship of religions. Secondly, I will put forward a theory of religion which, although primarily theological, attempts to do justice to the pluralism of faiths. Let me begin by anticipating my conclusion and propose, as a working definition of religion, that it can best be understood as a traditional symbolic framework of myth, ritual and personal piety which forms and gives substance to a community of faith. The 'essence' of any particular religion is not, therefore, some element which is held in common with all others; it is contained in the structure of theory and practice which grounds all religions and which makes them all, at once, similar and different.

Models of religion

Looking at the theologians we have already discussed, it seems that much of the 'problem' of religious pluralism is created by very different models of religion. Barth has a theological theory of religion as a human construct, a record of human projection, which is opposed dialectically to God's revelation which relativizes all human attempts to understand and grasp the divine. Rahner sees all religion as an expression of a fundamental human openness to the Divine, an awareness of God at the heart of creation which finds its expression in particular complexes of traditional symbols and rituals. Hick, following Cantwell Smith, sees the great world religions in personalist terms as the cumulative traditions which record the faith manifested by particular cultures over the centuries. All of these theories of the nature of religion embody important insights. There are clearly 'universal' or common elements in all religions; to some extent religion is the 'same' everywhere, but religions are also peculiar to particular cultures and cannot be reduced to a few stereotypes. Religions begin from different premises and emphasize different values. Anyone who has tried a little dialogue with Buddhism, at any level, will appreciate that; wherever else that dialogue may begin, it is not, as most Christians assume, with the concept of God. Hence the importance of understanding the particular context and background within which religions are formed.

But if we are looking for a theory of the relationship of religions, it makes sense first to consider what it is that our theologians *think* holds them together; in other words we need to take note of the philosophical or theological presuppositions which are at work. It is not just that religions appear to be different; theories about the differences are different. Thus – to follow up the example just mentioned – whether one thinks of Buddhism as a religion in the sense which I have outlined or as some sort of a 'philosophy of life', a term with all sorts of secularizing overtones, depends very much on one's theory of religion. Different theories have different roles for dialogue and different models for the relationship of religions. Thus an intellectualist theory, which emphasizes the cognitive aspect of religion, sees religion as primarily concerned with informative propositions or truth-claims about objective realities. In these terms religion is like a philosophy. Dialogue is aimed at reconciling such truth-claims, at arriving at objective truth. And the more one emphasizes the significance of truth-claims, the less one is concerned for the symbolic, the ritual and the experiential side of religion. The essential practice of theology consists either of a fundamentalist interpretation of certain key-texts or in a more or less sophisticated system of apologetics. Either way, religions end up being compared in terms of which one makes the most adequate truth-claims. I do not want to suggest that questions of truth and falsity are unimportant; but there is a danger that if our model of religion becomes too intellectualist we reduce our theology of religions to an exercise in comparative system-building.

If, on the other hand, we take as our model of religion that which I think is implicit in the Rahnerian approach, namely the experiential,

94

then dialogue is seen primarily as an attempt to discover and share in what is common to all religious experience. For Rahner all religions are expressive of a basic unity of experience, particular objectifications of a 'common core'. Christian theologians will thus be seeking for the form of Anonymous Christianity, the shape which the normative Christian mystery will be taking in other religious traditions. Such a model of dialogue demands more than an encounter at the level of truth and meaning. First we must learn to join in a common search, seeking out those concepts or symbols which prefigure or find their fulfilment in the Christian mystery.[6] Again this is obviously important to the promotion of dialogue and, as a supplement or corrective to the purely intellectualist approach, this model clearly has a lot to recommend it. But both have their limitations. If the former ignores the ritual and experiential, the latter presumes a common core experience which is inevitably very difficult if not impossible to describe except in the broadest terms. Such an experience has got to be sufficiently general to apply to a wide variety of existing religious traditions with the result, perhaps, that one risks losing that specific element which makes a religion unique and gives it a particular vitality. Moreover it begs the question about the relationship between language and experience. Can one experience something without knowing it, and can one know something without being able to name it?

Both these models are described, and largely dismissed, by George Lindbeck, the American neo-orthodox or, to give him his own title, 'postliberal' theologian. He proposes instead a third version which he calls the 'cultural-linguistic'.[7] It makes religion something like a cultural framework or language which shapes the life and thought of a particular people. Lindbeck is more than aware of the challenge being made to theology by religious studies and the social sciences. He makes it his special concern to attempt a reconciliation of theological and non-theological accounts of religion without opting for relativism. His criticism of the Rahner approach is especially significant. What he calls an experiential-expressive account of religion tends to dominate theology; traced right back to Kant and Schleiermacher, this locates all significant contact with the Divine in the pre-reflective depths of the individual and makes all public features of a religion, such as ritual and myth, expressive objectifications. This 'dominant' liberal theological tradition runs from Schleiermacher to Rahner and Lonergan and includes such diverse figures as Tillich and Eliade. It approximates to the liberal or pluralist side of our 'dialectical morass'. Typically in this paradigm a model of religion is used which is concerned to base all contact with the Divine in the inner experiences of the subject. 'Whatever the variations,' says Lindbeck, 'thinkers of this tradition all locate ultimately significant contact with whatever is finally important to religion in the pre-reflective experiential depths of the self and regard the public or outer features of religion as expressive and evocative objectifications (i.e. non-discursive symbols) of internal experience'.[8]

Theology must not be allowed to become isolated from the major currents of contemporary life. But if we reject the experiential-expressivism of the liberals then theologians must find some way of adapting the scope and method of their subject. We have already noted Cantwell Smith's prophetic call for a 'global' theology. Lindbeck, starting from a similar cultural model of religion, goes in another, yet parallel, direction. The scientific study of religion works from very different premises, emphasizing the modern awareness of cultural and historical relativity. Religions are not so much variations on a common theme as comprehensive interpretative schemes, embodied in myths and narratives and expressed in ritual, which structure human experience of the world. Here we may detect something similar to the Kraemer-Troeltsch insistence that religions are cultural 'totalities'. It is not enough to postulate some sort of general 'transcendental' experiential source of all religiosity. Religions emerge from, and can only be interpreted within, certain cultural frameworks; only there do they really make sense. Religion is 'that ultimate dimension of culture . . . which gives shape and intensity to the experiential matrix from which significant cultural achievements flow'.[9] Like Cantwell Smith Lindbeck begins with the religious traditions of people as a 'fact' of experience. People are religious not because they have particular experiences which are said to be 'religious' but because their *whole* experience as persons reared in particular societies is religious. Which is to say no more than that they have been formed in a religious framework. A religious tradition presents people with an acquired set of skills, a tradition of looking at, and dealing with, the world. In many ways it acts like a sort of Kantian *a priori*, forming a series of idioms which shape life and thought, or a language which makes possible the description of realities and the formulation of beliefs. This model is very different from Hick's, who considers the various religions as only specific, and therefore inadequate, versions of a common religious quest for the Divine, or even from Rahner's transcendental approach. But how different and how distinct?

Religion in society

Lindbeck's cultural-linguistic model accepts a certain plurality of religions even if, as a <u>christocentric theologian</u>, he cannot recommend pluralism.[10] 'Religion', he says, 'need not be described as some universal religious sense arising from the depths of individuals and diversely and inadequately objectified in particular faiths; it can at least as plausibly be construed as a class-name for a variegated set of cultural-linguistic systems that, at least in some cases, differentially shape and produce our most profound sentiments, attitudes and awarenesses'.[11] For this insight Lindbeck is clearly indebted to the anthropologist Clifford Geertz and, perhaps more fundamentally, to Wittgenstein. For Geertz the problem of understanding another culture is not solved by simply listing and analysing the core symbols around which the most significant relationships within a society are organized. We need to ask why such structures of meaning are significant and therefore look at the *context* within which they operate. Cultural analysis, he says, should not be abstracted from 'the informal logic of actual life'.[12] Rather than beginning with a grand theory of cultural interpretation we should be seeking to interpret that particular universe which is, however obscurely, painted by a particular set of symbols – the vehicles by which people interpret their world to themselves. In other words we must first generalize *within* particular instances, discerning particular structures of meaning, and only then generalize *between* them.

This means that our concept of religion must take its rise from its function or, as Wittgenstein would say, its *use* within society. Geertz defines religion as '(1) a system of symbols which acts to (2) establish powerful, pervasive, and long-lasting moods and motivations in men by (3) formulating conceptions of a general order of existence and (4) clothing these conceptions with such an aura of factuality that (5) the moods and motivations seem uniquely realistic'.[13] In Geertz's view religion not only describes and reflects the social order but also shapes and forms it. <u>Religion is thus not a model *of* society but a model *for* society.</u> A religion is a system of symbols by which Geertz means any object, act, event, quality or relation which serves as a 'vehicle for a conception'.[14] Such a system is innately meaningful insofar as it provides the structure within which persons can come to terms with their existence. This process of religious interpretation rests on a fundamental sense or awareness that life is not meaningless. It is possible to orientate ourselves within our particular world by learning to accept the symbols which society provides. Naturally we can find ourselves at the limits of our ability to cope with the sometimes enormous challenges which face us; the problem of evil appears in some shape or form in all religions. But when faced with what Geertz calls 'metaphysical anxiety', people do not ordinarily retire in confusion; rather they try to convince themselves that the phenomena of experience can be explained within the accepted order of things. The natural tendency is not to abandon one scheme or symbol-system for another or to give up altogether. A person's religion helps him or her to endure stress by providing emotional as well as intellectual support. In short, it teaches people not how to avoid suffering but precisely how to suffer. 'The effort', says Geertz, 'is not to deny the undeniable – that there are unexplained events, that life hurts, or that rain falls upon the just – but to deny that there are inexplicable events, that life is unendurable, that justice is a mirag` [5]

On this view of human religiosity there is a common purpose or function to be found in the plurality of religions. Religious practices, such as ritual or acts of prayer or worship, can be seen as formal occasions for expiating suffering in some way. The group which shares a particular symbol-system gathers to celebrate and relive the history of their protection from evil. From such ritual acts arises a theodicy which may be encapsulated in myth or legend or find more sophisticated expression in theological speculation. Religion begins with the acknowledgement of order in the universe and develops as people try to accept the manifestations of disorder. One of the most obvious threats to the cohesion, perhaps even to the very existence, of a society, is the suspicion that maybe there is no such thing as order, that it is all a mirage. Hence the need to formulate through a symbol-system an image of the world as ordered and of disorder as explicable and temporary. In religion there is no such thing as a purely intellectual answer to the problem of evil; people have to learn to live with the fact of evil in the present. And the fact that such an answer is elusive makes no difference to the way people continue to live now, convinced that an explanation is possible, albeit in the distant future when the inexorable demands of order or cosmic justice will be worked out. The point is that for the religious person nothing in the end can count against his or her fundamental belief that the world makes sense.

In Lindbeck's opinion this cultural-linguistic model of religion makes more sense of the diversity of religions than a model which puts experience to the fore and derives particular interpretations from it. Thus inner experiences are derived from the tradition, not vice versa.[16] To be religious is not primarily a matter of gaining the experience and then learning the language; rather one first becomes skilled in the language which itself shapes and produces our most profound sentiments and attitudes. Religions are different traditional ways of shaping whatever is most important to a people: major crises and problems are overcome through a variety of myths and rituals which are, in fact, socializing processes. To become a Christian, then, is a matter of learning the Christian language, the story of Jesus, and thus learning how to interpret one's world in these terms. Similarly to be a Buddhist means getting in touch with the cultural world of Buddhist tradition and seeing everything from that standpoint. Different Christian and Buddhist communities will have their own interpretations of the received tradition. A variety of patterns may be developed, but all will be ultimately dependent on the language of a particular tradition and community. Religion as the most significant element in human culture provides answers to and support for fundamental life-crises. Even if it is acknowledged that these answers may only arrive at the end of life, or the end of time, this does not detract from the very real structure which they give to human existence in the present. In the first place the tradition helps a community to cope, even if it does not stop there.

In speaking of religion in Lindbeck's cultural-linguistic terms we enter upon a difficult investigation into the relationship between language, culture and experience. If we are saying that the nature of particular experiences depends on the context or the conditions whereby we enter into that experience (that is to say, the cultural pattern through which the interpretation of experience is made) does this not mean that language influences – and perhaps even determines – the nature of that experience? Put in these terms, the answer must be 'Yes'. Language can, very generally, be seen as an attempt to organize and classify our patterns of experience. If so, then it follows that the language which we inherit from society has the leading role in forming our world-view. This is central to Lindbeck's thesis: religion introduces people into the shared language or story of the group. Thus stated, Lindbeck's model of religion coheres well with Cantwell Smith's cumulative traditions; it accounts for the total world-view and *practice* of a particular people, rather than abstracting from that world-view certain themes or ideas which can be directly compared with patterns elsewhere, outside the tradition. What such an account misses is the very different ways in which language can be used, both within culture and in communicating between cultures. If, as I have argued, the task of the theologian is not just to defend the tradition but to articulate it in an ever-changing world, we must pay attention not just to the elements of continuity within a tradition, what keeps it recognizably the same, but the elements of change. Religions are not just concerned with maintaining the tradition of the past but with accounting for, and integrating, the vagaries of present – and future – experience. To speak of religions, therefore, in purely cultural-linguistic terms is only half the story. The symbol-system may have primacy in forming experience but there is a true dialectic at work: language shapes us, but we also shape it. In order to develop Lindbeck's model of religion as the most satisfactory basis for a theology of religions we need to note the different forms in which language is used by a religious culture. Only then can we understand the extent to which it influences or determines that culture. This will introduce us to the structure of human religiosity.

Religion – integrative and transcendent

There is, in fact, a constant interplay between language and experience, a dialectic between the tradition and the challenge made to tradition by the very limits imposed by language. John Dominic Crossan, in his perceptive little book, *The Dark Interval*, attends to precisely this point. If story is what creates world, it 'becomes very important to differentiate the various ways or types or modes of story. It becomes especially important to see how story itself admits its own creativity, admits that it is creating and not just describing world'.[17] With his particular interest in the New Testament Crossan devotes most of his attention to the literary genre known as parable, to which he gives the function of *subverting* world. But parable can only be understood as operating within, as well as in opposition to, an already accepted world-view, a world-view which is established through the genre called myth. Christianity, coming from a thoroughly prophetic tradition, lends itself to this type of dialectical interpretation. Myth is constantly laying itself open to criticism just as Jesus fulfils the prophetic role by challenging the assumptions of a sinful and corrupt society. Religious awareness – that is, awareness of the nature and demands of God – grows through such a dialectic. But this interplay of myth and parable, institution and challenge, is at the heart of other religions too. In Hinduism there are no prophets of the Hebrew variety but the same dialectic of institution reacting to external challenge is present. The myth of cosmic order is represented by the concept of *dharma*, which might be said to represent

100

this-worldly value, while the parable or challenge is represented by *moksha*, which is usually translated as 'liberation' and which can loosely be rendered as 'other-worldly value'. Somehow these have to be reconciled in the lives of ordinary people. But how? Hindu mythology is full of stories in which gods and heroic holy men fulfil both ideals – that of the person in society who does his or her caste-duty and that of the ascetic who rejects society and strives for perfection in solitude. Such myths effect a reconciliation. Through entering into the story of Śiva, for instance, the god who combines in himself all opposites, ascetic-erotic, creator-destroyer, even male-female, the ordinary devotee can come to terms with the polarities and painful choices of existence. The Hindu wants to choose all, indeed become all, but is forced to choose one or the other. Śiva represents the one who by choosing both poles of the dilemma holds out the possibility of ultimate reconciliation.[18] Another example might be the celebrated story contained in the *Bhagavad Gita*. The youthful charioteer Arjuna is taught how to cope with the painful duties of life in the world by shifting his attention to the god Krishna, the perfect guru and example of 'desireless action'. The teaching of the *Gita* holds out to the devotee the possibility of reconciling life's painful choices.[19]

Other examples could be produced. Religion in these terms is less a series of answers than a strategy for coping with questions. Myth, the archetypal story, points the way to the ideal, assuring people that their fundamental belief in order is not misconceived. The problem of evil can be overcome. 'It is', as Crossan says, 'much more important to believe in the possibility of solution than ever to find one in actuality'.[20] Not even the best and most consoling of myths can account for the fullness of human experience, still less support people against inevitable life-crises and traumas. In fact an over-reliance on myth can make for complacency. One cannot go on living forever in the world created by myth for another world – perhaps we might call it the world of the Other – disturbs it by challenging the structures with which we try to order our experience. What happens to the world characterized by order when it encounters something new or different, still more when it comes face to face with the other, the one who by definition is not part of one's ordered world? This is the world represented in Crossan's terms by parable. 'You have built a lovely home, myth assures us; but, whispers parable, you are right above an earthquake fault'.[21] The world which is created by story has to accommodate and react to experiences both of stability *and* instability, or reconciliation *and* contradiction. The religious tradition enables people to do precisely this. Obviously it is possible to exist only in the world created by myth, and to avoid the world introduced by parable, as many people do. And such is the weakness of religion: that it can become a structure for escape and survival. The strength of religion, on the other hand, is that it enables human beings to integrate what is alien, to adjust to disorder and to live, however uneasily, with a world which simply refuses to fit into a single myth or pattern of experience. Once the other is accepted as a fact of life he or she becomes not a challenge to one's present security in an alien world but a possibility for growth into a fuller humanity in a shared world. The great world religions, for all their differences, are indisputably examples of the latter.

Religions are not just language, not just story, but complexes of different literary and symbolic forms, a dialectic of tradition and the challenge of otherness or – in Crossan's terms – of myth and parable. Is it correct, then, to say that religions are just, or even primarily, socializing processes, ways of initiating individuals into the shared myth of the community? Our cultural-linguistic model of religion develops the important insight that religion forms communities and, therefore, the human subject. But this should not obscure another insight: the equally creative task that both community and individual exercise in reacting to the tradition. If our humanity is formed by culture then it is equally true that culture is formed by human beings. To live in a community which seeks to come to terms with the world of which it is part demands a constant dialogue between our free creativity as human persons and the cultural and social context of experience in which that creativity operates. It is one thing to accept that religion must always be expressed in cultural forms and quite another to reduce religion to culture. Our human creativity is always seeking to transcend the boundaries that culture puts on religion. However much it is bound up with culture, religion always has a transcendent as well as an integrative function.[22] To put it another way, religion seeks to understand God as well as to understand the world of women and men.

All human beings are adept at turning the absolute demand of the transcendent into something they feel they can control. The history of religions is full of examples of how, once institutionalized, religion can become a tool by which dominant groups, whether Vedic brahmans or Jewish high priests, can manipulate society. A religion, however, is not determined by the cultural forms in which it is expressed even if it is necessarily conditioned by them. All religions at some stage clash with culture but any religion which has survived the struggle (and, of course, there are many which have not) has done so not by ignoring the claims of the wider society but by managing to adapt itself to them. Tradition is necessarily a conservative force. It may well stand as a bulwark against what is foreign, but it is also a power for the creation of value and the constant renewal of society, and can be, where necessary, a force for the assimilation and acceptance of what is foreign. The history of religions illustrates how religions can break out of the constraints laid upon them by political, economic or some such other vested interests of society. The prophets of the Old Testament are nothing if not a witness to the demands of the counter-culture, calling the people of Israel back to the pure faith of Yahwism. And the *sannyasi* in classical Hinduism is not so much a drop-out on the edge of society as a reminder to people living 'in the world' that there is such a thing as transcendent value, that even the upright moral life of caste-society has as its true fulfilment *moksha*, liberation.[23] Such examples point to the power a religion has to transcend itself, to be less a symbol of reaction and more an expression of the adaptability and resilience of human beings.

It is possible on a purely cultural-linguistic model to reduce religion to its integrative function. In this sense, however, any structure of social integration – whether it be a political ideology such as Marxism, a creed for the party faithful such as monetarism, or a cult associated with some modern folk-hero – can be given the name of a religion. The very core of religion, I have suggested, is the power it gives people to cope with change. A follower of one of the great religions would quite reasonably object that such pseudo-religions fail to give people a sense of the transcendent because they teach them only to accept certain values; they do not provide the motivation both to criticize and change the culture and to live with what cannot be changed. They may facilitate a certain integration into society but cannot provide that creative stimulus without which culture stagnates and society dies. The model of religion we are seeking must take into account that element of continuity within a culture which keeps it recognizably the same, even over countless generations, but it must also be alive to the changes which are taking place – both within and between cultures. Anthropologists and historians of religion are constantly preoccupied with the problem of change in religion and, therefore, with the question of how religions manage to retain an enduring sense of self-identity. Patterns of behaviour within a particular tradition may be similar but there is also a rich variety of expression as people learn to generate new patterns of meaning. A purely cultural-linguistic model of religion allows for the latter but finds it difficult to account for the element of discontinuity. It may ignore that creative moment of prophetic or revelatory insight which ensures continuing growth and vitality.

The transcendent dimension is what sets religion apart from culture. To understand the part that religions should play in a pluralist society, we must avoid the temptation to institutionalize them, letting the integrative dimension dominate. If myth represents the collective answer to the problem of living, then parable raises the question, the seed of doubt. When a society or culture owes allegiance to only one collective myth the danger is complacency. The forms of society as it exists acquire an absolute character and become part of a sort of civil religion with its own national myths and rituals. The integrative dimension of religion becomes ossified into an empty ideology for there is nothing to challenge it. In a rather subtle way this is what has already happened in the West. A technocratic and utilitarian society provides not just immediate and pragmatic answers to our everyday needs but effectively protects us against all but the worst effects of personal life-crises. Religion, if it means anything at all, is reduced to an empty ritual, a legitimation of the *status quo*. It does not answer our deeper questions; in fact it may even stifle them. It is easy to refer to our contemporary western society as post-Christian or even a-religious. In fact the continuing interest in eastern forms of meditation from Tantra to T'ai Chi, the various new religious movements, the flourishing of neo-paganism, not to mention the ever-increasing number of followers of the great religious traditions, all go to show that religion is far from dead. What has died is the sense of allegiance to the collective myth; what is alive is parable, the challenges and questions which the different religions are now putting to each other. If nothing else, today's pluralism witnesses to the extraordinary fertility of the human imagination and its power to integrate old and new cultural patterns.

The culture of our society has already become plural. How, then, is it to cope with many myths and many ways of integrating people into society as a whole? The *sine qua non* is tolerance; people from the different religions have to learn to respect each other's ways as legitimately different. Without mutual understanding there is no future, but a tolerance which would reduce all religions to the myths, customs and rituals of particular communities risks forgetting the transcendent dimension. All religions express the community-myth and enable people to integrate themselves into society, but religions also point beyond society and the concerns of the present. Somehow all religions must remain responsive – and allow others to become responsive – to the transcendent dimension, the prophetic freedom of the Spirit which very often operates outside established society. It is clear, as the pluralist theologians remind us, that for the various communities of faith to coexist in a single society they must have a certain familiarity with, and respect for, the integrative dimension, wherever it may appear. What is not so often stressed is that respect must also be accorded to that element of the prophetic in all religions which fulfils the basic human need for vision and hope. Prophets are often regarded as oppressive figures, awkward, overly critical and even deadening influences. But, in the account of religion I have given, the prophet, the one with the power to develop the language of faith, is the creative figure. Only lack of vision kills.

The relationship of religions

Let me try to draw the main lines of this argument together. The search for a harmony of religions usually proceeds on the basis of common essences or elements. The problem is that this can often restrict our account of human religiosity to its integrative function. However tolerant we are of different religions and however concerned to preserve them, it is no mark of respect to a community if we forget that religions have ever been subject to challenge and that it is only through challenge that the tradition is enriched and is empowered to face the future. Before it makes sense to look for individual points of similarity (and difference) we have to agree on a 'common structure'. This structure is dialectical or, better, dialogical: it is based on a tension which allows not just for the obvious continuity within religions but also for that tantalizing element of change and novelty which is so difficult to define. On this view all religions owe their fundamental 'shape' to a combination of ancient traditional myths, beliefs and rituals and to a certain measure of the prophetic or revealed truth. This, surely, is where the Barthian insight into the dialectical relationship between religion and revelation comes into its own. Religion may be a human construct and ever in need of reform and correction, but it is also the locus of God's revealing activity. It is, to use Barth's celebrated and ambiguous language, 'elevated' by that revelation. The problem, of course, is that dialectical theology limits this elevation to Christianity as the 'redeemed' religion, which can thus be set apart from all others by virtue of its explicit acknowledgement of the *mysterium Christi*. But is not such a dialectical structure to be found outside the Christian religion? The creative tension between the integrative and the transcendent dimensions is fundamental to various types of human religiosity. Tamil Śaivism, for example, is just as clear as Christianity in its confession of human sin, failure and distance from God and in its total reliance on the grace and goodness of God if one is to be released from the unhappy human condition.[24] The same can be said for various religions of grace, but even as different a religion as Zen Buddhism depends for its own vitality on such a tension. The Buddha established not 'another religion' but a critique of all religion; Buddhist meditation is nothing if not an attempt to achieve perfect mindfulness, which is not a striving for perfect recollection, but a balanced awareness of the world as it really is. *Nirvana* is not some 'thing' to be grasped; it is the peace which, in Barthian terms, allows God to be God and, in more pragmatic Buddhist language, accepts whatever comes with 'self-lessness' and equanimity.[25]

To talk in terms of this common structure has certain obvious advantages. It considers religions as dynamic structures which are wedded to particular cultural expressions but seek to transcend them. It allows for Lindbeck's social studies model of religion as dependent on traditional idioms or languages by which humans everywhere seek to come to terms with their world. Yet it also seeks to do justice to the experiential and revelatory or, as Rahner would put it, transcendental source of all religion. Finally it may well provide something of a middle ground between the two models of theology which we have been discussing. The christocentric operates from within the Christian tradition; the theocentric seeks to mediate between all traditions. But once we accept that all religions have both a transcendent dimension which is universal and an integrative dimension which is particular, and that *both* are present wherever we find a community of faith, the apparent opposition can be overcome. To do something like Cantwell Smith's global theology does not require Hick's neutral stance, deliberately avoiding the truth-claims of the christocentric theologian. We may take Rahner as an example. Like Hick he believes that there is a common ground to all religions; unlike Hick he thinks it is defined by God's revelation in Christ. There is thus a transcendental element in Rahner's understanding of religion as well as a categorial one.[25] That is to say, he gives primary importance to a pre-reflective experience which is then given expression through the language and culture of religion. This, as we have noted, is the reverse of Lindbeck's cultural-linguistic model, but if what I have said above is at all accurate, Lindbeck's distinction is misleadingly rigid. Language or culture may provide the form in which we come to experience Ultimate Reality, but in all religions there is an implicit demand being made to press beyond the limits of language, to enter eventually into a silence which recognizes that the Ultimate is more than can be spoken of in any human form of words. Whether we speak of the transcendent and the integrative, or the prophetic and the institutional, of parable and myth, or revelation and religion, the same point is being made: all religion has a common dialectical structure. The two have to be held together.

I began by speaking of the task of the Christian theologian in a pluralist society. In one sense that task remains what it has always been: the articulation of the tradition revealed in Christ. But today's context is different. It is full of parables: what may well be the prophetic voice of the Spirit speaking through the other. Thus theology must be different. To that extent Cantwell Smith is right: theology is a reflection on the Word of God wherever it may be spoken. The problem is then how to listen and how to recognize the signs of the Spirit. In Christianity we may be convinced that we have the 'shape' of God's Spirit-given activity; and we may be sure of finding in the other a 'mirror' which in some way reflects what God is doing everywhere. But there is more to dialogue than finding a common language with which we can speak to the other. The first requirement is always to listen.

Notes

1. cf. Hick, 'On Grading Religions', art. cit.
2. cf., for instance, the opinion of Steven Katz, in 'Language, Epistemology, and Mysticism', *Mysticism and Philosophical Analysis,* ed. Katz, Oxford: Oxford University Press 1978, pp. 22–74, that *'there are NO pure (i.e. unmediated) experiences.* Neither mystical experience nor more ordinary forms of experience give any indication, or any grounds for believing, that they are unmediated. That is to say, *all* experience is processed through, organized by, and makes itself available to us in extremely complex epistemological ways. The notion of unmediated experience seems, if not self-contradictory, at best empty' (p. 26). Tracy makes the point more trenchantly: 'Mystical experience, like all other experience, is also interpretation, and, like all other interpretation, mysticism participates in the discourse of highly particular traditions and societies' (*Plurality and Ambiguity,* London: SCM 1988, p. 92). Frank Whaling's second approach to 'global theology', *Christian Theology and World Religions,* pp. 112ff., which is based on

the *philosophia perennis* associated with such names as Aldous Huxley, Seyyed Hossein Nasr and Huston Smith, seems susceptible to Katz's criticism.

3. Thus in *God Has Many Names*, London: Macmillan 1980, Hick says that the Christian doctrines of Trinity and Incarnation are not 'precise metaphysical truths' but rather 'imaginative constructions giving expression – in the religious and philosophical language of the ancient world – to the Christian's devotion to Jesus as the one who has made the heavenly Father real to him' (p. 125). In his essay 'The Non-Absoluteness of Christianity' in *The Myth of Christian Uniqueness*, pp. 16–36, he seems content with a rather naive trinitarian modalism, God 'experienced as acting in relation to, and accordingly known by, us – namely as creator, redeemer, and inspirer' (p. 32). Hick seems here quite happy to cut short discussion at the epistemological level, while ignoring any ontological reference. Or, as Roger Trigg puts it in 'Religion and the Threat of Relativism', '. . . the emphasis is moved from a question about reality to one about our response to that reality' (op. cit. p. 301).

4. Karl Rahner, *Foundations of Christian Faith*, London: Darton, Longman & Todd 1978, pp. 176–321.

5. Wilfred Cantwell Smith, *Towards a World Theology*, London: Macmillan 1981, p. 87.

6. Rahner, *Foundations*, p. 321: '. . . the dogmatic theologian has to hand the question over to the historian of religion and to his Christian interpretation of the history of religion'. For Rahner dialogue is very much a conversation between *a priori* dogmatic principles and *a posteriori* evidence of the grace of the absolute saviour.

7. George Lindbeck, *The Nature of Doctrine, Religion and Theology in a Postliberal Age*, London: SPCK 1984.

8. op. cit., p. 21.

9. ibid., p. 34.

10. Kenneth Surin has contributed an exhaustive analysis of two aspects of Lindbeck's Chapter Three, 'Many Religions and the One True Faith' – namely 'Unsurpassability' and 'Salvation and Other Faiths' – to the symposium published in *Modern Theology*, vol. 4, 2 January 1988, pp. 187–209. In Surin's opinion Lindbeck 'makes possible an acknowledgement of the "facts" of religious diversity without propelling us down the *cul-de-sac* of "religious pluralism" ' (p. 190). It is not my intention to deal with these two facets of the old problematic; but the second part of this book (and especially the next chapter) could well be seen as a commentary and expansion of what Lindbeck, all too briefly, says about the 'interrelationships of religions' and dialogue (pp. 52–55).

11. Lindbeck, op. cit., p. 40.

12. Clifford Geertz, 'Thick Description: Toward an Interpretive Theory of Culture', in *The Interpretation of Cultures*, New York: Basic Books 1973, p. 17.

13. 'Religion as a Cultural System', in *Interpretation*, p. 90.

14. op. cit., p. 91.
15. ibid., p. 108.
16. cf. Gerard Loughlin, 'See-Saying/Say-Seeing', *Theology* vol. 91: 741 (May 1988), pp. 201–209, who discusses Lindbeck's thesis in the light of traditional post-Enlightenment thinking, most obviously exemplified in Hick's theology, that 'religion is see-saying'. 'First you see the world and sense the presence of God, and then you say it, in word and deed, praise and service' (p. 202). A second way of viewing religion, following Lindbeck, is as 'the experience of following after an already expressed way of life' (p. 207).
17. John Dominic Crossan, *The Dark Interval: Towards a Theology of Story*, Illinois: Argus Communications 1975, p. 9.
18. cf., for example, Wendy Doniger O'Flaherty, *Śiva, The Erotic Ascetic*, Oxford: Oxford University Press 1981, which applies a structuralist analysis to śaivite mythology. O'Flaherty concludes that the sometimes exceedingly obscure and contradictory myths about Śiva are simply one way of supporting people in their endless quandaries about life and ultimate destiny. 'How can one live *in* the world, enjoying the pleasures of life and perpetuating these in one's children, and yet renounce the world, thus freeing the spirit?' (p. 316).
19. R.C. Zaehner, in his edition of the *Bhagavad Gita*, Oxford: Oxford University Press 1969, pp. 24ff.
20. Crossan, op. cit., p. 54.
21. ibid., p. 57.
22. I am indebted to Michael Amaladoss for access to a pre-publication copy of a paper in which this distinction is explored. This has now been published as 'Befreiung: Ein Interreligioses Projekt' in Felix Wilfred (ed.), *Verlass den Tempel* (Freiburg: Herder 1988), pp. 146–178. cf. two articles of his which have appeared in *Vidyajyoti* 50 (1986), pp. 176–184; and 47 (1983), pp. 67–76.
23. cf. the thesis of Louis Dumont, expressed most fully in his celebrated essay 'Renunciation in India Religion', in *Religion, Politics and History in India*, Paris – The Hague: Mouton 1970, pp. 33–60, that the 'secret of Hinduism may be found in the dialogue between the renouncer and the man-in-the-world' (p. 37).
24. cf., for example, Glenn Yocum's *Hymns to the Dancing Śiva*, New Delhi: Heritage Publishers 1982. Yocum translates and comments on the hymns of the Tamil Nayanar saint, Manikkavacakar, stressing the relationship of love and dependence established between God and sinner. 'The nature of Śiva is not characterized by "either . . . or" but by "both . . . and". From Śiva's standpoint . . . antitheses . . . are no longer opposed but rather are, in fact seen to be, two aspects of the same reality. Likewise, the experience of his devotees, who are "possessed" by him and enjoy mystical union with God, is that of reconciliation, wholeness, non-fragmentation' (p. 129).
25. The debate about the meaning of Nirvana has occupied western scholars since the earliest colonial times. cf. Guy Richard Welbon, *The Buddhist Nirvana and its Western Interpreters*, Chicago: Chicago

University Press 1968, for a fascinating account. My unpublished M. Litt. thesis (University of Oxford, 1977) looks at the origin of meditative practice in the Theravada school and shows that what later developed into the schools of Vipassana and Samatha in fact represents a creative interaction of two distinct types of practice.

26. cf., for example, Rahner, *Foundations,* p. 153.

6 INTERIOR DIALOGUE:
LEARNING FROM THE OTHER

I ended the last chapter with a theological account of religion based on a dialectical structure of integrative and transcendent dimensions. This explains human religiosity in terms of a number of cumulative traditions which enable persons to come to terms with a sometimes confusing and challenging existence. Such a theory accounts for the elements of continuity and change in religion by emphasizing the function played by religious faith in sustaining communities. It also makes plain the extent to which individuals are dependent on the cultural and social setting for their sense of personal identity and, therefore, for their knowledge of God. But while it may provide a theoretical basis for inter-religious relationships does it actually enhance and develop inter-*personal* relationships? There is always a danger that any abstract theory remains irredeemably inclusivist, seeking only to extend the original umbrella and providing no incentive to develop the dialogue at the human and more personal level. In this chapter I want to shift the emphasis from this rather abstract dialectic of ideas to the more human dialogue of persons: the meaning-giving conversation in which words, symbols and concepts are actually used. In other words dialogue is to be understood as the process which unites the two dimensions. It may be that in this way we can develop a theology of religions which goes beyond the straitjacket of the exclusivist/ inclusivist and pluralist dichotomy.

Problems of dialogue

The chequered history of inter-faith relationships is beyond the scope of this study. Instead I want briefly to summarize some of the problems which face people when they attempt the inter-faith dialogue. Earlier I spoke of the shift of emphasis from the Church to the Kingdom. Dialogue seems an eminently acceptable and appropriate way to pursue this aim. A greatly enhanced missiology has developed, one less concerned for extending Church frontiers and much more aware of the basic Christian imperative to share a particular experience of the love of God with others. How far have we reflected on the demands which this shift imposes on us? My deliberate, if somewhat self-conscious, attempt to substitute the word 'conversation' does not solve all the problems, but it may help to focus our attention on the way in which the term dialogue has been used. It suggests something necessarily formal in structure and purpose. In practice, however, people do not meet in order to talk; they talk in order to meet. Or, to put it another way, the 'problem of the other' with which I began is often overcome in the actual process of getting to know people – not disembodied representatives of another tradition but persons with a particular, and perhaps very personal, experience of God. At that point the tradition comes alive; the conference model of dialogue gives way to the conversation model in which strangers become friends.[1]

This shift of perspective is not easily made, especially by people committed to a missionary faith. Traditional missiology has been imperialist and old attitudes die hard. Even in today's pluralist, post-colonial world-culture it is still all too obvious where the real power lies. Many communities find themselves threatened not just by the economic policies of the West but by influences which they see as fundamentally destructive of their ancient values and way of life. To that extent the *attitude* of dialogue rather than aggressive confrontation is much to be preferred. But how is this new mode of mission actually perceived by those we would dialogue with? What, if anything, has really changed?

People from other faiths often remark on the fact that only Christians seem concerned for dialogue. And it is a sad fact that dialogue in practice seems to be restricted to a few enthusiasts, mainly Christian academics. Can it be that only Christians feel sufficiently strongly the imperative to witness to their faith and that, given the impossibility of more traditional forms of evangelization, dialogue is the only viable alternative? There is something in this. When Francis Xavier arrived in India he learned the language and preached the gospel. His aim was to 'win souls for Christ'. The Jesuit missionaries of a later age established their mission-stations around schools, in order to raise educational levels and gradually to build up a Christian community. The strategy was different, but the aim was much the same. Today conversion can cause very real social problems, cutting Hindus off from their communities and provoking something of an anti-Christian backlash. In the circumstances dialogue seems to be the only way to reconcile the Christian's evangelical commitment to mission with the reality of the contemporary situation. Does dialogue do any more, then, than salve the Christian conscience? Unfortunately the current enthusiasm for dialogue does give the impression that it is simply another tool for proselytizing. Christians are accused of developing a more subtle way of proceeding; instead of being quite open about what they are up to, they achieve their conversions by going through the back door. Small wonder if Hindus, Buddhists and Muslims are wary of getting involved.

It may be no bad thing that the dialogue movement has, at any rate temporarily, stagnated.[2] Round-table discussions and the exchange of information about different traditions have fulfilled their purpose. Contacts have been made; ancient prejudices are no longer insurmountable obstacles to understanding and cooperation. There is much still to be done, and the contributions of the scholars and academics cannot be discounted. At a slightly less exalted level precious little is happening, and it is not difficult to see why. Our theology has traditionally been apologetic. Our main concern has always been to articulate, if not defend, the faith against those who think differently and therefore, so we imagine, wrongly. Some accounts give a rosy impression of both the practice of, and prospects for, dialogue.[3] The reality is often rather different. We are fast discovering that the demands of dialogue are enormous, that it is more difficult to practise dialogue in today's multi-religious world than it was to establish the Church in far-off countries five hundred years ago.

Part of the problem is that we have neither examined this situation critically nor been prepared to analyse the theologies implicit in very different approaches to dialogue. Between the participants in dialogue there is often a fundamental confusion about the very purpose of the encounter. Are the intentions of the two the same? How much common ground is presupposed? Do we acknowledge, are we even aware of, the hidden agendas? Now, more than ever, a more systematic examination is in order. Eric Sharpe has tried to draw some of the different definitions of dialogue together.[4] He distinguishes between discursive, human, secular and interior dialogue, and makes the point that the goals of dialogue are as varied as its forms. As an attempt to clear the ground his categories are helpful. What he does not do is to relate theory to practice, to ask, that is, what effect particular theologies of religion have on the approach to, and experience of, dialogue. Our theological presuppositions make a difference, both to our expectations of dialogue and to the way we practise it. An encounter with the other as a fellow human being, sharing the same anxieties and concerns of our one world, may be a more adequate model of dialogue than the purely intellectual, but such dialogue can be hopelessly vague or narrowly pragmatic, failing to engage the very real differences which, whether we like it or not, distinguish the various religions. Nor is it clear that Sharpe's fourth model, which would place all inter-religious encounter in a contemplative mould, is as value-free as some of its advocates presume. Not all Christians, let alone people of other faiths, are contemplative. Again, theology dictates the agenda. Sooner or later partners in dialogue must extract themselves from the actual encounter in order to consider the nature of dialogue itself, preferably together. At this point, once a certain equality between the partners is acknowledged, the agenda changes totally.[5]

The problems surrounding any serious inter-faith conversation ultimately reduce themselves to some version of our loyalty/openness dilemma. Holding both values means appreciating the other tradition for its own sake and appropriating that tradition without losing touch with our roots. Such an ideal is fraught with difficulty. Even talk of the 'other tradition' betrays a narrowly intellectualist view of religion. As Cantwell Smith ceaselessly reminds us, religions are expressions of faith, the developing self-consciousness of persons. They cannot be separated from the living context. Such traditions, however much they may be subject to conservative forces, are not inflexible. In fact their very vitality under the threat of vested interests from within, or secularizing forces from without, may be the greatest witness to the power of the transcendent dimension. Be that as it may, religions change and yet remain ever the same. Some are more adaptable than others; some are more tolerant than others; some are more obviously reasonable than others. But all are living under the same imperative: to adapt to the modern world. The problem is that perceptions of the nature of the threat to traditional ways of life are often quite different. A tradition which went through the intellectual maelstrom of the European Enlightenment two hundred years ago does not view the world in the same way as, say, contemporary Islam, to note only the most obvious example. Not all religions maintain the same neat balance between openness and loyalty which liberal Christians expect.

This is not to deplore the situation or to commend any particular ideology for mutual understanding, Christian or otherwise. It is just a statement of fact. But it should also make us wary of the way as Christians we continue to impose our perceptions on others. Nor is it to ignore the missionary nature of Christianity which, like any religion, has a perfect right to proclaim its vision of the truth to all people. Rather, we should note that dialogue is rarely between equals. Open, genuine, frank dialogue may strike us as the obvious way forward, the way of cooperation and service, but we need to be honest with ourselves and constantly examine our motives. Even the best of intentions can appear patronizing. To repeat what was said at the end of the last chapter: dialogue consists of more than exchanges in a common language. If we are not thoroughly rooted in the attitude of listening and learning, we should not be surprised if we are met with incomprehension and suspicion. Murray Rogers, himself a veteran of the Hindu-Christian dialogue, writes of one particular crisis he experienced.[6] It made him realize that the external dialogue is only a part, and perhaps the least important part, of a much more demanding process of inner dialogue. Personal conversion is essential. To be unprepared spiritually for the demands of encountering the Divine in the other, he says, is only to risk falling back into the empty polemics or easy syncretizing to which dialogue, wrongly conceived, may easily lead. We may be agreed that dialogue is not a more subtle way to persuade people that our signpost is the best, but neither is it a matter of fudging the distinctions between the different paths so that we can all agree about something or other. Dialogue is not just a more civilized form of mission; it is about learning who the other is in order to find out who I am.

This is the new experience: the acceptance of the other as other and of dialogue not as a means to *our* end, as opposed to theirs, but as an end in itself. Such a dialogue, not the barely suppressed monologue which seeks to justify itself as an attempt to convert the other to my opinion, must, in practice, contain elements of all four of the models distinguished by Sharpe. It goes beyond them, however, in making inter-religious encounter the point at which the partners move away from their immediate concerns to examine the implications of the relationship itself. To put it more bluntly, dialogue forces us – myself and the other – to find the ground of our common search in the Divine. Such dialogue requires a commitment, an honesty and a willingness to learn, qualities which are as difficult to sustain as the single-minded zeal which so much characterized the greatest of the old missionaries. There is clearly a lot to be learned from a model of dialogue which sees it as a more efficient form of communication. We stop treating the other as a *tabula rasa* on which our message can be impressed. We begin to see that he or she will learn more successfully by personal discovery rather than by having our message painstakingly explained in its every detail. Dialogue makes for better pedagogy. I manage to overcome my anxiety to teach something correctly; I let the Spirit do the revealing in God's way and in God's good time. There is sound theology, as well as psychology, behind this move. But still the presupposition is that I know some *thing* which I think the other ought to know. I do not want to suggest that witnessing to the Word does not entail a confession of faith *and* some attempt to pass on that faith to the other. The Good News has a content which every Christian should be willing and ready to share. I am concerned here with something quite different – a previous stage, perhaps: how we arrive at that faith, what sort of a content we think it has and what we think we are passing on. The old missionaries were dominated by a classical sense of culture which divided the world into privileged initiates and ignorant pagans. They felt the imperative to share their faith, but not the need to examine the cultural presuppositions on which that faith was based. Today's experience of dialogue teaches us that at the heart of our confident proclamation of the gospel there must also be a humility which admits that we do not know everything about the ways of God with humankind. The people we meet have their own messages, their own versions of the Good News, their own insights into truth. And they have as much right to communicate their message to us as we do to them. Once it gets beyond academic investigation at one extreme, or the neighbourly exchange of pleasantries at the other, dialogue introduces us into a real relationship with people who are also seeking to know. At that point dialogue becomes a common quest in which the distinction between teacher and pupil breaks down.

Is there a contradiction in speaking of 'confident proclamation' going hand in hand with humility? It all depends on what we think we are called to proclaim. The Good News is not a formula of words but a story of what God has done in a person like myself, a story of redeeming love. I am what God has made me. But how am I to know what that means for *me*, let alone what it might mean for the other? When the Church was a persecuted minority and had not fallen prey to the grandiose pretensions of state religion, mission meant simply a 'witness to the hope that is in you' (1 Peter 3.15). The mystery of the Kingdom, revealed in Christ, was not a commodity to be hoarded but a gift which of its very nature was to be shared with others. Now that we have returned at last to a post-triumphalist vision of the Church we can once again appreciate that understanding such a hope, let alone communicating it, is a matter first and foremost of coming to terms with the mystery of what God is doing in the world.

And that means not just in me, or in my Church or religion, but in the other who is also a subject of that mystery. Our partner in dialogue is accepted as one who shares a similar human predicament and, perhaps, a real experience of transformation and enlightenment. To communicate successfully with that person means first of all taking him or her seriously at the human level and being prepared to learn from another story and another religious vision. In such a sharing of experience new meaning is generated between us which is capable of overcoming the obstacles that would normally block such a relationship.[7] Dialogue is that interaction between persons where both seek to give themselves to each other and to know each other as they really are. Communication is born of self-understanding and vice versa.

The interior dialogue

The fear of such dialogue is the fear of losing one's identity. Experience, however, often teaches quite the opposite: that in honest and open encounter with the other, when the integrity of faith is respected, commitment to one's own tradition and understanding of the other's are both deepened. The inter-personal dialogue demands that both partners be prepared to learn, and relearn, as well as to teach.[8] This, of course, raises a number of issues, for, if religions are primarily communities of faith, how can anyone be expected to live in more than one?

I propose to examine this question by focusing first on the experience of Raimundo Panikkar. Commenting on his own pilgrimage of faith he speaks of 'leaving' as a Christian, 'finding' himself a Hindu, and 'returning' a Buddhist, without having ceased to be a Christian. To those who wonder whether such an attitude is 'objectively tenable or even intelligible' he replies with what amounts to a commentary on our 'openness-loyalty' dilemma: how to keep one's feet firmly planted on the ground while one's arms embrace the distant heavens. The problem, he says:

> was trying to live one's faith without an exclusivity that appears outrageously unjust and false . . . In other words, the whole idea of belonging to a chosen people, of practising the true religion, of being a privileged creature, struck me not as a grace but a disgrace. Not that I felt myself unworthy, but I thought it would ill become me to discriminate in such a fashion and I thought it would ill become God to do so. I am well aware of the innumerable theoretical ways to get around the objection. I do not claim this idea runs counter to God's goodness or justice, which

presumably is not affected by our revulsion; I contend only that this idea contravenes the freedom and joy I would look for in a belief that enables the human being to grow to full stature.[9]

Panikkar does not object to any particular concept of God as such, but to the very inadequate vision of redeemed humanity which such a concept entails. His point is that simple solutions to the 'salvation problem' do not go very far towards enhancing inter-faith relations. In fact Panikkar's life and experience, set between the Hinduism of his Indian father and the Catholicism of his Spanish mother, are as eloquent a statement as any of the new problematic.

Seen in these terms, the challenge put to the Christian is to integrate different religious cultures and, to some extent, different commitments within the framework of Christian theology – seeking the *Christian* meaning of other religions. This is what Panikkar refers to as 'interpenetration', a theory based on the profound conviction that, as we grow in sensitivity to the religiousness of our neighbours, the more we 'surmise that in every one of us the other is somehow implied, and vice-versa, that the other is not so independent from us and is somehow touched by our own beliefs'.[10] Experience teaches that religions are not foreign to each other, and that for all their differences they may well be saying mutually complementary or correcting things. And thus we may find it easy to indulge in a little constructive criticism of our own formulations of faith, especially where they make it more difficult to appreciate the insights of the other. Panikkar's sometimes very personal, not to say idiosyncratic, approach often draws attention to the fact that the concepts and language we use may well obscure the issues. This is the first fruit of dialogue: an awareness of the limits of our language. Even the familiar images which describe the process of inter-religious relations betray certain prejudices. The language of paths and pilgrimages, signposts and maps, makes some useful points – that all religions may be different ways to a single goal, that the goal itself is often hidden from view, that there are sidetracks and dead ends, and so on – but they are all largely concerned with easing the burden of the old problematic. The 'ways up the mountain' theory suits a pluralist or, in Panikkar's terms, 'parallelist' theory. But it does not get us that far once we enter the realm of dialogue.

The dialogue which is founded on an encounter of persons, in short a conversation, raises the possibility of developing a more useful metaphor: that implied in the very concept of dialogue itself, namely language. Like all metaphors it can, within certain limits, be highly illuminating. A language is capable of a variety of expression and nuance, is adaptable and open to change and refinement, but is also self-sufficient and representative of particular cultures and values. It is doubtful, however, whether an expression which is, by definition, unique can ever find the same life outside its own terminology and context. Similarly with religions; there is something unique in each one yet, at the same time, an infinite richness of vocabulary and expression which allows different traditions to intermingle and, to some extent, to influence one another. In the first place, therefore, the language model gives full weight to certain irreducible values within religious traditions. Just as a language is a series of interdependent signs and symbols, so a religion interprets itself and finds its own meaning.

Moreover, the very nature of language is that it can communicate with the outsider. Translation may be difficult but it is possible. Languages consist of words, yet are clearly so much more; only within a certain context do the words make sense. This, of course, is the difficulty with translation from one language to another: to convey the meaning of the author rather than merely find suitable equivalents for his words. And the same is true of religions. A point for point comparison often makes very little sense without some appreciation of the context of meaning in which concepts operate. Moving from one culture to another demands more from us than the simple seeking of verbal equivalents. *Nirvana* is not the same as 'liberation'; nor is *Brahman* to be translated simply as 'God'. Translation demands sensitivity to context; something of the inner spirit or life of a language has to be carried over. Just as language requires speakers and listeners, partners in the conversation, so perhaps what goes on within and between religions is a dynamic process of growth and mutual understanding; the other becomes, as it were, a mirror in which I see not a stranger but a reflection of myself.

To engage in dialogue, then, is to attempt a process of translation which must be interior before it can become exterior. If religions are understood as particular culture-specific traditions which sustain communities of faith, then dialogue consists of the act of sharing one's own language or idiom. Thus a Christian has been introduced by his religion to a divine mystery which is summed up in the story of the death and resurrection of Jesus Christ. This is the language which he speaks – very different from the particular forms used in another tradition, but not necessarily incompatible, as far as the general structure is concerned. The Buddhist speaks another language and it makes no sense to speak of a point-for-point comparison.

119

Nevertheless one can at least postulate a similar pattern within the Buddhist tradition: the inner dialogue which goes on between the ancient tradition and the new insight, between the cultural framework of the past and the word that breaks in and enlightens. The skill which mediates between the two is learned in particular religious cultures. We may, of course, think of them as different languages, but, if all languages have a similar dialectical structure, they also have a similar purpose: to communicate. Thus, once translated, interpreted and understood by the other, my language about the death and resurrection of Jesus may well find echoes in the heart of another tradition. Here I am speaking of something more than an attempt to find exact but inevitably crude correspondences, as might be the result if one operated on a purely experiential model of religion. Rather, what develops is a search for a common structure or a common dynamic pattern; perhaps, to pursue the metaphor developed above, a common grammar.

Learning from the other

Panikkar refers to this process of interior translation as the intra-religious dialogue. His is the most celebrated example but it is not unique. Wherever dialogue takes place people are learning to assimilate different concepts and values and to expand their horizons beyond the familiarity of traditional starting points. From this conversation there may arise in due time a new theology, one which releases from the heart of the Christian tradition new insights and a whole new way of interpreting our experience. However, if that is to happen we have to attend to the process by which we learn, and that is impossible without the recognition that theology in this context is not generated from the more or less private thoughts of the individual, however well-steeped in the tradition he or she may be. Theology emerges from the reflection by the community on the experience of the community. And that experience, in a multi-faith world, is in large part experience of the other. In a sense it was always of the other, since God is not some sort of personal property or innate idea but the Totally Other who calls us out of ourselves to a recognition of creatureliness and dependence. But today's religious experience has brought the point home with much greater force. The meeting of East and West, so easily and misleadingly depicted as a dialectic of ideas, theories or 'ways of thinking', actually takes place in much more humble circumstances: wherever two or more subjects attempt to share something of their common humanity the process of internal and external translation takes place. Dialogue makes us confront not objects or items of thought but fellow-subjects, engaged in the same search; not a series of 'its' but an I who is also a Thou.

To speak in such strongly personalist terms should not obscure the fact that dialogue implies communication; our subjects have to listen and speak about *something*. The intellectual content of our dialogue cannot be flippantly dismissed as an obstacle to cosy togetherness, as if dialogue consists only in a massive act of love and goodwill. We shall return to this point in due course. For the moment, however, I want simply to note that a model of dialogue as a purely intellectual activity is no longer valid. Dialogue is, first and foremost, something more profoundly religious and therefore more profoundly human: an encounter of subjects who, even if they are not strongly committed in any formal sense, do bring with them their own interests, preconceptions and cultural values. Dialogue, in short, is conversation, not just an exchange of comment and opinion but a meeting of persons who share a common humanity.

So far I have argued that the dialectical structure of religion should be understood as a learning process centred primarily on persons rather than on abstract ideas. Seen in cultural-linguistic terms religions operate like languages: not private activities for constructing an inner world but social engagements formed by the relationships which make up the life of a community. Now as long as that community remains a homogeneous unit the integrative dimension remains dominant; relationships are ordered, even defined, by the nature of the tradition. The other becomes a problem only because he or she does not fit into the normal processes by which persons learn their identity. Outsiders are either excluded altogether or found a place on the fringes through some sort of inclusivist theory. Whichever way, our theology suffers from being 'abstract ideas-dominated' rather than person-centred. The pluralist theory recognizes the problem, opts for the latter approach, but misses the crucial point: how we come to understand the other is going to depend very much on how we define a person. This becomes clear once we realize that the problem of 'the other' is much wider than the problem of other or 'non-Christian' religions. Missionaries in Third World Asia, pastors coping with those marginalized from the Church, women and men struggling to witness to Christ in an increasingly secularized environment, all have to cope with the stranger, the one who does not belong to 'our' group and who cannot simply be persuaded or coerced into joining. The other seems to demand a thoroughly pluralist style of theologizing – perhaps even syncretist or global. And yet, if Christian theology is to be faithful to its roots, it must retain something of the strangeness of the transcendent or prophetic dimension. This peculiarly modern problem demands more than a choice of the best items from our three paradigms; the problem of the other – a person like me – raises a question mark against the way in which we go about speaking of persons in the first place.

The new problematic is all about identity. It asks what the other has to teach me *about myself*. To that extent it challenges the way in which Christian theologians have tended to operate, putting the knowing self at the centre of the tradition and extrapolating meaning from a sort of basic 'given'. In a recent book Fergus Kerr has drawn our attention to this process.[11] He suggests that it can be traced as far back as Augustine but owes its philosophical provenance mainly to the influence of Descartes. In chapter two above I spoke briefly of the intellectual inheritance of western Christianity and, particularly, of the post-Enlightenment discovery of the nature of the self as a knowing subject. My main concern at that point was with the origins of relativism: knowledge in general must be seen as dependent on, or relative to, the conditions of the knower. Here it becomes central to our understanding of the new problematic. For Descartes the human person is to be defined primarily in terms of consciousness. The Cartesian perspective is 'completely *egocentric*': the human subject is a 'thing that thinks'. The result is a theology of the person as a 'pre-formed ghostly presence' contingently inhabiting a social and historical setting. Descartes and Kant together have left modern theology with a legacy of the knowing subject as self-reliant, self-conscious and all-responsible.[12] Kant's emphasis on the subject led, of course, to the fully-formed idealism of Hegel in which objects 'out there' are made dependent on our act of thinking. The evolutionary perspective of so much liberal theology was, as already noted, one result: faith in the power of reason. Nowadays, two world wars and one holocaust later and with the constant threat of nuclear disaster, we are less confident. The sublime authority of the solipsist subject, controller of the material world, is suspect. Dependence – of one individual, one society, one religious tradition on another – is increasingly recognized. The thinking individual does not dominate a particular social and historical setting any more than that setting dominates him or her. The two coexist – in relationship.

All this underlines the importance of Lindbeck's cultural-linguistic model of religion.[13] Insofar as a thinking subject can be

LEARNING FROM THE OTHER

said to control or dominate anything, it is only possible through the categories, concepts and language which are inherited from the tradition. Human beings do not start out with ready-formed concepts or ideas; they have to be learned from the social setting in which they are involved. Religious meaning lies in what people do *together* within a community and, increasingly, outside it as well, not in the basically private thoughts and mental experiences of separate individuals. Religions, to emphasize the point made in the last chapter, do not consist of detached thoughts about God, salvation and the after-life which are then celebrated in public ceremonies. Reflections about God arise from a tradition of worship, praise and lament which are the condition, not the result, of belief in God. The conversation puts people in touch with each other through the medium of these traditional meaning-giving activities. Religions, like languages, are not private possessions or activities. Rather are they the necessary focus for the conversation, a communion between subjects. The first act of dialogue involves the assimilation from another subject of a certain process of understanding, namely what it means to be human in a particular society or religious community. This is why dialogue can never be fully expressed in either purely intellectualist or purely experiential terms. Both are necessary. The meeting is between persons who express themselves and therefore come to understand *themselves* through the language which, in a very real sense, they give to each other, just as a mother gives to a child not just love but a certain way of responding to and articulating that love.

This rediscovery of the subject as essentially relational rather than the Cartesian 'thing that thinks' is not the result of the inter-faith dialogue alone. Modern technology, which has brought American gangster movies into Indian villages and threatens each and every one of us with instant destruction, is another significant factor. It all makes for a very small and interdependent world in which human persons, no longer omnipotent masters of all they survey, have to work within some very obvious limitations. Similarly the feminist movement can be seen as a reaction against a view of sexual relationships which makes the woman, if not an object, then at least a secondary partner in a male-dominated power game. No doubt one could list various factors, but religious pluralism, the existence of the other, raises a question mark, as perhaps no other contemporary experience does, over our western/Christian sense of self-sufficiency.[14] As long as we seek simply to fit 'them' into 'our' world we ignore the problem. For what happens when *we* become the foreigner, the infidel, the outsider, in *their* world? The fact is that 'they', who hold different views from us, who claim to argue on equal terms with us, who refuse to have their vision of truth turned into a cut-down version of ours, challenge not just our ideas and beliefs but the very way in which we claim to arrive at those beliefs and maintain them. This is today's experience and it is easy to see why Christians who experience this world for the first time find themselves caught on the horns of a dilemma: whether to retreat into the time-honoured fastness of orthodox exclusivity or to abandon such a position altogether in favour of some form of relativism. To say that these options are just the negative forms of our twin values of loyalty and openness is not to dissolve the problem. There is no way in which one can hold these values together without being prepared to reject a totally egocentric view of relationships. At some point I have to allow the other to penetrate my world, to dare to let myself be touched by him or her. Once one comes to accept the other not as 'them' but 'you', as a person who speaks another language, the nature of the problem changes. We create much of the problem for ourselves anyway, especially if we think of religion in intellectualist or propositional terms. But whatever the force of the imperative to defend the tradition – and to ignore this imperative must be to court some form of irrationalism – it may not be allowed to obscure another imperative: to respect the other as one committed to a similar pursuit of truth. This is not for purely pragmatic reasons, because we all have to survive somehow in our 'global village', but because I have discovered through dialogue that I only become complete by learning to participate in the life of another.

Faith and beliefs

How does such a person-centred version of dialogue address itself to the topic or subject of conversation? Here we return to the integrative and transcendent dimensions in another guise. Images of the Ultimate are very much specific to different traditions; concepts of completeness, perfection, individuation, salvation, have varied over the centuries and continue to vary from one religion to another. The pursuit of the ideal has not; it is part of what it means to be human. And the experience of the other which I am describing reminds us that while we are more than aware of difference and diversity, we remain convinced that there is a harmony, if not a unity, somewhere at the heart of it all. Moreover we know that the only way to appreciate that harmony is in company with the other, for none of us has the monopoly of truth. This, however, is not to recommend relativism and suggest that religions are true only within their own frameworks. It may be to acknowledge the relatedness and incompleteness of all our human knowing, but that is rather different. Pluralism does not imply relativism, but it does demand a radical reassessment of our claims for a privileged position over against those of the other. The rules of the game must be the same for both participants; if I make universal claims then I must allow the other to make universal claims too.

Some form of pluralism is essential. The experience of inter-faith dialogue emphasizes just how similar in all religions is the process by which human beings reflect on the pursuit of the ideal. This makes of the other not merely a pleasant companion on the way but the one who in some sense is responsible for leading us into ourselves. Once I, the subject, stop treating the other as an object we both have to change. Here I am referring to what in Christian terms is called conversion and to what I take to be an acceptable Buddhist equivalent, namely enlightenment. Conversion can come about through study, prayer and meditation. But rarely, if ever, can such activity be separated from contact with the other. Even in the arid and lonely landscape of Zen, enlightenment is never the result of sitting and meditating on the *koan* alone; the pupil needs the relationship with the Master who can provoke the necessary response. No one will want to argue seriously with the proposal that it is possible to be led more deeply into oneself by another as long as he or she is a co-religionist, a friend, confessor, spiritual director or even – in these more ecumenical days – a member of another Christian denomination. Such a person can promote the essential inner dialogue which must precede the outer one. But there is no reason in principle why the partner in the inter-faith dialogue should not perform the same function. All that is necessary is the part that the other person plays in human understanding. Genuine conversion always involves a renewed or deeper understanding of some essential of the tradition. And the catalyst may well be the parable which the other puts to our vision of the world. Dialogue is essentially an encounter between subjects, not a discussion about objects. As I said in the last chapter, the tension between change and continuity in any tradition is maintained by the balance between the transcendent and integrative functions in human religiosity. If one is ignored or emphasized at the expense of the other then clearly no dialogue is possible. Still more is this the case if we subordinate the dialogue of persons to the dialect of concepts, ideas and beliefs. The relationship is first and foremost a human encounter which depends on maintaining mutual respect and a balance of our key values of loyalty and openness.

The first task of the interior dialogue is to overcome the fear of losing identity. It requires not just trust of the other but an effort to understand. This is impossible unless we can first accept that all religions are at the same time universal and particular, that they are saying something important which is true for all people, and yet may not simply be reduced the one to the other. To maintain this principle is our most formidable task, but it is nothing new. As Panikkar points out, after centuries of human civilization we still find ourselves asking the fundamental question: 'What is there in Man which makes him irreducible to unity and yet unable to renounce the quest for it?'[15] There is, in other words, a certain fundamental dynamism which drives us to seek for that unity of religions even if we know that we shall never find it. At the same time we must remember that however much our conversation may be a communion of persons, it does not take place in a linguistic vacuum. The persons involved will certainly change. One must also ask: what about the *content* of the dialogue? Does that change too? Is it possible to safeguard the content of the tradition and still find a unity and harmony of faith?

Religions are not vague amalgams of devotions and rituals which can be picked up at will like so many packs of breakfast cereal from the supermarket shelf. No two statements of belief, still less the practices which express them, are the same, even if they perform much the same function within their respective traditions. Religions make sense only as comprehensive wholes or totalities. In one sense they are irreducible; remove one part and you change the whole edifice. Yet all religions agree that the superstructure is only a cover for the mystery of the Divine which cannot be encapsulated even in the richest of mythologies or the most sublime of rituals. Somewhere a distinction has to be made between the enigmatic universal and that which is particular to this or that tradition.

This in theory does not seem problematic. Cantwell Smith takes as his universal the act of faith, as does Panikkar.[16] And it is true that all religions, even Buddhism, demand some personal expression of the sense of relationship with whatever one takes to be the goal or ideal of life. From this universal attitude can be distinguished beliefs, the intellectual and cultural forms which faith takes within a particular tradition.[17] Such belief-forms obviously vary from culture to culture, and even within a culture. And it is these which change in response to the prophetic or transcendent element in human religiosity. Indeed such forms must change. As the expressions of faith, they must never be allowed to obscure faith or to identify it with what are only particular perspectives through which the goal of all human religiosity, salvation or liberation, is to be obtained. For once faith is seen as synonymous with belief it becomes exclusivist and even fanatical. Faith is reduced to a particular theological formulation and change is seen as a threat. There is no need to dwell on this point at length except to note that what are often taken to be crises of faith, whether personal or communal, may be more accurately described as crises of belief. We might prefer to see them more positively as real opportunities for growth. The realization that in its present form the tradition does not provide all the answers can be extremely salutary, reminding us of the relativity of all cultural forms of religion. A crisis of belief only becomes a crisis of faith when the believer fails, for whatever reason, to let him- or herself be enriched by the tradition. Faith is rarely, if ever, lost. It may well change. One hopes it will frequently be purified. The change of understanding which comes with conversion is often a profound revelation of what one has always believed. Perhaps it may be compared to learning a new language. The old does not disappear: it becomes more highly prized. The new appears as an alternative way of articulating that which one has always held most dear.

Faith, in other words, is that fundamental acknowledgement of creatureliness in the face of whatever one takes to be the transcendent; it represents the human response to the transcendent dimension in religion. It is present, and may be recognized, in all religions. Without that response we are left with a bare acceptance of community rituals and regulations – and certainly with no sense of the Divine Mystery at the heart of the other. Religion becomes no more than empty form, a response to the integrative dimension alone. Such belief, without faith, may be no more than superstition or idolatry. It is, therefore, both possible and necessary to distinguish faith from belief. My point here, however, is that while belief may exist without faith, faith cannot exist without belief. Moreover, as there is a dialectical relationship between the transcendent and the integrative, so there is one between faith and belief. This, however, is not a matter of belief revealing or showing forth faith in a human form – the sort of cultural clothing which can be swopped when one feels like a change. Still less is it analogous to the many paths up the single mountain. I have tried to argue that the universal can never be apprehended except in and through the particular. The belief structure is what faith always needs in order to find expression, the language (to return to my central metaphor) without which it cannot be articulated. A disembodied faith makes about as much sense as a disembodied person, the 'thing that thinks' and depends on no one.

Faith and meaning

The relevance of this distinction between faith and beliefs becomes obvious when we are forced to make the internal dialogue, when we discover what faith really means. To appropriate another religious tradition is not a matter of simple comparison, lining up aspects and items of belief and practice. At the very least dialogue demands personal reflection and conversion. But all this is to operate only at the level of belief, not at the level of faith: here we are asked to integrate a new experience, that of people from different religious communities meeting to form, in practice, a new community and new relationships. The mistake of the Cartesian subject-orientated approach to theologizing is that it turns faith into the mental functioning of the embodied rational animal. But once a person is understood as a member of a celebrating and worshipping community, the meaning of faith is seen not in rather static terms as a sort of lowest common denominator (what is left over when all the words of belief have been exhausted), but as arising from what people *do* together as human beings: the processes of communication which make up religious practice and lead to, but do not depend upon, reflections about the nature of the Divine. What happens, then, when our concept of community is broadened to include inter-faith relationships, in other words when hitherto acknowledged barriers break down? In the last two chapters I want to consider the loyalty side of the theologian's dilemma and to argue that learning from the other is quite compatible with faithfulness to the Christian tradition. Here I want finally to return to the imperative of openness, and to consider further this process of deriving Christian meaning from the different beliefs or languages of faith.

The interior dialogue follows the initial contact with the other as stranger. The first task is to accept this strangeness totally and then, by an exercise of the imagination and a suspension of judgement, to learn something of the coherence of the beliefs of the other. Gradually we learn that belief and practice only make sense within the overall pattern of faith. This leads, through argument and dialectic, to a different type of external dialogue in which the other is no longer a stranger but another person like myself, an 'I' who is also a 'Thou'.

The dialectic of objects-in-tension has become a dialogue of subjects sharing a common humanity. The key to overcoming the largely intellectualist model of dialogue is the recognition of that common humanity, which, in turn, means understanding the nature of our common religiosity. A religious person is one whose faith, something shared with all persons, has become active, fully explicit and articulate. Through contact with a particular tradition he or she is able to name the Divine Mystery. And through contact with other traditions that capacity is expanded. Since faith and belief are so intimately bound up together, it makes sense to think of the intrapersonal dialogue as an attempt to find within oneself different ways of referring to that mystery, in confidence that ultimately and, perhaps, in a way one can never hope to explain, they cannot be contradictory.

Such confidence can only come through human contact. It is not to be gained from even the most sympathetic and persuasive of scholarly studies and it marks the shift from dialectic to dialogue. Conferences and conversations may make for initial contact; monologues and lectures may give way to 'duologues' and a sharing of experience. Eventually the other will penetrate through the belief-structures to the person of faith. This, as Panikkar suggests, is the root meaning of the word dialogue: a 'going through the logos', a passing beyond the words with which we articulate and explain our collective or personal myths.[18] In dialogue our myths and stories, our theologies and philosophical conventions, are laid open to the parable which is the stranger. The intellectual horizons within which I normally come to terms with my experience, and even the time-honoured language which I use, are shown to be limited and based on all sorts of hidden presuppositions. If nothing else the intra-personal dialogue makes me own my *logos* for what it is: the rational elaboration of the conscious and semi-conscious attitudes and practices which make up religious belief. Dialectic touches only the level of doctrines, and more often than not ends up in the impasse which is created by incompatible vocabularies. Dialogue touches the level of motivation and acknowledges that different languages may sometimes share a common grammar. Krishna is not Christ and Christ is not Krishna. But it may be that Krishna performs much the same function within devotional Hinduism as Christ does in Christianity. Again, Muhammad is not Christ, nor does the prophet fulfil the same function within Islam. But the Qu'ran, as the revelation of Allah, the word of God, comes much closer to a Muslim equivalent. Such comparisons are never exact.

We cannot just substitute one form of words for another. We need to know how the words are used.

This is the heart of the interior dialogue, when we argue within ourselves not about the appropriateness of different words but about what the other intends, what he or she is trying to express. Such inner debates often begin in crisis. Is faith compromised? How much can I share without betraying Christ? Can I remain fully committed to the Christian language, which tries to express what God has done in Christ, and affirm the Hindu devotee's faith in Krishna? What sense can it possibly make to acknowledge *both* as saviour of humankind, *both* as the source of all truth and value? First, we note that the Christian imperative is to love our neighbour, not necessarily to agree with everything he may say or do. Love means being prepared to invite the other into a relationship which involves sharing and trust. This, as a minimum, demands a willingness on both sides to change. Anyone not prepared to take that risk is not ready for dialogue. But a second condition is that we are both prepared to look for ways of acknowledging that what the other takes to be true is indeed truth. Again, changing the words is never enough. I must look at the other's belief as another highly complex tradition of faith, performing the same function for him or her as my Christian tradition does for me. To object, therefore, that 'our' Christ is quite different from 'their' Krishna, since the former is a historical and the latter a 'mere' mythological figure, quite misses the point. Such value-judgements only reflect the limitations of our own religious presuppositions. Put like this, the two are not strictly comparable. Rather, from what I can experience of the faith of the other, I trust that what Christ does for me Krishna does for the other. At the same time I have to be willing to go on suspending judgement so as not to fall into the trap of imposing on the other the same sort of limits which I have only recently learnt to avoid in myself.

Beyond inclusivism

What, in the end, does it mean, to live in two traditions at once, to speak the language of the other? Does what I have described differ in any way from the inclusivist paradigm which we discussed and found wanting earlier? Here we must first remind ourselves that the various paradigms are trying to answer very different questions. Inclusivism is a response to the old problematic and represents a type of christocentric theology which seeks to show how other

religions may be included within the Christian d
burden of the new problematic is that we are tr
different question, one demanded by the particular
our age. Today's pluralist culture forces Christian
thesis of religions not on the basis of one religion alo
promoting the interpenetration of one by another. I ....m, as
described earlier in this book, sees the other as little more than an
extension of the self. Our dialogal theory of relationships questions
this. A religious tradition can no more see the other as a cut-down or
amended version of itself than a man can afford to regard a woman as
a sort of secondary image of his own 'superior' maleness. If psycho-
social – and now theological – thinking has made us rethink the
relationship of male and female on the basis of mutual support and
complementarity, ought we not to extend the same thinking to
inter-faith dialogue as well? As husband and wife come to understand themselves through understanding each other, so it is with
religions. To return to Panikkar's term, we need a theory of
interpenetration, not the theological colonialism of Anonymous
Christianity.

Religions are not competing ideologies. They represent different
ways of being human, each quite unique, yet as people grow in
understanding of each other, increasingly interdependent. Thus I
am asked to seek out the Christian meaning of other traditions while
at the same time admitting the Jewish, Muslim, Hindu and
Buddhist meaning of Christianity. We have to accept that if Christ
includes Krishna, then, from the Hindu's point of view, Krishna
includes Christ. Not that there is any need to revert to an Anonymous Christianity theory, even if we are prepared to go the whole
way and allow that Christians may well be Anonymous Hindus or
Buddhists or whatever. As noted already, the language of inclusivism always carries with it the implication that one tradition is
privileged or superior. Whatever the demands of loyalty and our
commitment to Christianity as the most adequate of all languages, it
is unhelpful to begin with the dialectic of beliefs. The only way to
meet the other is to accept him or her fully at the personal level. The
'other tradition', previously an object of polemic and suspicion, has
to be seen as incarnated in this person, a fellow-subject in dialogue.
At which point the other becomes for me a source of revelation and
self-knowledge, no longer a self-projection but the embodiment of a
tradition from which I can learn about myself.

otes

1. Tracy's suggestions for how conversation can be used as a model for interpretation are instructive: 'It is by conversion alone that we are freed from epistemological solipsism for a dialogical life, with others and with all the classics' (*Plurality and Ambiguity*, London: SCM 1988, p. 28).

2. The variety of approaches to the mission-dialogue tension within the Roman Catholic Church and in the World Council of Churches shows the complexity of the theological problem; cf. S.J. Samartha, 'The Cross and the Rainbow, Christ in a Multireligious Culture', in *The Myth of Christian Uniqueness*, pp. 69–88, especially pp. 71–72.

3. cf. for example, the article by Albert Nambiaparambil, 'Religions in Dialogue: Indian Experience Today', in *Meeting of Religions*, ed. Thomas Aykara, Bangalore: Dharmaram 1978, pp. 76–88; and *Pro Mundi Vita Bulletin* 88 (January 1982) on 'Hindu-Christian Dialogue in India'.

4. cf. his article 'The Goals of Inter-religious Dialogue' in *Truth and Dialogue*, ed. John Hick, London: Sheldon 1974, pp. 77–95.

5. Lindbeck, op. cit., pp. 52–55, alludes briefly to various models of dialogue. A cultural-linguistic approach to religion he thinks the most adequate to cope with the new agenda. The lack of a common understanding of what dialogue is about is 'a weakness, but is also a strength. It means, on the one hand, that the partners in dialogue do not start with the conviction that they really basically agree, but it also means that they are not forced into the dilemma of thinking of themselves as representing a superior (or an inferior) articulation of a common experience of which the other religions are superior (or inferior) expressions' (p. 55).

6. cf. H.J. Singh, ed., *Inter-religious Dialogue*, Bangalore: CISRS 1967, pp. 104ff., and 'Hindu-Christian Dialogue Postponed', an exchange between Murray Rogers and Śivendra Prakash, in *Dialogue between Men of Living Faiths*, ed. S.J. Samartha, Geneva: World Council of Churches 1971, pp. 21–31.

7. Rowan Williams, 'Trinity and Revelation', art. cit., does not refer specifically to meaning being derived from contact with the other, but the implication is there. Revelation, he says, 'is essentially to do with what is *generative* in our experience – events or *transactions in our language that break existing frames of reference and initiate new possibilities of life*' (p. 199) (my italics).

8. I am grateful to James Redington for clarifying for me the origin and meaning of the term 'Interior Dialogue'. He has developed the point, with examples from his own contacts, in his article 'The Hindu-Christian Dialogue and the Interior Dialogue', *Theological Studies* 44 (1983) pp. 587–603, especially p. 596.

9. R. Panikkar, *The Intra-Religious Dialogue*, Bangalore: Asian Trading Corporation 1978, pp. 40ff.

10. op. cit., p. 21.

11. Fergus Kerr, *Theology after Wittgenstein*, Oxford: Blackwell 1986. cf. especially Chapter 1, 'The modern philosophy of the self'.

12. Kerr, op. cit., pp. 22ff., finds a 'common paradigm' in a sample of modern theologians which includes figures as diverse as Rahner and Don Cupitt: 'One thing is beyond dispute: in each case the starting point is naturally assumed to be the individual. In every case . . . the model of the self is central to some important, sometimes radical and revisionary, theological proposal or programme. A certain philosophical psychology is put to work to sustain a theological construction. Time and again, however, the paradigm of the self turns out to have remarkably divine attributes'.

13. Gordon E. Michalson Jr., in 'The Response to Lindbeck', *Modern Theology* 4, 2 (January 1988) pp. 107–120, situates Lindbeck's cultural-linguistic approach in the context of 'recent criticisms of epistemological "foundationalism" and with an emerging anti-Cartesian mood in certain circles, epitomised perhaps by the work of Richard Rorty' (p. 113).

14. Panikkar, referring to the contemporary attitude of dialogue as the form which Christian interaction with the other will take today, draws our attention to dialogal thinkers whose prophetic insights may be valuable for 'this kairological moment': Ramon Lull, Nicholas of Cusa, Brahmabandhav Upadhyaya etc., *The Myth of Christian Uniqueness*, p. 96. In his essay 'The Dialogical Dialogue', *The World's Religious Traditions*, ed. Frank Whaling, Edinburgh: T. & T. Clark 1984, pp. 201–221, he draws our attention to the limitations of post-Cartesian idealism, and mentions the tradition of 'dialogical dialectic' running from Feuerbach to the personalist philosophy associated with Buber, Rosenzweig and Ebner (cf. p. 215).

15. 'The Myth of Pluralism: the Tower of Babel – a Meditation on Non-Violence', *Cross Currents*, XXIX, 2 (Summer 1979), p. 212. This whole issue is dedicated to the work of Raimundo Panikkar, being based on a seminar held at the University of California at Santa Barbara in February 1977.

16. cf. W. Cantwell Smith, *The Meaning and End of Religion*, London: SPCK 1978, especially chapters six and seven. In his article 'Idolatry in Comparative Perspective', in *The Myth of Christian Uniqueness*, Smith refers to his basic thesis that what we call 'religions' are fundamentally based on two components, faith and cumulative tradition, which interact, and, significantly, he adds a third: community. Together tradition and community have the capacity to 'elicit and to nurture faith, the term that I gave . . . to that relation of human beings to God' (p. 59).

17. Panikkar speaks of the distinction between faith and belief in *The Intra-Religious Dialogue*, pp. 40–61. For a useful discussion, drawing attention to the use Lonergan makes of this distinction (in *Method in Theology*, London: Darton, Longman & Todd 1972, pp. 108–111, 115–119), see Redington, art. cit., pp. 599–603.

18. cf. 'The Dialogal Dialogue' in *The World's Religious Traditions*, esp.

pp. 218ff. 'The very "rules" of this dialogue are not fixed "a priori",
they emerge out of the dialogue itself. The dialogue is not a "duo-
logue", but a going through the logos, *dia ton logon*, beyond the
logos-structure of reality'.

7 SPIRIT OF THE MYSTERY

In this study I have tried to build on what I see as a fundamental distinction between an old and a new problematic, a theology *for* dialogue and a theology *of* dialogue. The challenge to Christian theology is to go 'beyond inclusivism': to avoid the impasse created by the currently available spectrum of theological opinion and to build a theology of religions which is faithful to the Christian tradition, on the one hand, and open to the reality of God's revelation outside that tradition, on the other. But in suggesting that the 'problem of religious pluralism' lies in the nature of otherness I hope I do not appear to emphasize the new at the expense of the old. This study has not started with christology or soteriology precisely because it is unclear what the *Christian* meaning of other religions can possibly be. What does it mean to say that the other is fulfilled in Christ? Why and in what way does Christian self-understanding demand that Christ be present in other religions?

As long as we are trying to build a theology *for* dialogue we are unlikely to answer these questions adequately. I have worked the other way round, from the inter-faith conversation to theology, not out of any perverse desire to be different but in the conviction that a contemporary theology of religions cannot simply be based on the sort of *a priori* Christian principles which underlie traditional christocentric theology, the so-called exclusivist and inclusivist paradigms. This, in due acknowledgement of the seminal work of Wilfred Cantwell Smith and Raimundo Panikkar, is in order to underline the impact which the new problematic is making. In the last chapter I was concerned with the question of how the dialectic of integrative and transcendent dimensions may be expressed in terms of a dialogue between persons. Panikkar's intra-religious dialogue arises from the personal encounter with the other and the attempt to integrate that experience into the traditional Christian understanding of the ways of God. Theological argument or dialectic only makes sense within the wider context of inter-faith dialogue. A theology which begins with a Christianity-centred defence of orthodoxy mistakes the nature of that dialogue and misses the opportunity to engage in an enterprise which is truly cross-cultural and interreligious.

It would be wrong, however, to give the impression that theological reflection on the challenge to Christianity can be avoided. If this process of dialogue is conducted with goodwill and tolerance it is possible to marry respect with criticism; clearly this is the *sine qua non* of the conversation, and in the final chapter I want to develop further the conditions under which inter-faith encounter must take place. The immediate task, however, is to focus on the Christian side of the conversation at another level and examine the language of Christian belief. The symbolic 'content' of faith which makes up the integrative dimension has a central role to play in the conversation. The tradition must be formulated in such a way as to enable the Christian partner to remain open to the other while maintaining his or her own integrity as a confessing member of the Christian Church. To say that contact with the other will help us to understand the tradition does not mean that he or she somehow *forms* us in that tradition, only that we come to a deeper appreciation of its meaning *in relationship* with the other. I do not learn alone as an autonomous subject. Moreover, once the conversation with the other has begun, the relationship itself and the experience of otherness become the subject of reflection.

Beginning the conversation

An alternative model to the three-fold paradigm is Panikkar's idea of interpenetration, which attempts to safeguard the specific and irreducible quality of all religions, not just of Christianity. But what is this 'specific quality' which sets Christianity apart and how are we to avoid losing it in some sort of pan-religious mélange? Here my approach will not be apologetic in the sense of correctly articulating the credal formulations of the Christian Church in the face of contrary opinion. When we come to examine the effect that dialogue must have on the Christian tradition and to raise the question of the limits of legitimate change within that tradition, we have to resist the temptation to act like some latter-day Inquisition, prowling around in search of heresy. Of course a Christian theology of religions needs to be orthodox. But orthodoxy is not governed simply by adherence to the correct credal form, as might be the case if we stuck rigidly to a purely cognitive version of religion or the 'thing that thinks' account of the human person. Religions are dynamic processes which help understanding through the exercise of faith. It is precisely because we seek to understand the other as person that we cannot be content simply to equate religious faith with an unchanging set of rigid

same individual is prepared to enter into another dialogue, with another tradition, the horizon or frontier of the language of belief is extended. The questions which we inherit remain the same; the answers are bound to change. If we begin to understand through one type of conversation – within the tradition – we go on learning through a second – outside it. This is saying something important not just about how we learn but also about our nature as human beings. We are not born full of innate ideas which simply have to be brought to fruition; nor do we grow up in society as largely passive receptacles into which the tradition of the community is somehow poured. We learn in society, in relationship, in dialogue with the other. The two dialogues have, therefore, but a single purpose: the pursuit of understanding. The key symbols around which any tradition has developed demand an initial effort of the imagination if one is to begin to understand. But there is also need of the 'catalyst' or the parable of the other if that understanding is to grow.

The Meaning that is Christ

A religious tradition is an expression of faith, the conviction that the world is not ultimately irrational. It is nothing new for structures to be put under strain; they will inevitably change in some regards while the fundamental attitude of faith remains. The search for the rational goes on within a certain horizon of meaning which is constantly expanding. Thus the mystery of Christ represents the horizon within which the Christian tradition attempts to articulate itself. Other religions bring their own guiding symbols. At the level of beliefs they are using very different languages, but there is no reason to assume that at the level of faith they are incompatible; they share the same pattern of integrative and transcendent dimensions. In a very obvious sense the mystery of Christ can no more be exhausted than the nature of Nirvana can be explained.

The above remarks refer more to the new problematic than to the old, and to the dialogue with the other rather than to the dialogue with the Christian tradition. At the same time I repeat that once we have entered the intra-religious dialogue our approach to Christology is guided, if not conditioned, by the sort of demands which the other makes on us. Thus we must ask what the meaning of Christ is for us today *and* for the other. To put it in terms of the old problematic: what is a genuinely Christian spirituality and a truly Christian way of life in today's multi-cultural world? Or to use the terms of the new: how are the insights which the other may have gained into the revelation which God has made in Christ to be understood by *us* – let alone by him or her? The two go together; even if we are concentrating solely on the latter question, we cannot simply absolve ourselves from the christological dilemma of how not to fall into exclusivism or relativism. Once seen in dialogue with the other, the christological question appears in its starkest form. It echoes Jesus's original challenge to the disciples: 'Who do you say that I am?' and forces Christians not to seek out new titles to supplement Lord, Son of Man, Messiah and Suffering Servant, but to find new ways of entering fully into the mystery of what God has done in Christ. The Christian's self-understanding is always bound up with the answer to this question, and still more so when we are forced to re-evaluate our traditional response in the light of new experience. As Christians we are committed to recognizing that horizon as Christ; but is Christ the horizon for the other too? And if so, how?

This is a complex and controversial issue over which opinions tend immediately to become polarized.[5] Many Christians see in any acknowledgement of the religious values of other faiths a compromise as to the uniqueness of universality of Christ; for others the dogma of Christ's divinity is simply outdated and inappropriate to the contemporary religious situation. The danger is, as Cantwell Smith has pointed out, that such arguments become a distraction. The problem 'is not with whether the figure of Christ has served as a form in which God has entered history and been active within it. It is certainly not with *how* this has been done. Rather, our concern is whether this has been and is one form among others'.[6] To some extent the answer we give to this question depends on how much weight our Christology wishes to place on the crucial issue of the particularity of Christ. Jesus of Nazareth, son of Mary, in whom the Logos became incarnate, lived and worked in a particular place at a particular time. The Christ really appeared in history. Now the fact that there are historical links between Christianity and other religions, that Jesus appears in the Qu'ran, that Hindu reformers of the last century were inspired by his teaching, is an important reminder that cultures and religions do not live in separate worlds. Nor should we lightly ignore the impact which the story of Jesus continues to have on people of other faiths everywhere. But in itself this sort of contact only raises the problem more acutely. The Jesus of the Qu'ran is a messenger of God; the Jesus that so impressed Raja Ram Mohan Roy and Mahatma Gandhi is a moral giant.[7] The Hindu who keeps a picture of the Sacred Heart in his family shrine is not so

Christian tradition, and yet seeks to extend our understanding of the many routes by which the Spirit enables us to know the Divine.

Meaning given by the Spirit

To speak of the Third, rather than the Second Person, of the Trinity means shifting the whole debate into the doctrine of God. Instead of concentrating exclusively on the content of the act of faith and the language of Christian confession we look at the process by which we come to know anything, including God. Simply to take refuge in an all-powerful revelation avoids the issue. For how is that revelation to be discerned? A Christian God is known throughout Christ who alone leads us to the Father: 'No one knows who the Son is except the Father or who the Father is except the Son and anyone to whom the Son chooses to reveal him' (Luke 10.22). Such language, the language of confessional belief, immediately takes us away from a static world of theological definitions and back to the practice of faith: 'Who do *you* say that I am?' Christianity as religion introduces people to a way of articulating faith. This is one particular language of belief. In Christian terms we may say that it is the meaning of Christ. But the structure of *all* religions describes something universal. This was the point of our distinction between faith and belief. All religions make universal claims. The key symbol of the Christian tradition – Christ – represents that universal and, therefore, what must be considered true in an absolute sense. If this is so, then that universal must be present in some way in other religions. But to repeat, how is it possible to speak of a sort of 'latent' presence of Christ where he is not known or explicitly acknowledged? Still more, how can we say that Christ is present where he is made one of many *avatars*, as in Hinduism, or a compassionate *bodhisattva*, as in Buddhism, or one of the messengers of God, as in Islam? These figures may not just be equated together. They represent different functions in the different traditions.

We are unlikely to get very far if we do not, at the same time, remember what the Christ-symbol is trying to *do* in Christian theology, let alone in other religions. What we have called the 'shape of grace' lies in the dialogal structure by which we are brought into contact with the Divine. Now I have suggested earlier, in arguing for a common structure in religions, that a way forward would be to understand the phenomenon of religious pluralism in terms of different cultural-linguistic systems in which the key experiences of a particular community are summed up and passed on in a more or less developed system of symbols. Structurally the key faith experiences would be the same and would be evoked by the different symbols or the idioms of the tradition. Thus, rather than beginning with a comparison of Christ and Krishna as equally valid symbols of God's revelation (for they must of course differ in many respects), we look at the *single process of divine activity in the world*. This is described in different and perhaps strictly incomparable ways through Christian and Vaishnava theology. But our fundamental conviction is that the *meaning* of the Christ-event cannot be limited to one particular historical revelation, any more than the meaning of Krishna can be limited to Vaishnavism. However unique or special we might want to make the Christian way we must never forget that God 'did not leave himself without witness' (Acts 14.17). Christ is the symbol which represents the integrative dimension in Christianity just as Krishna does in Vaishnavite Hinduism. In this sense they are different because they exercise different functions within their respective traditions. But both are also representative of the *single* transcendent dimension. And there is no reason to suppose that this dimension is restricted to one tradition. Through Christ God may challenge all our preconceived ideas about the Divine and introduce a measure of strangeness and the unexpected into our deliberations. And similarly through Krishna: the meeting with another symbol of the Divine may well raise the same questions, not just in Vaishnavism but also in Christianity. This is one effect of dialogue. In this sense no religion has a monopoly of the truth nor can one religion alone exhaust the meaning that is Christ – or Krishna. Dialogue makes us aware of what we know about God, and equally of what we do not know. The Spirit promised by Jesus, the Spirit who will 'lead you into all the truth', continues his work of pointing the way to the Father. But no one can know all the ways of the Spirit, just as Jesus said of the wind that 'you do not know whence it comes or whither it blows' (John 3.8).

A Spirit-centred theory of the interpenetration of traditions can help us to solve the loyalty-openness dilemma. Instead of asking how other religions are related to Christ, and raising the inevitable conundrum of his 'latent', 'unknown' or 'hidden' presence, we look to the way the Spirit of Christ is active, in all religions, in *revealing* the mystery of Christ – the mystery of what God is doing in the world. Such an approach begins with the conviction that this world is already in principle redeemed in Christ, that a new creation has been inaugurated with the outpouring of the Spirit and that the glorification of Christ cannot therefore be limited to the confines of

of believers enables us to cry out, with Jesus, 'Abba Father' (Romans 8.9ff.). Thus the Spirit which worked in Jesus is the same Spirit which is now present and active in the whole of creation and 'intercedes for us with sighs too deep for words' (Romans 8.26f.). If 'God was in Christ reconciling the world to himself' (2 Corinthians 5.19), God is also working as Spirit at the heart of creation which groans inwardly in the hope of final salvation (Romans 8.22).

It is not my intention here to develop a Spirit christology, a project which has its own peculiar problems.[15] Our interest is in the role of the Spirit in the extension of God's salvific action to the whole of creation. Enough has been said to indicate that there is one major theme running through both Old and New Testaments: the Spirit as making God present in the world. Creation and salvation are two aspects of the same mystery. The function of the Spirit is to continue the work of Christ. Thus, in their different ways, both John and Paul speak of the close connection between what God has done in Christ and what he continues to do in the Spirit. In Paul the 'Spirit of God' and the 'Spirit of Christ' are one and the same; the Christ raised from the dead is now a life-giving Spirit (1 Corinthians 15.45). The risen Lord is now so filled with the Spirit that he has become the source of God's Spirit for all those called to be saints (1 Corinthians 1.2, 6.11). And yet Christ and Spirit are not to be merged into one; they exist in relationship and it is through their essential relatedness that God's presence is made known. Those who knew God only indistinctly, as if a veil were placed before their minds, now see clearly, for 'the Lord is the Spirit, and where the Spirit of the Lord is, there is freedom' (2 Corinthians 3.17). To return to the image with which we began, the 'Lord who is the Spirit' is the means of access to God, without whom the many languages of the world would remain little more than the confusion which resulted from Babel.

Even such a selective use of scriptural evidence about the early Church's experience of the Spirit leads us to the conclusion that however closely Christ and Spirit may be related, they are not to be identified, as if the Spirit were Christ in a new guise. There is still a distinction. And it is in the working out of the relationship that any trinitarian theology, let alone a theology of religions, is to be developed. As in the Old Testament the *ruach Yahweh* gives us an image of God active in the world, so in the New the Spirit is not Christ's *alter ego* but the means by which God's self-revelation in Christ becomes actively present within the world. A simple identification of Christ and Spirit misses the point. Thus at the end of John's Gospel, Jesus breathes on the disciples, passing on the gift of the Spirit (20.22). Here the sending of the Spirit is a consequence of the resurrection; indeed, John goes so far as to say that before the glorification of Jesus the Spirit was not given (7.39). And yet the Spirit is also the one who blesses Jesus at his baptism, who fills him with power during his encounter with Satan and accompanies him in his public life. It is through the Spirit that Jesus is known and identified. The Spirit belongs to the process of identifying who Jesus is, provoking the answer to the christological question, 'Who do you say that I am?' Thus we should note that, although Jesus is clearly the *giver* of the Spirit, he never points to the Spirit; he witnesses to the Father (16.25). Similarly the Spirit points the way to the Father, to God's action in Christ. This is not to turn the Spirit into a sort of heavenly messenger or, to bring the image up to date, the great cosmic interpreter. But it is to emphasize that in addressing our central problematic – how do we know God? – the Spirit plays a major role, guiding us into the mystery of God's love made explicit in Christ.

A Spirit-centred theology

If this Spirit-centred theology is to take us beyond inclusivism successfully then we must ask if it can address both old and new problematics. There is no great difficulty with the salvation of the other. The Lucan theology of the Spirit in particular makes it quite clear that the Spirit is poured out on Jew and Gentile alike. The real problem is that, in an age of religious pluralism, such a theology of fulfilment has manifest weaknesses. What does it do to the identity of the other? Secondly, what of the definition of Christian identity and its understanding of the meaning of Christ and the nature and mission of the Church? I have suggested that 'inclusivism' – which, as the surveys show, has a long and distinguished pedigree – is only one version of christocentric universalism. Rahner's Anonymous Christianity thesis differs from Reformed theology more in the value it gives to the sacramental than in any *a priori* approval or dis-approval of 'the religions'. To that extent such a theology is more welcoming to a Spirit-centred understanding of grace and to an eschatological model of salvation. It makes Christians aware of the 'signs of the Spirit' in other religions. At the same time I have argued strongly that inclusivism represents a particular type of theology which, in defining the other by way of self-projection, renders itself inadequate as a grounding for a theology of dialogue. The difficulty is that christocentric theology effectively limits the sphere of action

define what is specific to Christianity. A Spirit-centred theology of
salvation expresses one side of the New Testament revelation: that
God's promises are fulfilled despite human sinfulness, that the 'new
creation' is the greatest manifestation of God's self-giving to
humankind, but does not negate what has gone before. In which case
what are we to make of such clear statements as we find in John's
Gospel: 'There was no Spirit yet because Jesus had not yet been
glorified' (7.39)? Does our theology of the Holy Spirit present us
with a new awareness or a new reality? Durrwell opts for the latter.
But why should we not accept both? Again, the question arises: how
do we know God? To reply that it is through his activity in the world
only recasts the terms of the question. What is the relationship between the new awareness and the new reality? At this point we may
begin to wonder whether we are not paying the price for the sort of
abstract theologizing which turns dynamic activities into static
'things'. A juridical conception of redemption, as Durrwell points
out, almost inevitably leads us to think of grace as a sort of commodity
for which Christ has paid the price and which can be distributed by
God just as easily before the death of Christ as after it, both inside and
outside the Church. The alternative, understanding grace as the gift of
the Spirit to humankind, stresses another model of salvation: deifica-
tion, the process by which humankind grows into the image of God
for which we were originally intended. Such an idea focuses on the
creative and redemptive activity of God who has made known his
purposes specifically in Christ but whose love for all people is
continually being made known by the activity of the Spirit.

To develop such an inter-religious theology of the Holy Spirit
need not fudge all distinctions and produce a gloriously vague
concept of divine activity as some sort of esoteric initiation. Nor is a
theology of the divinization of the world through the Spirit an
alternative to the theology of incarnation, a convenient way to
account for God's revelation to the other. My point is that we need
some way of holding together pneumatology and christology.[18] This
is no place to emulate Durrwell with his exhaustive exegesis of the
New Testament. But a brief perusal of the scriptural evidence, such
as I have already presented, would seem to indicate that alongside
theologies which would make the coming of Christ a 'new creation'
cancelling out the old, there are those which see the relationship in
more dialectical terms. Paul's Epistle to the Romans, wrestling not
just with the overthrow of the Law but with the fate of those still
committed to it, is the most obvious example. The distinction
between the new reality and the new awareness, between the gift of

grace and the revelation of grace, is itself a dialectic, not a dichotomy. The two necessarily go together. Which brings us back to a
model of grace – God's free communication of himself – as dialogue
and the exigencies of the new problematic.

God communicating Godself

When we follow Rahner's *a posteriori* search for the 'shape of grace'
in other religions we would do well to show less concern for some
sort of abstract essence and more for a sense of the inter-personal
structure which characterizes the Mystery of Christ made present in
the here and now through the Holy Spirit. A dialectic of opposites
has always been a feature of the different schools of Christian
theology, both Catholic and Protestant. Perhaps it is typical of
human religiosity in general; certainly it is difficult to explain the
elements of change and continuity in a tradition without accepting
some version of the dialectic of the integrative and transcendent
dimensions. But we cannot stop there; the dialectic of the two
horizons, represented (in Christian terms) by the Christian tradition
and by the tradition of the other, meet in a single inter-personal
process called dialogue. Although a fairly new experience within the
self-awareness of Christianity, this should not obscure the fact that
understanding in religion has always been provoked by contact with
the other – even if that otherness is simply expressed in terms of the
strangeness of a new experience. The question or the challenge of the
new, or simply a new relationship, has to be integrated into the
pattern of the old; I learn how to appropriate my horizon and you
learn to appropriate yours, but, more importantly, I learn how to
appropriate yours and you mine – at least to the extent that we each
enter more profoundly into the mystery which is represented by that
horizon.

It is precisely this idea, that inter-faith encounter and dialogue
leads to a deepening of awareness of identity, which provides the
basis for our theology of religions. A satisfactory theology of
religions must find a way to unite Word and Spirit. Strictly christocentric *or* theocentric theories only compound the problem. A
Spirit-centred approach at least has the advantage of broadening the
terms of our enquiry but pneumatocentrism only makes sense
within the wider framework of the central Christian doctrine of the
Trinity.[19] As Christians our first conviction is that the key Christian
symbol, the person of Christ, defines the Christian horizon. But we
also want to say that in some way it informs the horizon of the other.

the Father into the 'Thou' which is the Son; they are eternally one and yet eternally different – the 'we' which exists between them. Thus the Spirit is the bond or source of relationship within the Trinity which makes for the continuous expression 'in the world' of the relationship of Father and Son. The Spirit, in these terms, is the link that binds Father and Son together in love, the immanent presence of the transcendent.

Does this approach enable us to answer the question with which we began this chapter: what does it mean to say that the other is fulfilled in Christ? The problem with the statement of trinitarian theology advanced so far is that the Spirit's role appears to be secondary, *introducing* us to the mystery of the Father-Son relationship, but not appearing to give the Spirit any substantive role in the continuing relationship. Do we not end up with another form of fulfilment theology in which the other remains 'outside' until fully incorporated into the mystery of Christ? In other words, inclusivism again?

Whatever we may understand by the imperative to faithfulness, it does not entail promoting the ontological inclusivism which underlies the Anonymous Christianity thesis. There are other ways of affirming the universal relevance of the Christian revelation. Beginning with the recognition of the divinization of the whole world through the action of the Holy Spirit we enter into the mystery of divine-human communication which is expressed theologically as the Father's self-giving. What I have referred to as the mystery of Christ represents the horizon within which Christians identify themselves *and* make sense of what they see happening increasingly outside their own community. Christ is the Word, the self-revelation of the Father, who articulates God's meaning for the Christian community. The symbolic system which makes up the Christian language of faith centres on the confession that 'Jesus is Lord', but we cannot simply extrapolate from this the conditions by which the other may be included within the Christian dispensation without attending to the question of how *Christians themselves* are empowered to make this confession. In other words, to make Christ the cosmic principle which somehow includes all people of good will begs the question of what as Christians we expect Christ to do for *us*.

Once the other becomes central to our *Christian* experience and not just a peripheral nuisance to be incorporated into the all-embracing 'system', the limitations of a strictly christocentric theory of inter-religious relationships become clear. The latter reflects a theology of revelation which is essentially monologic and oracular:

the Word is spoken unambiguously to a hearer who, almost by definition, is receptive and ready to understand. The 'dialogue-as-conference' model is based on such a vision of the human person, the Cartesian 'thing that thinks'. The 'dialogue-as-conversation' model is based on a different concept of the person and the process by which identity is assumed. Here there need be no dichotomy between what we believe the mystery of Christ does for us and what we expect it to do for the other. Christ is the Word who both affirms and challenges, putting the question to all people who would seek to know God, a God who is to be known through the strangeness of what is other as well as in the familiar and comforting words of the ancient tradition. A dialogic theory of revelation emphasizes the relational element in the process of learning; the Spirit is at work both within and outside the Christian community developing an ever-growing richness of interpretation of the constant dialogue between language and experience.

This theology of the Spirit does full justice to the element of continuity *within* the tradition. It also accounts for the element of change, when the divine is revealed in parable, paradox or in the experience of otherness. If we want our trinitarian theology to reflect a truly open-ended dialogue the Spirit cannot simply be turned into a pale shadow of the Son, any more than we can allow the other to be turned into a lesser version of the self, as tends to happen with inclusivist christocentrism. Here we find a trinitarian theology in which the Father speaks of himself in Christ who is shown forth to human beings as the perfect revelation of the Father's love. There is no room for the other as other. But if the Father is giving the *whole* of himself to the Son and the Son is returning the *whole* of himself to the Father then *there can be no limit to that gift*. Nor is there any limitation within the divine 'we' which marks the eternal giving of 'I' and 'Thou'. A Spirit-centred theology of religions which gives as much weight to the new as to the old problematic must do more than present us with a role for the Spirit as the relation of love which binds Father and Son together.[23] The scriptural evidence speaks of the Spirit as pointing to Christ but this is only possible because the Spirit is *already* at work in creation. Once we think of revelation in broader terms, as conversation rather than proclamation, the Spirit assumes a certain freedom and personality. To quote Panikkar again:

> Could one not say that in spite of every *effort* of the Father to 'empty himself' in the generation of the Son, to pass entirely into his Son, to give

154

him everything that he *has*, everything that he *is*, even then there remains in this first procession, like an irreducible factor, the Spirit, the non-exhaustion of the source in the generation of the Logos?[24]

To believe that revelation takes place through the other, of course, raises an immense question mark over our attempts to understand the Divine; but so too does the ultimate paradox that the Father's love for the Son is revealed on the cross. Dialogue, as I have described it, is such an invitation: to enter into the eternal communion of the Godhead. But it is also, and more importantly, a reminder that God is not a duality of persons held together by a third but properly a trinity of persons forever seeking to communicate in and through what is other.

Thus our theology of the unity of religions lies in the inter-personal structure of human religiosity, not in common elements but in a common experience of dialogue. The conversation is revelatory not in the sense that it provides us with further knowledge or even an enhanced awareness of our identity but because the process reflects something of the mystery of God's self-revelation. The Christian religion is based on the mystery of the Trinity, a constant communication between Father and Son in the Spirit. The language spoken by the Father is the language of love and it is obvious that the basis of inter-religious dialogue is love: that esteem and respect which sees the image of God, the signs of the Spirit, in the other. God is to be recognized in the ways in which we try to communicate with the other, in our personal relations, in the sometimes painful ways in which human beings identify themselves and others and grow, however slowly, in harmony together. God is to be recognized, therefore, in the very language of dialogue itself. If the particular language spoken by Christians has a trinitarian structure or grammar, this is not to make it any different in kind from that spoken by someone who practises another faith-tradition. What holds them all together is precisely a similar grammar. In Christian terms this is identified with the Spirit as the continuing outpouring of the Father to his people, all his people, not just those who have explicitly confessed their faith in Christ. The great religions, insofar as they are characterized by a grammar of communication, reflect exactly the same pattern. The Spirit can thus be said to be active within all religions.

Dialogue, as we have seen, can be understood in a number of different ways, but primarily it implies a conversation between two people which is an *end in itself*. This is not to say that conversation is basically aimless but that the end is the human process of *self-communication*, not necessarily the passing on of information. Dialogue-as-conversation is not intended to solve the problems of the universe, still less to enfold the other in a Christian system which runs the risk of limiting our appreciation of the continuing story of God's outpoured love. If we are content to see our contact with the other as a sharing of traditions, an attempt to understand different ways of looking at our world, then we begin and end in the Spirit of the love of God: not a 'fact' which we have to communicate, still less a 'truth' to which we think we have sole access, but that common ground in which we live and move and have our being.

Notes

1. An edition of *Modern Theology* (4.2, January 1988), has been devoted to various aspects of Lindbeck's book; cf. especially the articles by Geoffrey Wainwright, 'Ecumenical Dimensions of George Lindbeck's "Nature of Doctrine"' (pp. 121–132), and Lee Barrett, 'Theology as Grammar: Regulative Principles or Paradigms and Practices?' (pp. 155–172). cf. also the Review Symposium in *The Thomist*, 49 (July 1985), especially the comments of David Tracy, (pp. 460–472), who has 'some lingering questions as to the adequacy of Lindbeck's rule theory interpretation of doctrine . . . Nevertheless, the interpretation of doctrine as *'regula fidei'* is generally illuminating'.

2. Kenneth Cracknell, *Towards a New Relationship*, pp. 65f., draws our attention to the British Council of Churches document, *Towards a Theology for Interfaith Dialogue*, London: CIO Publishing, 1984, which develops a trinitarian perspective, but in none of our surveys is the Spirit given more than a cursory mention. There are some interesting suggestions in J.V. Taylor's insightful *The Go-Between God*, London: SCM 1972, especially pp. 179–197 where he speaks of the Spirit as the capacity to participate in what is other. One of the few articles which specifically addresses itself to the significance of pneumatology for a theology of religions is J. Dupuis, 'The Cosmic Influence of the Holy Spirit and the Gospel Message' in *God's Word Among Men*, ed. George Gisbert Sauch S J, Delhi: Vidyajyoti 1973, pp. 117–138.

3. John Hick, *The Myth of Christian Uniqueness*, pp. 30ff., takes this somewhat modalist line, accepting a dyad of forms of the divine reality but clearly finding a Trinity hard to appreciate in the inter-faith context. In theory, says Hick, it would have been possible to account for the divine presence outside the life of Jesus 'with a more economic binitarian doctrine by attributing what came to be regarded as the work of the Holy Spirit to the eternal Christ-spirit or Logos . . . However, eventually the trinitarian pattern became established and now per-

vades Christian theological and liturgical language'. Hick sees the Holy Spirit as the third of 'three distinguishable ways in which the one God is experienced as acting in relation to, and is accordingly known by, us – namely, as creator, redeemer, and inspirer'. Hick fails to ask what a pneumatology, let alone a christology, is trying to *do* in the first place.

4. Panikkar, in *Myth of Christian Uniqueness*, pp. 109ff., goes so far as to say that 'the mystery of the Trinity is the ultimate foundation for pluralism'. Panikkar's version of pluralism affirms that truth is neither one nor many. Thus we can be content neither with a pluralist 'system' (a contradiction) nor with the relativism which denies the perichoresis or 'mutual indwelling' of different religious views of Reality. In Panikkar's highly addictive trinitarian vocabulary, 'The theanthropocosmic insight (which sees the unity between the divine-human-cosmic) suggests a sort of trinitarian dynamism in which all is implied in all'.

5. cf. in particular Schineller, art. cit. 'In terms of Christology, all affirm that Jesus Christ is *a* way to salvation, a mediator of authentic existence'. But they differ on the 'relation of Jesus to other mediators of salvation' and on 'the degree of dispensability and the normative value of Jesus Christ' p. 549.

6. In *The Myth of Christian Uniqueness*, p. 63.

7. cf. M.M. Thomas, *The Acknowledged Christ of the Hindu Renaissance*, London: SCM 1969, in which the author attempts a response to Panikkar's *The Unknown Christ of Hinduism*, London: Darton, Longman & Todd, 2nd edition, 1981. The Indian acknowledgement of Christ is 'no doubt partial and very inadequate' (p. xiv) but it is essential to appreciate it for its own sake if a genuinely Indian Christian theology is to grow.

8. *God and the Universe of Faiths*, pp. 151ff.

9. cf. D'Costa, *John Hick's Theology*, pp. 48–60; 119–133.

10. Panikkar, *The Trinity and the Religious Experience of Mankind*, New York: Orbis; London: Darton, Longman & Todd, 1973, pp. 53–54.

11. cf., for example, the comments of Stanley Samartha in *The Myth of Christian Uniqueness*, p. 79. 'The distinctiveness of Jesus Christ does not lie in claiming that "Jesus Christ is God". This amounts to saying that Jesus Christ is the tribal god of Christians over against the gods of other peoples.'

12. This is the lingering doubt hanging over such christologies as Panikkar's *The Unknown Christ*. His thesis, that the 'cosmic Christ' principle is the goal and ultimate meaning of Hinduism, lays itself open to the criticisms levelled earlier against Rahner's inclusivism.

13. cf. Schineller, art. cit., for the normative/constitutive distinction; Paul Knitter, 'Catholic Theology of Religions at a Crossroads', in *Christianity among the Religions, Concilium* 183 (1986), edited by H. Küng and J. Moltmann, produces a highly schematic account of changes in Catholic christology, shifting the preposition from Christ 'against' to Christ 'with' the religions. More persuasive is the programme he suggests for

a Liberation Theology of Religions in which the two most creative contemporary expressions of Catholic thought respond to each other. cf. his article in *The Myth of Christian Uniqueness*, pp. 178–200.

14. cf. Raymond Brown, *The Gospel According to John*, London: Chapman 1971, pp. 644ff. and Appendix V on The Paraclete, pp. 137ff.

15. cf. Hick, *Myth*, pp. 31ff. and the reference to G.W.H. Lampe; *God as Spirit*, Oxford: Oxford University Press, 1977. J.O'Donnell, in a *Theological Trends* article, 'Theology of the Holy Spirit I: Jesus and the Spirit', in *The Way*, 23 (1983) pp. 48–64, is highly critical of what he sees as Lampe's adoptionist approach. Against Lampe's unitarianism O'Donnell recommends the more orthodox trinitarian approach of Eberhard Jüngel in *The Doctrine of the Trinity: God's Being as Becoming*, Edinburgh and London, 1976.

16. F.X. Durrwell, *The Mystery of Christ and the Apostolate*, London: Sheed and Ward, 1972, p. 122.

17. op. cit., p. 124.

18. Where does the process of Christian theologizing begin? In *Karl Rahner in Dialogue, Conversations and Interviews 1965–1982*, ed. Paul Imhof and Hubert Biallowons, translated by Harvey Egan, New York: Crossroads 1986, Rahner says that 'the divinization of the world through the Spirit of God is humanly and speculatively the more fundamental basic conception for Christianity, *out of which the Incarnation and soteriology arise as an inner moment* [my italics]. This is so because the divinization of the world must manifest itself in a historical way and must come in its history to an irreversible point' (p. 126).

19. C.M. Lacugna and K. McDonnell, 'Returning from "The Far Country"': Theses for a Contemporary Trinitarian Theology', *Scottish Journal of Theology*, 41 (1988) pp. 191–215, suggest that the way to overcome the 'general malaise' in trinitarian theology is to return to its proper context in liturgy and doxology – the language of praise. Their scheme is broadly based and ecumenical, incorporating Orthodox insights into the relationship between Father and Spirit. They propose as part of their 'programmatic statement' that 'Christology and pneumatology must be counterpoised in a comprehensive trinitarian perspective' (p. 214).

20. My thanks to John McDade for clarifying many of the more awkward points of trinitarian theology for me. For a penetrating analysis of the economic/immanent distinction see his 'The Trinity and the Paschal Mystery', *Heythrop Journal*, XXIX (1988), pp. 175–191.

21. Panikkar, *Trinity*, p. 46.

22. cf. Lacugna and McDonnell, art. cit., p. 195: 'The path of glory is the path of God's own personal exodus and return *through* history. The personal exodus of God through history is also our way back to God. The personal exodus of God has a threefold pattern: from God through Christ in the Spirit; as does our return: in the Spirit through Christ to God'.

23. cf. Rowan Williams, 'Barth on the Triune God', in *Karl Barth, Studies in his Theological Method*, ed. S.W. Sykes, Oxford: Oxford University

Press 1979, pp. 147–193. 'The Spirit, then, is the relation of Father and Son, but is not to be thought of as some kind of common possession which the Father takes from himself and bestows upon the Son for the Son to return to him. He is not the same as the Father or the Son, *or* the two together' p. 183.

24. Panikkar, *Trinity*, p. 60, quoted in Williams, art. cit., pp. 183–184.

Christian "system of thought" should not be avoided, simply reconfigured.

PRACTICE OF DIALOGUE
D THE LIBERATION OF
THEOLOGY

The last chapter in a book always presents a problem. Is it to be the final item in a cumulative argument, a summary of what has gone before, or suggestions for a future now totally transformed by the author's thesis? No doubt readers will find traces of all three possibilities in what follows, but my intention, as in the whole of this book, is to urge something rather different: that we resist the temptation to cope with the other, a *person*, by inserting him or her into a *system of thought*. The first part of this study, based on the conviction that the threefold spectrum of opinions can act as a straitjacket, has tried to promote a more nuanced conversation between Christian theologians. The second has tried to build a Spirit-centred theology of dialogal relationships which seeks to avoid the sort of programmatic approach typical of the inclusivist 'middle way'. That theologians cannot ignore the challenge to Christian self-understanding addressed by Rahner is clear; it is not so obvious why an answer cannot be found within the *actual process* of dialogue. In this last chapter I want to address two issues which, I believe are closely related. The first is to return to the process, the actual practice of dialogue, to consider the liberation theology perspective to which it gives rise, and to ask how our concepts of Church and mission – the heart of Christian identity – respond to this practice. Secondly, building on practice, I want to develop my trinitarian perspective into a theology of dialogue which allows the other a properly creative and revelatory role in the conversation of religions.

Living with the other

The problem of the other is not confined to the meeting of faiths, even if it becomes noticeably more acute in this area.[1] Every human institution has to exercise judgement over the terms of its membership, define its own identity and work out its relationship with those either on the fringes or belonging to other, perhaps similar, institutions. In the first part of this study I tried to show that different theologies reflect different versions of what the 'problem' is taken to be. The titles we use – whether Rahner's 'Anonymous Christian' or Barth's 'other words' – say as much about our theologians' self-understanding as they do about the identity of the other. But otherness is not a category of deviance from a Christian norm; the other is Hindu or Muslim, homosexual, coloured, poor, female, divorced – people with a particular identity of their own. No doubt one can draw distinctions between large organized groups such as the world religions and marginalized individuals, but the distinction is more one of degree than of kind. However varied the threats which the Christian Church has experienced over the centuries, more often than not it has prevailed over the other through the exercise of power. And the temptation to continue to behave in a totalitarian fashion is obviously enormous. But while the Church has the right to proclaim its own beliefs and to argue against heterodoxy or deviance wherever they may be perceived, the other also has rights: to freedom of conscience, belief and religious practice. For all that Christian mission has often imposed itself unfeelingly on different peoples, the gospel message is about service, not power. Reconciliation may present us with many a practical or ethical dilemma, but it is still an absolute imperative.

A theology of religions which concerns itself only with the salvation problematic fails to appreciate this situation. We dispose of the other by identifying him or her in terms of closeness to, or distance from, ourselves. In other words we explain what is unknown in terms of the known, the other in terms of the self. A Hindu or a Muslim is a *non*-Christian. In so doing we may well fail to ask how we come to know our *own* identity, and therefore the other's, in the first place.[2] Dialogue in practice convinces the Christian Church of the need to look seriously at what we claim to know about God and about *how* we claim to know it. From the dialogue there arises the theological question: if God may be known by peoples of other faiths what are we to say of the way in which Christians know God? If we contend that it is different then we risk driving a wedge between the religions; if the same we are left wondering about the nature of Christian identity. This commitment-openness tension is only to be resolved in the actual meeting with people of other faiths and in theologically informed reflection on that encounter. Only insofar as we recognize the force of this new problematic can we expect to build an adequate solution to the old. In other words our two conversations are interdependent. At this point the theology of religions ceases to be a solution to a dogmatic problem and takes on a life of its own: theology which is done not in isolation but in dialogue with the other.

The theology of religions developed in the course of this book recognizes that while all religion is deeply dialectical an important distinction is to be made between dialectic and dialogue. The former is based on a distinction of ideas or concepts; the latter on a distinction of persons. The purpose of dialogue is not, therefore, the development of an apologetic structure which enables us to 'place' the other in our conceptual scheme; the conversation between persons remains always a highly complex, because deeply human, process. Nor can we be content to produce a mutually acceptable 'middle way' in which differences are ignored and the excess residue somehow siphoned off and quietly forgotten. We are speaking of a mutual search for truth, in which theology has a crucially important role to play. But before theologians get to work and coherent syntheses begin to emerge, there is practice and experience. And, again, after theologians reflect on the problems of being Christian in today's world, there is further practice to be pondered and more experience to be articulated. All that I have attempted is an exploration of the possibilities. It may be a cliché to say that all faiths have much to learn from each other, but we also have a lot to learn about the process of learning. There is no point in Christians seeking to learn from this or that item of Islamic theology or Buddhist metaphysics until we have reflected on the problem of actually living with the other. My initial contention is that we have worried too much over the problems raised by the word 'global', as if it meant taking stock of each and every item of religious experience (clearly an impossible undertaking), when the real issue is over what it means to do theology in an inter-faith context.

Dialogue in practice

What will make for fruitful dialogue? What guidelines are to be followed if we are both to communicate in love the hope that is in us (1 Peter 3.15) and to receive something of that same love from the other? Some of the principles have already been stated in the earlier chapters of this study. I have stressed a number of obvious points such as tolerance, openness and willingness to learn, but we must also note that any encounter between persons begins with respect for such persons as they are. We have to learn to hear what people say of themselves, not what we might like them to say or what we think they ought to be saying. If Buddhists speak of the doctrine of *anatmavada* – the lack of self or soul – as central to their understanding of Buddhism, it is no mark of respect to regard this as a fundamental misunderstanding of the Buddhist tradition. I may think the interpretation flawed or inaccurate; I may in the end be forced to regard the doctrine as simply untrue. But to the Buddhist it says something of major significance for the interpretation of that tradition. And essentially it is the *significance of the tradition for the Buddhist* which I must respect. Similarly a Muslim will deny the divinity of Christ and the theologically educated Christian may well be tempted to regard Islam as guilty of promoting a sort of latter-day Arianism. Again I may eventually reach the point where I am forced to choose. Questions of truth cannot be eradicated from the dialogue; apologetics has its proper place in the inter-religion encounter. Before reaching that point, however, I must try to understand the context of meaning which gives a coherence to Muslim or Buddhist belief: the tradition *as a whole*. Without this fundamental commitment to understand what the other is saying for its own sake there is no dialogue and no communication.

Panikkar speaks of two principles which need to be coordinated if dialogue is to be fruitful.[3] There is first the principle of homogeneity. A concept, he says, can be properly understood and evaluated only from within a homogeneous context. To fasten on to 'hurried syntheses or superficial parallelisms' is guaranteed to destroy dialogue. This is where theology comes into its own; we may describe its function, in general terms, as providing the self-understanding of a religion as it is lived. All too easily ideas and images are isolated from the total framework in which they become fully meaningful. Theology, whether the formal judgement of the scholar or the more open-ended reflection of the local community, links the second horizon, that of immediate contact with the other, to the first, the wider horizon of Church tradition. This is the work of the Spirit in the Church. Without our trinitarian theology of religions our language would not be able to cope with the new experience of religious pluralism. Nevertheless Christian theology cannot just be limited to an exercise in integrating different experiences within a Christian framework. Not everything can, or should, be fitted into a pre-existent scheme, however flexible the latter can be made. This leads Panikkar to speak of a second, the dialogical, principle. 'Applying the principle of homogeneity with strict rigor or exclusivity would paralyze a critical approach and halt any progress toward mutual understanding'.[4] Understanding the position of the other does not solve our theological problem. It is one thing to appreciate the beauty of ritual or to understand the meaning of certain symbols within the context of a particular faith; it is quite another to ignore the incoherence, incongruity or false assumptions of a particular practice or belief, wherever it may originate.

Ultimately, of course, it is the coordination of these two principles which is the measure of the success of dialogue. There are many styles or ways of doing theology. Once set within their own contexts all have important insights into theology of religions. In my survey of the spectrum of theological opinion I drew attention to the differences within the christocentric tradition: Protestants tend to a rhetorical model, Catholics prefer an integrative wisdom-based way of doing theology. The former, with their roots in the Reformation, look for the discontinuity between the prophetic Word of God and the sinfulness of humanity; the latter find no absolute distinction between the realms of Nature and Grace.[5] Now we must add the insights of the theocentric model to these two. Its insistence that the revelation of God may be found outside the historical form of Christianity takes it closer to the Catholic model; but the pluralist approach is not just the logical extension of Catholicism. By constantly stressing the particularity of context it warns us of the danger of assimilating one faith to another. At the same time it must also assimilate the Protestant insight; religions do presume to judge one another.

Panikkar's two principles are the basis for any sound hermeneutical method: the Catholic sense of homogeneity and continuity must be coordinated with the Protestant demand for a reconciliation which is dialectical and recognizes discontinuity. Only a theological praxis which accepts both will do justice to the claim of all religions to speak, on the one hand, of what is universal and, on the other, of what is particular and specific. Dialogue must allow both to exist in different traditions, however difficult, in practice, this may be.

Dialogue probes both partners in all aspects of their humanity and religious commitment. It cannot be selective. Nor can it afford to ignore the tragic misunderstandings of the past, the bigotry, downright hatred and inevitable chauvinism of people concerned only to defend their patch against the incursions of 'them'. Our history is part of our present, as indeed are the interpretations which we put on that history and on the history of the other. We bring all this and so much more to the dialogue and sooner or later it all has to be acknowledged. This is the stuff of the human encounter: our memories of the past as well as our hopes for the future. It would be naive, therefore, to suggest that a theology of religions demands only a certain degree of 'adjustment' to our traditional Christian concerns. A more expansive or open christology, theology of revelation of mission, of Church is a beginning but never enough. While as Church Christians must bear the burden of the continuity of the tradition so we must also be willing to accept the challenge to change in the light of our experience of the other. There is an otherness which needs to be integrated with the familiar, a newness which expands our sense of continuity with the past.

The experience of dialogue with which I began this study sees the conversation as an end in itself only insofar as the partners seek to be genuinely open and self-critical. The ideal – so rarely achieved – is to take on board not just some sort of core or essence but to accept the whole tradition for what it claims to be: a reflection of what is of ultimate value to people of different faiths. Such a dialogue brings us face to face with many unpalatable facts: our fears and unwillingness to take risks for the sake of growing in faith, not to mention sheer sinfulness and our inability as human persons to find a pattern which fits perfectly our respective patterns of experience. At this point the Christian's interior dialogue, which finds it impossible to integrate ideas or particular formulations of the other, must enter the external dialogue. This is not just a matter of recognizing sin for what it is – the aberration of human self-seeking which is inevitable in all religiosity – but part of the search for a deeper understanding of the other and of oneself. 'We are all learning to welcome light and criticism, even when it comes from foreign shores'.[6]

Reflecting on practice

The 'map' provided by the paradigms and the discussion to which they have given rise suggest that both inclusivism and pluralism provide important insights while retaining major weaknesses. Theologizing from an inter-faith perspective must mean more than simply adding all the religions together, but neither does it make sense to insist on some form of ethnocentric absolutism. When Rahner speaks of Christianity as the 'absolute religion' he is careful to distinguish between the historical form which that religion has taken and the ultimate mystery to which it is pointing as sign and sacrament.[7] Nevertheless an 'inclusivist' theology still retains an ethnocentric bias. Culture and religion, however intimately related, are not the same.

At the radical end of the spectrum, pluralism is often taken to entail the acceptance of a variety of opinions, none of which are privileged. Christianity and Buddhism appear as just lonely planets in Hick's universe of faiths, both equally close to, and therefore equally far from, the distant sun. According to this line the only way forward for Christian theology is to operate within a global perspective and to include the whole data of religious experience. There are at least two good reasons for rejecting this form of theological pluralism. The first is that it ignores the conviction, found in varying forms in all religions, that they speak of what is true in an absolute sense. The second is that it fails to take note of the effect which the experience of dialogue, with the various forms of modern culture as much as with the great religions of the world, has had on today's Church.

To reject the theocentric or pluralist paradigm does not mean closing our minds to the facts of religious pluralism. The new problematic is already being addressed both in the theologians' study and in the relationships being formed between Christians and people of other faiths. Panikkar's version of the Copernican Revolution seems much more convincing than Hick's original.[8] He gives the lie to the notion that to do theology is simply to engage in a private encounter with the tradition. The experience of the Church is prior. A missionary Church has itself learned, however painfully, to develop its understanding of 'the problem' of religious pluralism, away from the old-style missiology of conquest, even away from a missiology of translation and inculturation, to the more acute question of how different people from different backgrounds (minorities and majorities) can communicate and coexist in a shared world. In admittedly rather halting ways the interior dialogue, of which Panikkar speaks with such eloquence, has already become a feature of the life of the Church, especially, though not exclusively, in the Third World.

These are the fundamental issues to which the Church must always be addressing itself. They are not further examples of self-obsessed navel-gazing but problems arising out of the original question with which all Christian theology begins: 'Who do *you* say that I am?' We have already noted that the problem of religious pluralism is often taken to be about how one brings Christ *to* a culture. This is the heart of the old problematic: the 'other' religious tradition is seen to lack Christ. The new problematic begins *with* culture and, by seeking out the signs of the Spirit, asks how one can speak of Christ being *already there*. The starting-point has changed because the Church's experience has changed. Or perhaps it has only recaptured a lost yet so familiar perspective? In practice our theology of the Spirit provides the basis for today's self-understanding of the missionary Church, just as it did for the early days of the Church's life as described in the Acts of the Apostles. Thus we notice a very real development in missiology. Theologians and communities attempting to construct a theology appropriate to their local situation are less concerned with importing the Gospel tradition from outside, as it were, than with building it on the foundations already provided by the all-pervading action of God's Spirit. The ever-necessary task of translation is seen to involve not so much a search for appropriate linguistic equivalents as the reconstruction of the total context in which theologizing is to be done. The fusing of the two horizons – ancient tradition and contemporary experience – demands analysis of what is, in reality, a complex web made up of the claims of the gospel message, the wider community of the Church and, of course, the culture and society to which the Good News is addressed.[9]

Panikkar's experience of living in different cultures has led him to question the premise that religious traditions are so much locked into the first or foundational horizon that they must necessarily ignore the second. His might seem to be no more than the extraordinary experience of an unusually well-qualified and highly gifted individual; but it forces us to ask how far the Church may follow his example both of interior and exterior dialogue. Can communities and local churches enter this process of conversion? Here we may learn something from the experience of building local or contextual theologies.

The Church learns through dialogue to articulate both what is old and what is new. And theology is forever reflecting on this process, seeking to understand the Word. The traditional estimate of theology is that it is 'faith seeking understanding'. Yet even within that seemingly innocuous phrase is contained a rich variety of different, even conflicting, positions. Both the 'exclusivist' and 'inclusivist' paradigms have this much in common: they see theology largely as an academic science of interpretation, an activity necessarily limited to a very few highly trained individuals. Such a theology seems inappropriate for today's needs, and does not answer the problem of the other. In the first place, as an intellectual activity theology need not be limited to academic speculation or largely defensive apologetics. As David Tracy has so wisely pointed out, there are at least three different 'publics' for whom theologizing is done.[10] The academy is only one, while the Church and society at large are the others. What I earlier noted as the rise of local theologies has been responsible for one of the most remarkable shifts in Christian self-understanding in recent years.

In India, for example, where all religions are considered public property and the distinctions between faiths and spiritualities are not absolute, the place of society as a 'public' is becoming increasingly important. Theological debate is not the property of an educated Christian elite, an exercise confined to learned tomes and journals. Theologizing in India today is a complex debate about the place of Christian revelation in the wider debate about India itself: communalism, poverty, injustice, secularism, religious pluralism. There is some truth in saying that Indian theologians have recently shifted from religious pluralism to theology of liberation; certainly one cannot ignore a popular bandwagon for liberation theology which is represented by a certain social activism. A more perceptive analysis would note, however, that the Indian situation is really extremely complex. Inter-faith relationships and dialogue have proved problematic, the demands for a liberation perspective in theological education irresistible. But the two remain different sides of the same coin: the Indian context which the gospel confronts.[11]

Another very different example might be Central and South America. Here theology addresses the same public, but in a Christian environment. Religious pluralism is not a problem; economic oppression and injustice certainly are. Hence the phenomenon of liberation theology challenges the pretensions of a 'classical' European form of theologizing. The first principles are to be found in the way that ordinary people, usually the poorest of the poor, live out the gospel message. The role of the professional theologian is to help a community to articulate its experience and to relate that experience to that of other communities – in short, to keep it in touch with the wider Christian tradition. But the inspiration comes from within the experience of the local Church; that is where the Word is spoken and where the dialogue begins.

Everyone – expert exegetes, pastoral workers, humble parishioners – does his or her theologizing from a particular perspective. Today we are used to theology being done in slums and barrios rather than in seminar rooms and through international publishing houses. No longer the cloistered expert but the local community and the society in which it is immersed are made the focus of theological activity. The excitement caused by liberation theology stems less from its revolutionary iconoclasm than from its prophetic call to *all* Christians to do theology: not to produce yet another doctoral thesis but to state the meaning of Christ in today's world.[12] It does not follow that there is no place for the professional scholar-theologian. Nor does it mean that judicious academic study becomes otiose; rather such judgement becomes more necessary than ever. In reality the three 'publics' work together: academy, Church and society are not mutually exclusive. The theology which addresses itself to the wider community emerges from the local scene, but it must also be coherent with Church tradition and be based on sound principles of exegesis and argumentation. Nevertheless it is unreasonable to expect of 'local' theology the precision of the academy. A theology which emerges from *practice* cannot be expected to command the same level of exactness and intelligibility of expression as that which emerges from the study of the trained theologian. The experience of western Christians in a multi-faith world, raising questions about their identity as Church and their role in society, is exactly analogous to that of the Latin American Church or to the struggling Christian minorities of Asia and Africa.

Witnessing to Christ

How do our concepts of Church and mission relate to this account of dialogue in practice? Engagement in this process is what gives the Church its identity as the bearer of the Good News, the witness to what God has done in Christ. The argument of the last chapter was that christocentric and theocentric approaches find a resolution within a trinitarian theology of religions which is formed through the practice of dialogue. That dialogue, based on the conversation which goes on constantly between persons giving and receiving of each other, reflects the constant communication which makes up the inner life of the Trinity. The two problematics do not need two theologies. The same idea, which links christology and pneumatology, applies to ecclesiology and missiology. It is not that God speaks through the Word and *then* lives in the Church through the action of the Spirit; rather the Spirit is witness to the fact that the Father *goes on* giving himself to the Son, and *goes on* receiving the Word back. The conversation which is the Trinity is everlasting, for such is the nature of the work of the Spirit. A trinitarian theology of religions allows us to speak of the way God's action 'goes on' in the world, amongst all peoples, Christian and other. The dialogue demands freedom and commitment if the eternal 'We' is to be revealed in all its fullness. Both 'I' and 'Thou' are equally important. Thus the twin imperatives, to openness and to loyalty, are maintained.

The Church is involved in the conversation not as the object of the Word, a sort of relay-station passing on the message to the other, but as the human forum – literally a 'market-place' – where persons, Christians and others, learn the many languages of God. The mission to the other is essentially a sharing of languages, an attempt to communicate something of the way in which God goes on giving himself away to the other. The identity of the Church as the embodiment and sign of God's grace present to the world is not compromised by a missiology founded on witness to the loving activity of God. Christians will always want to make known the truth about God and humanity which is revealed in Christ. The establishment of Christian communities will be the most obvious sign of this truth, its manifestation in an historical and social form. The implication of a trinitarian approach is that salvation is achieved through God's activity of self-revelation, an activity of the Spirit at work in the people who make up the Church. But that activity cannot be limited to the Church any more than Church can be defined in terms of insiders and outsiders. The purpose of Christian mission is not to make outsiders insiders but to improve the situation in which salvation can be achieved for all; once we are consciously aware of who we are, the likelihood that we will arrive at self-fulfilment is greater than if we merely possess and fulfil that humanity at an unconscious level. As Rahner says, 'love strives for what is greater . . . it is precisely this striving which constitutes that love which is an absolute duty'.[13] The Christian must proclaim that love; the other will always be seeking for its deepest meaning and the demands which it makes on him or her.

Witness to the love of God is at the heart of all mission. And love can never be expressed in purely institutional terms. There is, as Moltmann reminds us, a 'qualitative' side to mission as well as a 'quantitative'.[14] Dialogue, for Moltmann, is all about spreading the spirit of hope, love and responsibility for the world. Mission in this day and age is not a matter of exporting the 'atmosphere of the Christian West' but of producing a certain ethos of mutual understanding in which solutions to the serious problems which face all people today can be found. Mission is not self-proclamation, or even Church-proclamation, but the announcement that the Kingdom is 'at hand', that the Spirit of God is already at work liberating creation from sin and division; the confusion of Babel is being replaced by the harmony of dialogue and cooperation. Conversation need not be vapid or defensive, but it does demand a willingness to make oneself vulnerable to change as well as eager to share something of the richness of one's tradition. People who can combine confidence in their own identity with a desire to know the other for his or her own sake may expect to give as well as to receive, to affect the other as well as being changed by the encounter.

Zeal to share our answers with the other is more typical of Christians than an enthusiasm to ask questions of ourselves. But we need not think that in learning from the other we are selling our missionary vocation short. If I expect the other to learn from me I must also expect to learn from the other. For in the end none of us are teachers. We are all taught by the love of God. Any dialogue which involves the transcending of personal horizons may be considered an experience of the love of God, however different one's language or expression of that experience. The openness and willingness with which we enter this new relationship with the other is based on the act of love, in due fulfilment of Christ's command to love one's neighbour as oneself. It is this sense – admittedly difficult to describe but nonetheless real – that the love of God is not something we *give* to the other but something which we *receive* from him or her, that turns the external dialogue of human relationships from a pleasant gathering of like-minded individuals to a process of mutual transformation.[15] This surely is the challenge which the parable of the Good Samaritan puts to our complacent pigeon-holing of religious types and attitudes. It is often the person we least expect, and perhaps least admire, who acts in the most neighbourly fashion. Parable challenges myth. It is the stranger who reveals the love of God to us, the stranger in whom we know God and in whom God is known to us.

A theology of dialogue

If Christians are to build truly local theologies – let alone a theology of religions – then ethnocentric ecclesiology has to give way to some such dialectical model. Looking to a future transformed by what Panikkar calls this 'kairological moment' our identity as Church may be found less in providing the correct 'system' of answers and more in our ability to present Christ as the question put to all systems. Such an approach could have a truly liberating effect on the way we do theology.

Theology is not an arcane science of Christian self-justification but an attempt to articulate the experience of participating in the constant movement between Word and Spirit which is the life of the Trinity. Whether we use the metaphor of debate, dialogue or

171

conversation we come back to the question of how the Christian language about God is learned and communicated. The answer that we must return to the foundational experience of the earliest community only states the problem rather than solving it. The horizon of the gospel, the frame within which the Church situates itself, is only half the story. There is a second horizon, that of contemporary experience, which forms the context from which we must interpret the first. The interpenetration of the two – something which is embodied today in the meeting of peoples of different faiths – is at the heart of Panikkar's theory. Historically, as Cantwell Smith points out, this interpenetration has been happening for hundreds of years anyway. To object that such a theory risks descending into the chaos of syncretism raises an obvious problem but rather misses the point. The second horizon only overwhelms the first when a tradition loses touch with its roots. And that, of course, is the point: we have to be sensitive to the unique character and demands of a tradition and the limits of adaptation to any particular culture. Admittedly not all the recent experiments in local, indigenous and contextualized theologies have proved immediately successful. Nor has the practice of dialogue always cleared away the clouds of suspicion and ignorance which have for far too long inhibited the harmony of faiths. On the more positive side, there is now a fair amount of experience on which to build. Theology emerges from the attempt to fuse our two horizons together; this is the heart of the inter-faith conversation.

Let me attempt to summarize the dialogal theology worked out in the last few chapters. The model which I have tried to develop is based on Panikkar's concept of interpenetration. Beginning from the encounter with the other, Panikkar seeks to analyse the conditions which are necessary if we are to enter into dialogue, literally 'to go through the word', 'beyond the logos-structure of reality' in order to uncover and understand the respective myths of the partners.[16] This demands what he calls a prior 'intra-religious dialogue', an inner dialogue or process of assimilating the imagery, symbols, basic concepts and structures of another tradition, into one's own. Thus one finds that what may appear at first sight to be conflicts of interest and interpretation can usually be transformed into creative or dynamic polarities. This is the beginning of a theology of dialogue. Such a model forms the basis for the only viable 'global' theology – one which is, at the same time, committed and open. Provided I am ready to accept the other on his or her terms and resist the temptation simply to rewrite the other faith-tradition in my own language, it is possible to pass over the divide and to return enriched by the experience, knowing something more about the ways of God than when I began.

Now the suggestion that we should be prepared inwardly or spiritually for the encounter with the other is not itself controversial. Without the effort of the imagination to understand and appreciate the stranger who is so different from, and even alien to, our ordinary experience the outer dialogue is likely to descend into empty polemics or facile syncretizing. And models of dialogue which turn the other into an object have already been rejected. It is not the purpose of the inter-religious dialogue to preach or patronize, still less to proclaim the superiority of one creed or the equality of all. What may well be controversial, however, is the implication behind the inner dialogue, that the inter-faith theologian has to risk change. By becoming more appreciative of the riches of the Hindu or Buddhist does one thereby become less Christian?

Earlier I tried to answer this point by drawing a distinction between faith and belief as the correlate of the dialectical interplay of the two dimensions of religiosity. This, I suggested, may help us to build a theory of the relationship of religions which broadens the options beyond the extremes of fundamentalist absolutism and a sceptical relativism. The 'dialectical morass' – the constant debate between forms of the Christianity-centred model and various versions of liberal theology – does not commit us to one or other horn of a dilemma any more than a concern to preserve a sense of true Christian identity must lead to European culture dominating the Third World churches. Is there not a form of pluralism which fulfils the demand to safeguard that identity without falling into the arrogant intolerance which the more liberal approach quite rightly criticizes?

Although superficially similar to Rahner I have argued that Panikkar's theory is in reality very different. Rahner's fulfilment theology, with its stress on the continuity of all religions, is clearly an advance on much exclusivist thinking, but it still represents a type of theologizing which is inappropriate to today's multi-faith world. Panikkar manages to avoid 'theological imperialism' by building a theory of interpenetration in which persons in dialogue seek to understand themselves through understanding each other. But can one justify his vision of a reciprocal interchange of symbolism in Christian dogmatic terms? The theological framework necessary for the development of such a programme was the subject of the last chapter. My aim was to show that there need be no conflict between

the meaning of Christ, to which the Christian theologian is committed, and the forms which the revelation of that mystery may take in
other faiths. Such is the aim of a Spirit-centred theology of religions.
My basic premise is that the ground of all Christian theologizing is
trinitarian as much as it is christological. That is to say that we begin
not with the historical Jesus Christ who points the way to the Father
but with the *Spirit* of Christ through which the world was brought
into being and who continues the work of God's ever-present
self-revelation to humankind. A trinitarian theology of religions may
begin to unite the salvation, or old, problematic with the theology of
revelation which is at the heart of the new.

Religions and revelation

It is not too much of a caricature to suggest that fifty years ago
theologians looked on 'religion' either in Barthian terms as an
essentially human construct opposed to the Christian revelation or in
liberal terms as some sort of a universal of human nature. But even
such diverse figures as Kraemer and Troeltsch were agreed that
religions are, first and foremost, cultural 'totalities'. They can only
be understood and interpreted holistically. Today's theologians,
who are much more self-consciously 'post-classical', would take the
same line; they are ready to accept the assessment of anthropologists
and historians of religion that all religions are unique and that direct
comparison of one tradition with another is fraught with major
conceptual difficulties. Hence I drew attention to the point made by
Lindbeck, following Geertz, that religions have to be recognized, in
cultural-linguistic terms, as meaningful symbol systems through
which people form a picture of their world and thereby learn how to
come to terms with the exigencies of existence in that world. It is not
that religions are all relative to history but, if anything, the other way
round; the fundamental dynamism of the faith of persons, ever-
changing but ever the same, with all the richness of its vision and the
sinfulness of actual practice, leads to that interaction of traditions
which is now – as Cantwell Smith says – becoming the very 'stuff' of
theology. Thus the first requirement of a theology of dialogue is not
the discerning of common elements or even the recognition of a
common structure but a sensitivity to the way in which we interpret
traditions, first to ourselves and then to the other. To put it another
way, dialogue is less about learning another language than it is about
reflecting on the way in which that language is learned.

The practice of dialogue only serves to bring this point home with greater force. Every theology is set within a particular cultural and social matrix; the language which we use relates to specific contexts and the attempt to adapt and translate that language must, at the very least, make us conscious of the assumptions behind any particular interpretation which we put on the other tradition. First attempts to develop a local theology in India, for instance, made use of the Advaita categories of Śankaracarya. But such pioneering efforts failed to see that the way of thinking which accommodates Śankara to Thomas Aquinas ignores the extent to which the data of Hinduism have been read through Roman Catholic theological spectacles. The recent upsurge of scholarly interest in Tamil religiosity, which has demonstrated so clearly the creative role of devotional bhakti cults in the development of the classical Hindu tradition, is a useful corrective to the somewhat simplistic western abstractions which make Hinduism little more than a set of variations on the Vedanta.[17] No religion can be reduced to a single school or tradition, however exalted. But if this applies to the Indologist, seeking to gain a more comprehensive interpretative scheme for Hinduism, it also goes for the theologian reflecting on the Christian tradition. At the very least we have to find an interpretation of the other's tradition which the other can recognize. But, secondly, we must examine our own theological presuppositions. The interplay of the external and internal dialogue forces us to acknowledge that however much we may want to speak of the language by which we refer to God as in some way privileged, it cannot simply be abstracted from the cultural and historical milieu in which it has been formed. It is very easy for theologians to give the impression that the language which they use is not only privileged but autonomous, subject to no other authority than its own. The assumption is that the tradition is simply given; the horizon of its meaning is set. All that is required is a suitable hermeneutical tool to unlock its riches, a tool which is not subject to rational scrutiny or analysis.

This is where strict exclusivists and liberal pluralist theologians make strange bedfellows.[18] For the former, truth is divinely sanctioned. But, as I noted earlier, any theology which looks to a specific revelation to solve the problem of how we may know God faces enormous difficulties. Why should not the Word of God be spoken other than in historical Christianity – and even elsewhere than in the historical Jesus of Nazareth? Might it not be that the mystery which Christians find expressed in the language and symbolism of Christ is revealed in very different ways and very different languages in other religions or, indeed, through other persons encountered in open yet committed dialogue? The major problem with any evangelical theology is that it has a very restricted notion of the nature of theological discourse. If theology is seen as an extrapolation from the Word gratuitously revealed in Scripture, there can, by definition, be no revelation elsewhere. Hence only the most rudimentary and grudging acceptance of the other. Any theology which emphasizes the proclamation of an authoritative tradition is through and through monologic. There is no possibility of the other contributing to the process of understanding since the locus of knowledge of God is already given by God himself – definitively in Christ.

Such a theology is manifestly incapable of dealing with the new problematic. But does the liberal theology of religions fare any better? Whatever its many merits, an approach which seeks to establish some 'common core', some preconceptual inter-religious phenomenon or experience, to be discerned beneath the ever-shifting particularities of the historical traditions, begs too many questions. If the authoritarian convictions of evangelical theology cannot disentangle the complexities of the learning process then the same can be said for the empiricist model of truth which underlies the liberal approach. Experience is always socially and culturally conditioned; there is no such thing as an unmediated experience, whether of God, facts or persons. To speak, therefore, of some pre-linguistic awareness of the Ultimate which grounds and forms our religious consciousness seems to have misunderstood the nature of that process. It is obviously true that we learn through experience; but at whatever stage and in whatever form persons apprehend the data of experience – whether through the sensate awareness of the child or the more abstract conceptualizing of the adult – learning is an activity of deriving meaning from certain determined contexts. It makes no sense to speak of some semi-autonomous transcultural, no doubt mystical, experience which can be separated from particular forms.

As stated, neither of these positions has an answer to the question of how Christians can continue to speak of a definitive revelation in Christ without begging the question of how God may be known at all. Most of the energy in the theology of religions has focused on the salvation issue when what is really at stake is a prior question: how does *anyone* come to know anything about the Divine? In discussing the nature of human religiosity I came to the conclusion that religions are to be related not as different versions of a common experience but as comprehensive symbol-systems which form a necessary precondition for religious understanding. Such a position, however, with its strongly holistic emphasis, runs the risk of a certain type of cultural relativism. Thus I went on to argue that religions have a prophetic or transcendent, as well as a social or integrative, function; they act as an agent or catalyst which provokes or deepens faith. The radical exclusivist will see faith as a special experience of Christ, a sort of enlightenment; the radical pluralist may speak of 'Reality consciousness'. Both suffer from the same problem: they are based on an experiential model of religion and the experiences of which they speak are regarded as self-authenticating. In the model of religion which I have tried to develop faith is certainly a response to revelation but such a response is part of a continuing process of learning, in which the 'newness' is less novelty and much more an activity – a struggle, perhaps – of renewal. Hence the dialectic between the two dimensions or functions of religion. It may be true that only in faith can we claim to know God, that we speak of God through what God has revealed to us of himself. But it does not follow that revelation must be seen simply in terms of new experiences. Rather it is the process of generating new meaning, new possibilities, new categories within which the ancient tradition is ever being made present to people prepared to listen. In these terms any inter-religious encounter is an invitation to explore the Divine Mystery in which all relationships are grounded.

Religions are not faceless systems, cultural embodiments of some vague mystical entity called 'faith'. Faith is the God-given life of persons prepared to listen for the Word of God wherever it is spoken and struggling always to live out the demands of the transcendent in an ambiguous world. The other is part of that ambiguity. An enemy? An alien? Possibly both; but no Christian can afford to ignore another possibility: that the other may provoke the insight which generates new meaning. The time-honoured strategies of exclusion, conquest and assimilation have obscured the most radical challenge of the gospel: to start a conversation with the other and thereby run the risk of changing our own self-understanding. This is not to relativize the truth of Christianity. It is simply to recognize that the mystery of Christ in which God reveals himself cannot be tied down to a formula of words or to a few, albeit privileged, experiences. In this new situation we have to find some way of speaking of God's initiative. The traditional metaphor of 'lifting the veil' is not the only, nor the most appropriate, model. If what is at stake is the truth that it is God who is forever making all things new, may we not also speak of revelation as renewal and regeneration, not the destruction of our sense of belonging but its very reinforcement? No contemporary theology of revelation can afford to base itself on a monologue – the enunciation and defence of certain truths, ideas and positions which are somehow to be found in the Christian story. We first have to ask what that Christian story is in today's world. New experiences have to be integrated into the whole; the traditional language which is Christianity has to interact with new questions. Thus Christian culture learns to criticize itself and to allow the other a part in that criticism. Experience does not so much lead to a new language; the language is expanded in order to speak of a new experience.

The very heart of the Christian experience is the conviction that God has spoken to human beings. The doctrine of the Trinity is founded on the mystery of a God who is known yet unknown, who is present through his action in the world and yet clearly remains beyond all comprehension. Paradox and dialectic are at the heart of all human religiosity; we only come to know God by being prepared to struggle with ambiguity and insecurity.[19] There is no room for exclusivist arrogance in the Christian life, but neither need we sink into the hopelessness of relativism. It is the heart of Christian identity to accept God's Word and to be prepared to share it while, at the same time, in conversation with the other, learning the deepest meaning of that revelation. If what we are seeking to promote is a vision of dialogue as a learning process in which all peoples are engaged then the Christian community has its own contribution to make to this vision: first through the task of *self*-transformation, learning from the other, and only then through its peculiarly prophetic function of transforming, but not dominating, culture. Such a witness – to what the Spirit can accomplish in the Church – is itself a witness to the Good News of the love of God revealed in Christ. So far from dialogue destroying faith it positively enhances the sense of Christian identity.

The spirit of the conversation

The practical guidelines outlined above arise directly from our account of human religiosity as rooted in the living communities which support ancient traditions of faith. Dialogue is neither a form of self-defence nor a platform for detecting heresy; it is expressive of the life of persons who are always seeking to articulate more adequately their ever-changing experience of the Divine Mystery. If the description of religions as languages or interpretative frameworks is anything like correct, one would expect the same process of constant reinterpretation – the internal dialogue – to be going on amongst all peoples of faith. This is the heart of the matter. A person who enters dialogue with the intention of arguing for one religion in particular or even for religion in general (presumably inveighing against unbelief or secularism or the irreligiousness of modern society) has rather missed the point. This is not to say dialogue may not arise from the activity of building common fronts and developing modes of cooperation between the people of different faiths. Such is the motivation which often draws people together – a common cause for peace, for example. Dialogue may well *begin* with a particular interest just as real communication may occur between two persons when the attempt to 'convert', or at any rate to prove who is right and who is wrong, has been quietly forgotten. But dialogue is not a beginning in this sense. With whatever mixed motives it begins – and that usually includes a fair measure of arrogance and fear as well as love and humility – dialogue proper is an end in itself. There is a world of difference between a dialogue which has a particular aim in view, such as cooperation over some social or cultural project, and one which is totally uninterested in anything except the relationship which is established between human persons and, through them, what they understand of the Divine Mystery. In using the metaphor of the conversation to describe the inter-religious encounter it has been my aim to show that the Spirit works as often in informal friendly contact between human persons as in the large-scale rhetorical set-piece. In many situations, especially in today's world, the florid sermon is no substitute for sympathetic silence.

God reveals himself at the moment when people learn to trust one another, when argument relaxes into conversation. This, of course, is not easily achieved, but if a considerable amount of time and energy is expended on the rather tedious business of learning how to listen to people and to learn about their joys, hopes, worries and fears, that is all to the good. The analogy of human relationships has been very much to the fore in this book and no human relationship, whether between husband and wife or between Christians and their Sikh or Hindu neighbours, is established without effort, perseverance and a fair measure of failure. I have spoken of faithfulness and openness. The two are not opposites, ever liable to be broken apart under the strain of trying to live in two worlds at once, but two sides of the single search for truth. I bring into every inter-religious contact the sum total of my experience as a religious person, as someone aware of the riches of one particular tradition, but also conscious of how much more there is to know. To be more precise, my contact makes me realize how limited is the articulation of my own experience. Faithfulness to the past entails an openness to the future and vice versa; perhaps it is only in the present attempt to speak of myself to another that the apparent dichotomy begins to break down. Like any human activity, conversation will include argument and misunderstanding but, if conducted with respect for the dignity and freedom of the individual, it will allow people to change themselves under the guidance of God's Spirit rather than simply being manipulated by the louder voice or the more sophisticated argument.[20]

The general guidelines I have enunciated and the theology of revelation to which they give rise are a beginning. What is it that keeps the conversation going? We are talking about a process of *mutual* transformation in which two or more persons, from very different traditions and backgrounds, attempt to come to terms with their respective identities. Without the conviction that my identity as Christian is not fundamentally at variance with that of the other as Hindu, Buddhist or whatever, there would be no possibility of communication, let alone transformation. Identities, however, are not something we possess but something we become. Religions are more than socializing processes; they introduce people to a way of coming to terms with themselves as members of human society but they also open people to the prophetic voice of the Spirit of God. To be Christian or Hindu, Jew or Sikh, Muslim or Buddhist, is to learn to speak the language of an ancient tradition – a process of growth rather than a state of being. Dialogue is based on the principle that the other has a crucial role to play in the learning of that language for it is only when I have someone prepared to listen to me that I learn how to speak. And only when I learn how to speak do I know what it is that I have to say. The conversation helps both partners to articulate their experience, to become not 'other' but truly self.

Notes

1. cf. Panikkar, 'The Myth of Pluralism: The Tower of Babel – a Meditation on Non-Violence', *Cross-Currents* 29 (1979), pp. 197ff. For Panikkar pluralism 'is rooted in the deepest nature of things' (p. 203). Which is not to recommend pure pragmatism or agnosticism. Pluralism is a myth in the sense that it is the necessary horizon within which all our theories of inter-human relationships are to be situated.

2. Assimilation or destruction are the usual ways of coping with the other. On the other hand, as Nicholas Lash says, in 'Understanding the Stranger', *Theology on Dover Beach*, London: Darton, Longman & Todd 1979, pp. 60–76: 'If . . . we decide to treat [the stranger] as a friend, as a potential partner, then we are taking the risk of having our self-understanding radically transformed' (pp. 1–72).
3. Panikkar, 'The Rules of the Game', in *The Intra-Religious Dialogue*, p. 69.
4. ibid.
5. I am grateful to Anne Murphy for enlightening me on the subject of the historical context of theological styles. For an admirably lucid and penetrating historical perspective on this topic see John O'Malley, 'Erasmus and Luther, Continuity and Discontinuity as Key to Their Conflict', *Sixteenth Century Journal*, V. 2 (1974), pp. 47–65.
6. Panikkar, *Intra-Religious Dialogue*, p. 70.
7. 'Christianity and the non-Christian Religions', *TI* 5, pp. 115–134.
8. Panikkar's expanded version of the Copernican Revolution in *The Myth of Christian Uniqueness*, reflects his trinitarian theology, based on the interpenetration and *perichoresis* of traditions. He says that '. . . each solar system has its own center, and every galaxy turns reciprocally around the other. There is no absolute center. Reality itself is concentric inasmuch as each being (each tradition) is the center of the Universe . . .' (p. 109).
9. cf. Schreiter, *Constructing Local Theologies*, London: S C M 1985, esp. pp. 22ff.
10. David Tracy, *The Analogical Imagination: Christian Theology and the Culture of Pluralism*, London: S C M 1981; cf. chapter 1 (pp. 3–46).
11. While there is as yet no such thing as a systematic Indian Liberation Theology, liberation themes play a major and influential part in most current thinking. cf., for example, *Liberation in Asia: Theological Perspectives*, ed. S. Arokiasamy SJ and G. Gispert-Sauch SJ, Gujarat Sahitya Prakash, 1987, a collection of articles from the Jesuit monthly, *Vidyajyoti*. A masterly and informative summary of much current thinking about the interface of Liberation Theology and theology of religions is contained in George Soares Prabhu's *Inculturation, Liberation, Dialogue*, Pune: Jnanadeepa 1984, translated from *Problemi e Perspettivi di Teologia Dogmatica*, ed. Karl H. Neufeld, Brescia, 1983. A number of articles in the collection, *Theologizing in India*, ed. M. Amaladoss, G. Gispert-Sauch and T.K. John, Bangalore: Theological Publications in India 1981, address the same themes; cf. especially the concluding essay, 'Diversity of Religions in the Context of Pluralism and Indian Christian Life and Reflection', by Ignatius Puthiadam, pp. 383–438.
12. cf. Knitter, 'Toward a Liberation Theology of Religions', in *The Myth of Christian Uniqueness* esp. p. 195.
13. *TI*, 12; pp. 178ff.
14. J. Moltmann, *The Church in the Power of the Spirit*, pp. 150ff.
15. cf. Panikkar, *Intra-Religious Dialogue*, p. 74.

16. Panikkar, 'The Dialogical Dialogue', in *The World's Religious Traditions*, ed. Frank Whaling, Edinburgh: T. & T. Clark 1984, p. 218.

17. A review article, focusing specifically on Friedhelm Hardy's *Viraha Bhakti: The Early History of Krsna Devotion in South India*, Delhi: Oxford University Press 1983, by Vasudha Narayanan, in *Religious Studies Review*, 11,1 (January 1985) pp. 12–20, assesses the present state of Tamil studies, including a very full bibliography. Hardy's book forms a major focus in an important symposium article, edited by James Laine, which witnesses to the increasing cooperation between theologians and historians of religion: 'Catholic Theology and the Study of Religion in South Asia: Widening the Context for Theological Reflection', *Theological Studies* 48 (1987), pp. 677–710.

18. Rowan Williams, 'Trinity and Revelation', *Modern Theology* 2 (1986), pp. 197–212, reminds us of the centrality of the hermeneutical question; theology, he says, 'is perennially liable to be seduced by the prospect of bypassing the question of how it *learns* its own language' (p. 197).

19. cf. Lacugna and McDonnell, art. cit., p. 199: 'We do not approach nor do we worship a "sitting God", enthroned on high, but we accompany and worship a "walking God". *Knowledge of God is journey with God*' (my italics).

20. As Tracy concludes, the Christian hope emerges from the belief that 'revelations from God have occurred'. Such a hope will express itself in both 'conversation and solidarity'. 'That hope is this: that all those involved in interpreting our situation and all those aware of our need for solidarity may continue to risk interpreting all the classics of all the traditions' (*Plurality and Ambiguity*, London: SCM 1988, pp. 113–114).

BIBLIOGRAPHY

The two subjects with which this book is concerned, the theology of religions and inter-faith dialogue, do not reduce themselves to a straightforward bibliography. I would refer readers in the first place to the surveys mentioned in the text, especially to the encyclopaedic work of Paul Knitter. Below I have provided two bibliographies, neither of which pretends to be exhaustive. *Christianity and Other Religions* covers all the major books and articles on the theology of religions referred to in this book, plus many other works which are essential to any account of contemporary Christian relationships with people of other faiths. *Theology and Inter-faith Dialogue* is a more detailed bibliography under the chapter headings of Part Two. This consists of various books and articles, many of them cited in the text, which I hope will be a stimulus to further reading.

Christianity and other religions

Aagaard J., 'Revelation and Religion', *Studia Theologica* 14 (1960), pp. 148–85.

Abbott, Walter M. (ed.), *The Documents of Vatican II*, with commentary and notes, London: Chapman 1966.

Abhishiktananda, *Hindu-Christian Meeting Point*, Delhi: ISPCK, revised ed. 1976.

—— *Saccidananda*, Delhi: ISPCK revised ed. 1984.

Almond, P., 'John Hick's Copernican Theology', *Theology* 86 (1983), pp. 36–41.

Amaladoss, M., 'Dialogue and Mission: Conflict or Convergence?' *International Review of Mission* 75 (1986), pp. 222–40.

Andersen, W., 'Dr Kraemer's Contribution to the Understanding of the Nature of Revelation', *International Review of Mission* 46 (1957), pp. 361–71.

Anderson, G.H., and Stransky, T.F., eds., *Christ's Lordship and Religious Pluralism*, New York: Orbis 1981.

Anderson, J.N., *Christianity and World Religions*, Leicester: Inter-Varsity Press new edn 1984.

Ariarajah, W., *The Bible and People of Other Faiths*, Geneva: World Council of Churches 1985.

Ball, J., 'Missiology I: Incarnational Christianity', *The Way*, January 1985, pp. 54–61; 'II: Liberation Theology', ibid., April, 1985, pp. 140–48; 'III: The World Religions', ibid., January 1986, pp. 53–60.

von Balthasar, Hans Urs, *Cordula oder der Erntsfall*, Einsiedeln, 1966; ET *The Moment of Christian Witness*, New York: Newman Press 1969.

—— 'Catholicism and the Religions', *Communio* 5 (1978), pp. 6–14.

Barth, K., *Church Dogmatics*, Edinburgh: T. & T. Clark, vol. 1/2, 1956; vol. 3/4, 1962.

—— *Evangelical Theology*, London: Collins, 1965.

Bleeker, C.J., 'Comparing the Religio-Historical and the Theological Method', *Numen* 18 (1971), pp. 9–29.

Braybrooke, M., *Together to the Truth: Developments in Hindu and Christian Thought since 1800*, Madras: ISPCK 1971.

British Council of Churches, *Relations with People of Other Faiths: Guidelines for Dialogue in Britain*, London: British Council of Churches 1983.

Bühlmann, W., *The Coming of the Third Church*, Slough: St Paul's 1976.

—— *All Have the Same God*, Slough: St Paul's 1979.

—— *The Chosen Peoples*, Slough: St Paul's 1982; published in the US as *God's Chosen Peoples*, New York: Orbis 1983.

Byrne, P., 'John Hick's Philosophy of World Religions', *Scottish Journal of Theology* 35 (1982), pp. 289–301.

Camps, A., *Partners in Dialogue: Christianity and Other World Religions*, New York: Orbis, 1983.

Choan-Seng Song, *The Compassionate God*, New York: Orbis; London: SCM 1982.

Clayton, J.P., ed., *Ernst Troeltsch and the Future of Theology*, Cambridge: Cambridge University Press 1976.

Coakley, S., 'Theology and Cultural Relativism: What is the Problem?', *Neue Zeitschrift für Theologie und Religionsphilosophie* 21 (1979), pp. 223–43.

Cobb, J., 'Is Christianity a Religion?', *Concilium* 136 (1980), edited by David Tracy and Mircea Eliade, pp. 3–11.

—— *Beyond Dialogue: Towards a Mutual Transformation of Christianity and Buddhism*, Philadelphia: Fortress Press 1982.

Coward, H., *Pluralism, Challenge to World Religions*, New York: Orbis 1985.

—— *Sacred Word and Sacred Text: Scripture in World Religions*, New York: Orbis 1988.

Cracknell, K., *Towards a New Relationship, Christians and Peoples of Other Faiths*, London: Epworth 1986.

Cracknell, K., and Lamb, C., *Theology on Full Alert*, London: British Council of Churches 1986.

Cragg, K., *The Christian and Other Religions*, Oxford: Mowbray 1977.

—— *Muhammad and the Christian*, London: Darton, Longman and Todd 1984.

—— *The Christ and the Faiths: Theology in Cross-Reference*, London: SPCK 1986.

Daniélou, J., *The Advent of Salvation*, Glen Rock: Paulist 1962.

—— *Le Mystère du salut des nations*, Paris: 1948.

—— *Holy Pagans of the Old Testament*, London: Longman 1957.

Davis, C., *Christ and the World Religions*, London: Hodder and Stoughton 1970; New York: Herder and Herder 1971.

—— 'Theology and Religous Studies', *Scottish Journal of Religious Studies* 2 (1981), pp. 11–20.

D'Costa, G., 'John Hick's Copernican Revolution: Ten Years After', *New Blackfriars* July/August, 1984, pp. 323–31.

—— 'Karl Rahner's Anonymous Christian – A Reappraisal', *Modern Theology* 1;2 (1985), pp. 131–48.

—— *Theology and Religious Pluralism*, Oxford: Blackwell 1986.

—— '20th Century Christian Attitudes to Other Religions: a Bibliographical Guide', *Anvil* 4,2 (1987), pp. 175–85.

—— *John Hick's Theology of Religions*, New York and London: University Press of America 1987.

Dhavamony, M., ed., *Evangelism, Dialogue and Development*, Rome: Gregorian University 1972.

Drummond, R.H., 'Christian Theology and the History of Religions', *Journal of Ecumenical Studies* 12 (1975), pp. 389–405.

—— *Toward a New Age in Christian Theology*, New York: Orbis 1985.

Dudley, G., *Religion on Trial*, Philadelphia: Temple University Press 1977.

Dulles, A. *Models of the Church*, New York: Doubleday 1974; Dublin: Gill and Macmillan 1978.

—— *The Catholicity of the Church*, Oxford and New York: Oxford University Press 1985.

Eminyan, M., *The Theology of Salvation*, Boston: St Paul's 1960.

Farquhar, J.N., *The Crown of Hinduism*, Oxford: Oxford University Press 1913.

Gispert-Sauch, G., ed., *God's Word Amongst Men*, Delhi: Vidyajyoti 1973.

Glasser, A.F., 'A Paradigm Shift? Evangelicals and Interreligious Dialogue', *Missiology* 9 (1981), pp. 393–408.

Griffiths, B., *Return to the Centre*, London: Collins 1976.

—— *The Marriage of East and West*, London: Collins 1982.

—— *The Cosmic Revelation*, London: Collins 1983.

Griffiths, P., and Lewis, D., 'On Grading Religions, Seeking Truth and Being Nice to People – a Reply to Professor Hick', *Religious Studies* 19 (1983), pp. 75–80.

Gualtieri, A.R., 'The Failure of Dialectic in Hendrik Kraemer's Evaluation of Non-Christian Faith', *Journal of Ecumenical Studies* 15 (1978), pp. 274–90.

Haight, R.D., 'The "Established Church" as Mission: the Relation of the Church to the Modern World', *The Jurist* 39 (1979), pp. 4–39.

Hallencreutz, C.F., *Kraemer Towards Tambaram: a Study in Hendrik Kraemer's Missionary Approach*, Lund: CWK, Gleerups 1972.

Hebblethwaite, P., 'The Status of "Anonymous Christians" ', *Heythrop Journal* 1977, pp. 47–55.

Heim, S.M., 'Thinking about Theocentric Christology', *Journal of Ecumenical Studies*, 24 (1987), pp. 1–16.

Hick, J., *God and the Universe of Faiths*, London: Macmillan; New York: St Martin's 1973.

——, ed., *Truth and Dialogue*, London: Sheldon; Philadelphia: Westminster 1974.

—— 'Jesus and the World Religions', in *The Myth of God Incarnate*, London: SCM 1977, pp. 167–87.

—— *God Has Many Names*, London: Macmillan 1980.

—— 'On Grading Religions', *Religious Studies* 17 (1981), pp. 451–67.

—— 'On Conflicting Religious Truth-Claims', *Religious Studies* 19 (1983), pp. 485–91.

—— 'The Theology of Religious Pluralism', *Theology* 86 (1983), pp. 335–40.

—— 'The Philosophy of World Religions', *Scottish Journal of Theology* 37 (1984), pp. 229–36.

Hick, J., and Hebblethwaite, B., eds., *Christianity and Other Religions: Selected Readings*, London: Fount 1980.

Hick, J., and Knitter, P.F., eds., *The Myth of Christian Uniqueness*, New York: Orbis 1987; London: SCM 1988.

Hillman, E., *The Wider Ecumenism: Anonymous Christianity and the Church*, London: Burns and Oates; New York: Herder and Herder 1968.

Hocking, W.E., *Rethinking Missions: A Laymen's Inquiry After 100 Years*, New York and London: Harper 1932.

—— *Living Religions and a World Faith*, London: Allen and Unwin 1940.

Hooker, R., and Lamb, C., *Love the Stranger, Christian Ministry in Multi-Faith Areas*, London: SPCK 1986.

Hunter, A., *Christianity and Other Faiths in Britain*, London: SCM 1985.

Jathanna, Origen Vasantha, *The Decisiveness of the Christ-Event and the Universality of Christianity in a World of Religious Plurality*, Berne: Lang 1981.

Jenson, R.W., 'Religious Pluralism, Christology and Barth', *Dialog* 20 (1981), pp. 31–8.

King, U., *Toward a New Mysticism, Teilhard de Chardin and Eastern Religions*, London: Collins 1980.

Klostermaier, K., *Hindu and Christian in Vrindaban*, London: SCM 1969.

Knitter, P.F., 'European Protestant and Catholic Approaches to the World Religions: Complements and Contrasts', *Journal of Ecumenical Studies* 12 (1975), pp. 13–28.

—— *No Other Name? A Critical Survey of Christian Attitudes Towards the World Religions*, London: SCM; New York: Orbis 1985.

—— 'Christianity as Religion: True and Absolute? A Roman Catholic Perspective', *Concilium* 136 (1980), edited by David Tracy and Mircea Eliade.

—— 'Catholic Theology of Religions at a Crossroads', *Concilium* 183 (1986), edited by Hans Küng and J. Moltmann, pp. 99–107.

Koyama, Kosuke, *Mount Fuji and Mount Sinai*, London: SCM 1984.

Kraemer, H., *The Christian Message in a non-Christian World*, London: Edinburgh House Press 1938.

—— *Religion and the Christian Faith*, London: Lutterworth 1956.

—— *The Communication of the Christian Faith*, London: Lutterworth 1957.

—— *World Cultures and World Religions*, London: Lutterworth 1960.

Kulandran, S., 'Kraemer Then and Now', *International Review of Mission* 46 (1957), pp. 171–81.

—— *Grace: A Comparative Study of the Doctrine in Christianity and Hinduism*, London: Lutterworth 1964.

Küng, H., *On Being a Christian*, New York: Macmillan 1976; London: Collins 1977.

—— *Christianity and the World Religions*, London: Collins; New York: Doubleday 1987.

Lash, N.L.A., *Theology on Dover Beach*, London: Darton, Longman and Todd; New York: Paulist 1979.

Lipner, J.J., 'Christians and the Uniqueness of Christ', *Scottish Journal of Theology* 28 (1975), pp. 243–58.

—— 'Truth-Claims and Inter-Religious Dialogue', *Religious Studies* 12 (1976), pp. 217–30.

—— 'Does Copernicus Help? Reflections for a Christian Theology of Religions', *Religious Studies* 13 (1977), pp. 243–58.

—— 'The Study of Comparative Religion', *Epworth Review*, January 1978, pp. 110–20.

—— 'Hick's Resurrection', *Sophia* 17 (1979), pp. 22–34.

—— 'Theology and Religious Studies: Thoughts on a Crisis of Identity', *Theology*, May 1983, pp. 193–201.

Loughlin, G., 'Paradox and Paradigms: defending the case for a revolution in theology of religions', *New Blackfriars*, March 1985, pp. 127–35.

Mattam, J., *Land of the Trinity: a Study of Modern Christian Approaches to Hinduism*, Bangalore: Theological Publications 1975.

Neill, S., *Christian Faith and Other Faiths: The Christian Dialogue with Other Religions*, Oxford and New York: Oxford University Press 1970.

Panikkar, R., *The Trinity and the Religious Experience of Mankind*, New York: Orbis; London: Darton, Longman and Todd 1973.

—— *The Intra-Religious Dialogue*, Bangalore: Asian Trading Corporation; New York: Paulist 1978.

—— *Myth, Faith and Hermeneutics*, New York: Paulist 1979.

—— *The Unknown Christ of Hinduism*, London: Darton, Longman and Todd; New York: Orbis new edn, 1981.

Pannenberg, W., *Basic Questions in Theology*, vol. 2, London: SCM; Philadelphia: Fortress 1971.

Parrinder, G., *Avatar and Incarnation*, London: Faber 1970.

Pedley, C.J., 'An English Bibliographical Aid to Karl Rahner', *Heythrop Journal*, 1984, pp. 320–60.

Race, A., *Christians and Religious Pluralism*, London: SCM; New York: Orbis 1983.

Rahner, K., *Foundations of Christian Faith*, London: Darton, Longman and Todd; New York: Seabury 1978.

—— *Spirit in the World*, 2nd ed., London: Sheed and Ward 1968.

—— 'Christianity and the non-Christian Religions', *Theological Investigations* 5, London: Darton, Longman and Todd; New York: Seabury 1966; pp. 115–34.

—— 'Thoughts on the Possibility of Belief Today', *Theological Investigations* 5, pp. 3–22.

—— 'Anonymous Christians', *Theological Investigations* 6 (1969) pp. 390–98.

—— 'Anonymous Christianity and the Missionary Task of the Church', *Theological Investigations* 12 (1974), pp. 161–78.

—— 'Anonymous and Explicit Faith', *Theological Investigations* 16 (1979), pp. 52–9.

—— 'The One Christ and the Universality of Salvation', *Theological Investigations* 16, pp. 199–224.

—— 'On the Importance of Non-Christian Religions for Salvation', *Theological Investigations* 18 (1984), pp. 288–95.

—— 'Church, Churches and Religions', *Theological Investigations* 10 (1973), pp. 30–49.

—— 'Jesus Christ and the Non-Christian Religions', *Theological Investigations* 17 (1981), pp. 39–50.

Riches, J., ed., *The Analogy of Beauty*, Edinburgh: T. & T. Clark 1986.

Robinson, J.A.T., *Truth is Two-Eyed*, London: SCM 1979.

Rosato, P.J., *The Spirit as Word*, Edinburgh: T. & T. Clark, 1981.

Rouner, L.S., *Religious Pluralism*, Indiana: University of Notre Dame Press 1984.

—— 'Theology of Religions in Recent Protestant Theology', *Concilium* 183 (1986), edited by Hans Küng and J. Moltmann, pp. 108–15.

Saldanha, C., *Divine Pedagogy: A Patristic View of Non-Christian Religions*, Biblioteca di Scienze Religiose 57, Rome: LAS 1984.

Samartha, S.J., *The Hindu Response to the Unbound Christ*, Madras: Christian Literature Society 1974.

——, ed., *Dialogue between Men of Living Faiths*, Geneva: World Council of Churches 1971.

Schineller, J.P., 'Christ and Church: A Spectrum of Views', *Theological Studies* 37 (1976), pp. 545–66.

Schlette, H.R., *Towards a Theology of Religions*, London: Burns and Oates 1966.

Sharpe, E., *Comparative Religion*, London: Duckworth 1975.

—— *Faith Meets Faith*, London: SCM 1977.

Smart, N., *The Yogi and the Devotee*, London: Allen and Unwin 1968.

—— *Beyond Ideology: Religion and the Future of Western Civilization*, London: Collins 1981.

Smith, W.Cantwell, *The Faith of Other Men*, New York: Harper, new ed., 1972.

—— 'A Human View of truth' in *Truth and Dialogue*, ed. John Hick, London: Sheldon 1974, pp. 20–44.

—— *Religious Diversity, Essays by Wilfred Cantwell Smith*, ed. Willard G. Oxtoby, New York: Harper and Row 1976.

—— *The Meaning and End of Religion*, New York: Macmillan 1962; London: SPCK, new edition, 1978.

—— *Towards a World Theology*, London: Macmillan; Philadelphia: Westminster 1980.

Staffner, H., *The Significance of Jesus Christ in Asia*, Anand: Gujarat Sahitya Prakash 1985.

van Straelen, H., *The Catholic Encounter with World Religions*, London: Burns and Oates 1965.

Swidler, L., ed., *Toward a Universal Theology of Religions*, New York: Orbis 1987.

Sykes, S.W., ed., *Karl Barth – Studies in his Theological Method*, Oxford: Oxford University Press 1979.

Thomas, M.M., *The Acknowledged Christ of the Hindu Renaissance*, London: SCM 1969.

Thomas, O.C., ed., *Attitudes Towards Other Religions*, London: SCM 1969.

Tillich, P., *Christianity and the Encounter of the World Religions*, New York: Columbia University Press 1963.

Tracy, D., *Plurality and Ambiguity: Hermeneutics, Religion, Hope* New York: Harper and Row 1987; London: SCM 1988.

Trigg, R., 'Religion and the Threat of Relativism', *Religious Studies* 19 (1983), pp. 297–310.

Troeltsch, E., *The Absoluteness of Christianity and the History of Religions*, London: SCM; Richmond, John Knox Press; 1972.

—— *Christian Thought: Its History and Application*, London 1923.

Veitch, J.A., 'The Case for a Theology of Religions', *Scottish Journal of Theology* 24 (1971), pp. 407–22.

—— 'Revelation and Religion in the Theology of Karl Barth', *Scottish Journal of Theology* 27 (1974), pp. 1–22.

Vempeny, I., *Inspiration in the Non-Biblical Scriptures*, Bangalore: Theological Publications 1973.

Viyagappa, I., *In Spirit and in Truth*, essays dedicated to Ignatius Hirudayam, Madras: Aikiya Alayam 1985.

Vorgrimler, H., ed., *Commentary on the Documents of Vatican II*, London: Burns and Oates/Herder 1967.

Ward, J.S.K., *Images of Eternity*, London: Darton, Longman & Todd 1987.

Whaling, F., ed., *Contemporary Approaches to the Study of Religion*, Paris – The Hague: Mouton 1984.

—— *The World's Religious Traditions*, essays in honour of Wilfred Cantwell Smith, Edinburgh: T. & T. Clark 1984.

—— *Christian Theology and World Religions: A Global Approach*, Basingstoke: Marshall Pickering 1986.

Zaehner, R.C., *Concordant Discord*, Oxford: Oxford University Press 1970.

Theology and inter-faith dialogue

1. RELIGION AND RELIGIOSITY

Berger, P., and Luckman, T., *The Social Construction of Reality*, New York: Doubleday 1966; Harmondsworth: Penguin 1967.

Crossan, J.D., *The Dark Interval: Towards a Theology of Story*, Illinois: Argus Communications 1975.

Dumont, L., *Religion, Politics and History in India*, Paris – The Hague: Mouton 1970.

—— *Homo Hierarchicus*, London: Paladin 1972.

Geertz, C., *The Interpretation of Cultures*, New York: Basic Books 1973.

Katz, S., 'Language, Epistemology, and Mysticism', in *Mysticism and Philosophical Analysis*, ed. Katz, New York: Oxford University Press; London: Sheldon 1978.

Lindbeck, G., *The Nature of Doctrine: Religion and Theology in a Postliberal Age*, London: SPCK; Philadelphia: Westminster 1984.

Loughlin, G., 'See-Saying/Say-Seeing', *Theology* vol. XCI, 741 (May 1988); pp. 201–9.

O'Flaherty, Wendy Doniger, *Śiva, The Erotic Ascetic*, Oxford: Oxford University Press, paperback ed., 1981.

Surin, K., 'Many Religions and the One True Faith', *Modern Theology* 4,2 (January 1988), pp. 187–209.

Thornhill, J., 'Is Religion the Enemy of Faith?', *Theological Studies* 45 (1984), pp. 254–74.

Tracy, D., 'Lindbeck's New Program for Theology: a Reflection', *The Thomist* 49 (July 1985), pp. 460–72.

Turner, V., *The Ritual Process*, Chicago: Aldine Publishing 1970.

Welbon, G.R., *The Buddhist Nirvana and its Western Interpreters*, Chicago: Chicago University Press 1968.

Yocum, G., *Hymns to the Dancing Śiva*, New Delhi: Heritage Publishers 1982.

Zaehner, R.C., *Bhagavad Gita*, Oxford: Oxford University Press 1969.

2 INTERIOR DIALOGUE: LEARNING FROM THE OTHER

Aykara, T., ed., *Meeting of Religions: New Orientations and Perspectives*, Bangalore: Dharmaram 1978.

Buber, M., *I and Thou*, Edinburgh: T. & T. Clark 1959; New York: Scribner 1970.

Cousins, E., 'Raimundo Panikkar, A Brief Bibliography', *Cross Currents* XXIX, 2 (1979), p. 130.

Gispert Sauch, G., 'Guidelines for Inter-religious dialogue', *Vidyajyoti* 42 (1978), pp. 96–8.

Howe, R., *The Miracle of Dialogue*, New York: Seabury 1963.

Kerr, F., *Theology after Wittgenstein*, Oxford: Blackwell 1986.

Klostermaier, K., 'Hindu-Christian Dialogue', *Journal of Ecumenical Studies* 5 (1968), pp. 21–44.

Lipner, J.J., 'Dialogue and Encounter', *Downside Review* 93 (1975), pp. 58–63.

Lonergan, B.J.F., *Method in Theology*, London: Darton, Longman and Todd; New York: Crossroad 1972.

Nambiaparambil, A., 'Religions in Dialogue: Indian Experience Today', in *Meeting of Religions*, ed. Thomas Aykara, pp. 76–88.

—— 'Dialogue in India: a challenge to redeem hope', *Vidyajyoti* 39 (1975), pp. 111–26.

Panikkar, R., 'Inter-religious dialogue; some principles', *Journal of Ecumenical Studies* 12 (1975), pp. 407–9.

—— 'The Rhetoric of the Dialogue', in *The Intra-Religious Dialogue*, pp. 15–37.

—— 'The Rules of the Game in the Religious Encounter', ibid., pp. 63–75.

—— 'The Myth of Pluralism: the Tower of Babel – a Meditation of Non-Violence', *Cross Currents* XXIX, 2, pp. 197–230.

—— 'The Dialogical Dialogue', in *The World's Religious Traditions*, ed. Frank Whaling, pp. 201–21.

—— 'Tolerance, Ideology and Myth', in *Myth, Faith and Hermeneutics*, pp. 20–36.

—— 'The Jordan, the Tiber and the Ganges', in *The Myth of Christian Uniqueness*, pp. 89–116.

Pro Mundi Vita Bulletin 88 (January 1982), on 'Hindu-Christian Dialogue in India'. See especially the bibliography.

Redington, J., 'The Hindu-Christian Dialogue and the Interior Dialogue', *Theological Studies* 44 (1983), pp. 587–603.

Rogers, C. Murray, 'Hindu-Christian Dialogue Postponed, an exchange between C. Murray Rogers and Sivendra Prakash', in *Dialogue between Men of Living Faiths*, ed. S.J. Samartha, pp. 21–31.

Samartha, S.J., 'The Cross and the Rainbow, Christ in a Multireligious Culture', in *The Myth of Christian Uniqueness*, pp. 69–88.

Sharpe, E., 'The Goals of Inter-religious Dialogue' in *Truth and Dialogue*, ed. John Hick, London: Sheldon 1974, pp. 77–95.

Singh, H.J., ed., *Inter-religious Dialogue*, Bangalore: CISRS 1967.

3 SPIRIT OF THE MYSTERY

Brown, R., *The Gospel According to John*, New York: Doubleday 1966; London: Chapman 1971.

Congar, Y.-M., *I Believe in the Holy Spirit*, 3 vols, London: Chapman; New York: Seabury 1983.

Dupuis, J., 'The Cosmic Influence of the Holy Spirit and the Gospel Message', in *God's Word Among Men*, ed. George Gispert Sauch, pp. 117–38.

Dunn, J.D., *Jesus and the Holy Spirit*, London: SCM 1975.

Durrwell, F.X., *The Mystery of Christ and the Apostolate*, London: Sheed and Ward 1972.

Gaybba, B., *The Spirit of Love*, London: Chapman 1987.

Heron, A., *The Holy Spirit*, London: Marshall 1983.

Imhof, P., and Biallowons, H., eds., *Karl Rahner in Dialogue, Conversations and Interviews 1965–1982*, translated by Harvey Egan, New York: Crossroad 1986.

Jüngel, E., *The Doctrine of the Trinity: God's Being is in Becoming*, Edinburgh – London: Scottish Academic Press 1976.

Kasper, W., *Jesus the Christ*, London: Burns and Oates; New York: Paulist 1976.

—— *The God of Jesus Christ*, London: SCM 1984.

Lacugna, C.M., and McDonnell, K., 'Returning from "The Far Country": Theses for a Contemporary Trinitarian Theology', *Scottish Journal of Theology* 41 (1988), pp. 191–215.

Lampe, G.W.H., *God as Spirit*, Oxford: Oxford University Press 1977.

McDade, J., 'The Trinity and the Paschal Mystery', *Heythrop Journal* XXIX (1988), pp. 175–91.

Moltmann, J. *The Church in the Power of the Spirit*, London: SCM 1977.

—— *The Trinity and the Kingdom of God*, London: SCM 1981.

Mühlen, H., *Una Mystica Persona*, Paderborn, 1968.

—— *A Charismatic Theology: Initiation in the Spirit*, London: Burns and Oates 1978.

O'Donnell, J., 'Theology of the Holy Spirit I: Jesus and the Spirit', in *The Way* 23 (1983), pp. 48–64.

Rahner, K., *The Trinity*, London: Burns and Oates 1970.

Taylor, J.V., *The Go-Between God* London: SCM 1972.

Williams, R., 'Barth on the Triune God', in *Karl Barth, Studies in his Theological Method*, ed. S.W. Sykes, Oxford: Oxford University Press 1979, pp. 147–93.

—— 'Trinity and Revelation', *Modern Theology* 2 (1986), pp. 197–212.

4   THE PRACTICE OF DIALOGUE AND THE LIBERATION OF THEOLOGY

Amaladoss, M., Gispert-Sauch, G., and John, T.K., eds., *Theologizing in India*, Bangalore: Theological Publications 1981.

Amalorpavadass, D.S., *Approach, Meaning and Horizon of Evangelization*, Bangalore: National Biblical Catechetical and Liturgical Centre 1973.

——, ed., *Research Seminar on non-Biblical Scriptures*, Bangalore: NBCLC 1975.

——, ed., *The Indian Church in the Struggle for a New Society*, Bangalore: NBCLC 1981.

—— *Theology of Evangelization in the Indian Context*, Bangalore: NBCLC 1984.

Arokiasamy, S., and Gispert-Sauch, G., *Liberation in Asia: Theological Perspectives*, Anand: Gujarat Sahitya Prakash 1987.

Boff, L., *Jesus Christ, Liberator*, New York: Orbis 1978; London: SPCK 1979.

Boyd, R., *An Introduction to Indian Christian Theology*, Madras: Christian Literature Society 1969.

—— *India and the Latin Captivity of the Church: the Cultural Context of the Gospel*, Cambridge: Cambridge University Press 1974.

—— *Khristadvaita, A Theology for India*, Madras: Christian Literature Society 1977.

Gutierrez, G., *A Theology of Liberation*, New York: Orbis 1973; London: SCM 1974.

Jesudasan, I., *A Gandhian Theology of Liberation*, Anand: Gujarat Sahitya Prakash 1987.

Knitter, P., 'Toward a Liberation Theology of Religions', in *The Myth of Christian Uniqueness*, pp. 178–200.

Laine, J., 'Catholic Theology and the Study of Religion in South Asia: Widening the Context for Theological Reflection', *Theological Studies* 48 (1987), pp. 677–710.

Pathrapankal, J., ed., *Service and Salvation*, (Nagpur theological conference on evangelization, 1971), Bangalore: Theological Publications 1973.

Pieris, A., *An Asian Theology of Liberation*, Edinburgh: T. & T. Clark; New York: Orbis 1988.

—— 'The Buddha and the Christ: Mediators of Liberation', in *The Myth of Christian Uniqueness*, pp. 162–77.

Pinto, Joseph Prasad, *Inculturation through Basic Communities: an Indian Perspective*, Bangalore: Asian Trading Corporation 1985.

Rayan, S., 'Indian Christian Theology and the Problem of History', in *Society and Religion*, ed. Richard W. Taylor, Madras: Christian Literature Society 1976, pp. 187–93.

—— 'The Justice of God', in *Third World Liberation Theologies: A Reader*, ed. D.W. Ferm, New York: Orbis 1986, pp. 348–55.

Schreiter, R., *Constructing Local Theologies*, London: SCM 1985.

Segundo, J.L., *The Liberation of Theology*, New York: Orbis 1976; Dublin: Gill and Macmillan 1977.

Soares Prabhu, G., 'Jesus Christ amid the Religions and Ideologies of India Today', in *Ecumenism in India*, ed. Mathai Zachariah, Delhi: ISPCK 1980.

—— 'Jesus the Teacher: the Liberative Pedagogy of Jesus of Nazareth', *Jeevadhara* 69 (May–June, 1982), pp. 243–56.

—— *Inculturation, Liberation, Dialogue*, Pune: Jnanadeepa 1984, translated from *Problemi e Perspettivi di Teologia Dogmatica*, ed. Karl H. Neufeld, Brescia, 1983.

Tracy, D., *The Analogical Imagination: Christian Theology and the Culture of Pluralism*, New York: Crossroad; London: SCM 1981.

Index